More Praise for
Active Value Investing

"Whether a self-styled seat-of-the-pants day trader or the kind of investor who intends to buy and hold forever, you're operating at a distinct disadvantage if you lack the skills to break a company down into its financial nuts and bolts. Vitaliy "Red" Katsenelson is one of the best on the Street at analyzing a business and putting that knowledge to work to make money. In *Active Value Investing*, Red shares the skills and strategies that allow him to cut through the noise and build a long-term portfolio of winners. Bull and bear markets come and go, but the 'secrets' shared in this book are forever. This book is a must-have guide for any market!"

—Jeff Macke
Contributor to Minyanville.com
and CNBC's *Fast Money*

"Vitaliy has done the world a significant favor; he shows, in erudite fashion, that value investing (the one tried and tested investment approach) holds in range-bound markets. This should matter for all investors as in a world of low returns, ensuring the avoidance of permanent loss of capital is paramount. But he doesn't stop there, Vitaliy manages to go even further and provides you with a working process for evaluating investment in such a world."

—James Montier
Global Equity Strategist, Dresdner Kleinwort

"In a world of uncertainty, Vitaliy's investing techniques help calm the storm."

—James Altucher
Author of *Trade Like a Hedge Fund*
Founder of Stockpickr.com

"Vitaliy Katsenelson wears two professional hats: As a successful money manager, he has the responsibility to clear out the noise and center upon what makes a market-beating investment. As an educator, he's honed his ability to distill complex concepts into the explainable. With *Active Value Investing*, he's managed both the clarity of thought and the clarity of investment to bring to you an outstanding investment resource."

—Bill Mann
Advisor, *Hidden Gems* newsletter
The Motley Fool

"*Active Value Investing* provides a laconic vision of how the individual or institutional investor can successfully navigate a market that is neither a bull nor a bear. Unlike most stock market authors who automatically posit the stock market's prospects as knowing only one way (up), Katsenelson provides a refreshingly honest and, sometimes, humorous approach to a less defined future."

—Douglas A. Kass
President, Seabreeze Partners Management Inc.

"Vitaliy's passion for value investing and teaching others makes *Active Value Investing* enjoyable as well as insightful. It is required reading for the investment team at Second Curve Capital."

—Thomas K. Brown
CEO, Second Curve Capital

Active
Value
Investing

Founded in 1807, John Wiley & Sons is the oldest independent publishing company in the United States. With offices in North America, Europe, Australia, and Asia, Wiley is globally committed to developing and marketing print and electronic products and services for our customers' professional and personal knowledge and understanding.

The Wiley Finance series contains books written specifically for finance and investment professionals as well as sophisticated individual investors and their financial advisors. Book topics range from portfolio management to e-commerce, risk management, financial engineering, valuation, and financial instrument analysis, as well as much more.

For a list of available titles, visit our Web site at www.WileyFinance.com.

Active Value Investing

Making Money in Range-Bound Markets

VITALIY N. KATSENELSON

John Wiley & Sons, Inc.

Published by John Wiley & Sons, Inc., Hoboken, New Jersey.
Published simultaneously in Canada.

Wiley Bicentennial logo: Richard J. Pacifico.

For general information on our other products and services or for technical support, please contact our Customer Care Department within the United States at (800) 762-2974, outside the United States at (317) 572-3993, or fax (317) 572-4002.

Wiley also publishes its books in a variety of electronic formats. Some content that appears in print may not be available in electronic books. For more information about Wiley products, visit our Web site at http://www.wiley.com.

Exhibits sourced Ibbotson Associates are from: *Stocks, Bonds, Bills and Inflation*® 2007 *Classic Edition Yearbook.* © 2007 Morningstar. All rights reserved. Used with permission. Copies of the *Yearbook* may be acquired directly from Morningstar. For more information, please visit global.morningstar.com/SBBIYrBks.

Library of Congress Cataloging-in-Publication Data:

Katsenelson, Vitaliy N.
  Active value investing : making money in range-bound markets / by Vitaliy N. Katsenelson.
p. cm.– (Wiley finance series)
Includes bibliographical references.
ISBN 978-0-470-05315-7 (cloth)
1. Speculation. 2. Investments. I. Title.
HG6041.K36 2007
332.6–dc22

2007013701

Printed in the United States of America.

10 9 8 7 6 5 4 3

For my parents:
My father Naum and in memory of my mom Irene
Thank you for always believing in me

Contents

Preface

R eaders of investment books are right to be skeptical. Hundreds of new titles hit the shelves of bookstores every year. It is hard to navigate them and determine which are worthy reads and which undeservingly consume bookshelf space.

I wrote this book for skeptics who look for opportunity but have a healthy dose of "the glass is half empty" mentality and a great passion for investing. Whether you are an "I'd rather do it myself, damn it!" investing weekend warrior or an "I do it 12 hours a day and eat lunch at my desk—I love this job!" professional investor (the latter category is where I fit in), you should find this book worthwhile. It takes common and traditional investing concepts and modifies and applies them in some surprising and profitable ways to the enigma of the range-bound market.

If you properly take the role of a skeptical reader, I'll answer questions you'd want to ask me before you buy this book.

> **Skeptical Reader: How is *active* value investing different from just value investing?**
>
> **Vitaliy Katsenelson:** *Active* value investing is the necessary modification for traditional value investing strategies to make them effective in range-bound markets. Although principles of fundamental analysis are agnostic to the long-term direction of the market, stock analysis and investment strategy should be *actively recalibrated* to adapt to changing market environments.
>
> **SR: What are these "range-bound markets" you're talking about?**
>
> **VK:** The most vivid analogy is to a roller coaster. After all the excitement of dramatic up, down, sideways, and pin-your-back-to-your-seat thrill-ride gyrations, no matter how long the ride lasts, you (and your portfolio) end up back where you started. This is the fate of the *in*active value investor, the buy-and-hold and passive index investor, during range-bound markets—close to zero stock returns plus meager dividends, with time having passed but little progress toward retirement nest-egg goals.

SR: This is a bear market, then?

VK: On the surface that certainly seems how it appears, but this is a common misconception. We are used to thinking about markets in binary terms: bull and bear. But if you look at the U.S. stock market during the entire twentieth century, most of the prolonged (greater than five years) markets were actually bull or range–bound markets. Prolonged bear (declining) markets happened in the past only when high market valuation was coupled with significant economic deterioration, similar to what was going on in Japan from the late 1980s through 2003 or so.

SR: And you think we are in one of those range-bound markets?

VK: Yes. If two centuries of stock market history are a guide, every protracted bull market (and we just had one of those from 1982 to 2000) was followed by a long-lasting range-bound market. Range-bound markets are the payback times—investors are paying with their returns and with lost time for the valuation excesses of prior bull markets.

SR: I see the first part of the book is entitled "What the Future Holds." That doesn't sound like value investing to me. What's that about?

VK: This book is a practical guide to value investing in range-bound markets. But to buy into and incorporate these strategies into your own investing process will require some convincing. I know I would need to be convinced. Therefore, in the first part of the book we examine historical performance of the U.S. market over the past two centuries and discuss what caused prolonged bull, bear, and range-bound markets. We look at the emotions that have dominated each of these markets, and why there is a high probability that a range-bound market has descended upon us and is here to stay for another good dozen years.

I'll then provide a framework that will help you forecast how long this market will last, and explain why I believe that corporate earnings growth over the next several years will lag gross domestic product (GDP) growth.

SR: If the market is not going anywhere, just up and down and sideways, you'll probably just tell me that I need to become a market timer.

VK: I won't. I promise. And what I do instead is offer a major new alternative mind-set. It is hard, if not impossible, to create a successful market-timing process. A market timer's buy and sell decisions are made based on predicting the short-term direction of stock prices, interest rates, or the condition of the economy. Aside from the fact that this demands that you be correct twice—when you buy and when you sell—emotions are in the driver's seat of the market, especially at the tops and bottoms. You don't need to time the market; you need to time the valuations of individual stocks.

SR: You are saying don't time the market, time stocks. How is that different from timing the market?

VK: Timing stocks is not much different from what you are accustomed to doing, except it has to be more proactive. If you don't like the word *timing*, call it *pricing*—you need to price individual stocks. Then you actively engage in a strategy that helps you buy when they are undervalued and sell when they approach becoming fully valued. As a market timer your cash balance is a function of what you think the market is about to do. However, the stock timer's (pricer's) cash balance is a by-product of investment opportunities you see in the market.

SR: I hope you are not saying that I need to be a day trader!

VK: Not at all. But you need to be a more active investor during range-bound markets than in a pleasant bull run. The traditional buy-and-hold strategy of the last bull market is not dead, but close—it is in a coma.

Buy-and-hold is really just a code name for the "buy and forget to sell" strategy. A stock is usually *bought* with a discipline, but *hold* is really just a disguise for absence of a concrete sell discipline—unless you call "I'll own it until death do us part" a discipline. "Buy and forget to sell" works great in a prolonged bull market, when P/Es keep expanding from much below to much above average; stocks of so-so companies rise, and stocks of great companies shoot to the stars. Passive investing—buying and never selling—is rewarded.

The opposite takes place during a range-bound market, as P/Es go from much above to much below average (it happened every single time during the twentieth century). We need a new thinking paradigm to replace what we subconsciously learned in 1982–2000!

SR: And you'll tell me what to do, right?

VK: Definitely. In Part II, the practical application section of the book, we discuss stock analysis and active investing strategy for range-bound markets.

In the Analytics section, we discuss a Quality, Valuation, and Growth (QVG) framework that lies at the core of the approach, and which should add clarity to stock analysis. We look at a stock from this systematic, three-dimensional view and assess each dimension separately; we then explore interactions among them. We identify what constitutes a good company, and how to determine at what price these good companies turn into good stocks worth owning.

The Quality and Growth dimensions of the analysis require some tweaking in range-bound markets, but it's not that much different from any market analysis. The Valuation dimension, however, requires the most recalibration for the range-bound markets.

SR: Why Valuation?

VK: Constant P/E compression, a staple of range-bound markets, requires a good understanding of stock valuation and a reassessment of valuation tools. Relative valuation tools generate false buy signals in times like this and should be used only in conjunction with absolute valuation tools. Absolute valuation becomes increasingly important in range-bound markets, however; this is discussed here in depth, and I introduce some new tools.

SR: What if I am a growth investor—do I care about all this?

VK: You very much should! Throughout prolonged range-bound markets, investors are willing to pay progressively less for earnings growth. P/Es of higher-growth companies contract at a much faster rate for higher-valuation stocks than for low-P/E stocks. I performed a study of what happened to low- and high-P/E stocks throughout the 1966–1982 range-bound market. In the beginning, investors were willing to pay a 200 percent P/E premium for high-growth companies versus low-growth companies. However, that premium consistently shrank, ending up at only 40 percent by the end in 1982. Growth investors must understand this dynamic to navigate these markets.

SR: But the higher earnings growth rate of growth stocks overcompensated for P/E compression, right?

VK: Not at all! Low-P/E stocks outperformed high-P/E stocks on a consistent basis throughout the 1966–1982 range-bound market.

SR: What if I'm a growth investor—what do I do about this?

VK: Be absolutely sure that the earnings growth and dividends of the higher-P/E stocks will overcompensate for their likely P/E compression. In the Valuation chapter I provide several adjustments that will help you deal with that.

SR: Does your strategy change as the market evolves?

VK: You need to *become an active buy-and-sell investor*. I cannot overemphasize the importance of the selling process. You need to sell when your stocks hit their predetermined sell valuations, which will be emotionally difficult, since often it will happen when everybody else is buying and excited about the market again. I'll share some strategies that will help you become a better seller.

This brings us to the importance of *being an independent thinker, a contrarian.* In fact, it is so important that I dedicated a chapter to contrarian strategies: taking advantage of media myth amplification, time arbitrage, how to use myth busting to find undervalued stocks, generate new stock ideas, and more.

It is more difficult to invest during the trendless range-bound market than in the bull market; no question about it. So a look overseas at other markets should help you to increase the incremental opportunity cost of each decision. This is the subject of Chapter 11.

SR: Amen! But what if I don't buy your range-bound market argument?

VK: Although I've written this book specifically to address investing in such markets, a lot of the concepts discussed have solid application at other times as well. In fact, I use the concepts from these sections (minus modifications for the range-bound markets) to teach Practical Equity Analysis class at the graduate school of the University of Colorado at Denver. I also added two chapters, "A Different View of Diversification" and "A Different View of Risk," in the Risk and Diversification section that apply to analysis in any market.

SR: What if the range-bound market you describe is not in the cards and we'll have a prolonged bull or bear market instead?

VK: Every strategy should be evaluated not just on a "benefit of being right" basis, but at least as importantly on a "cost of being wrong" basis, and I intend to do just that. The Active Value Investing strategy has the lowest cost of being wrong! It is superior to buy-and-hold or high-growth strategies in the range-bound and bear markets. In a very unlikely case of a full-fledged prolonged bull market, Active Value Investing should provide strong returns but may underperform buy-and-hold and high-beta strategies. The small level of underperformance is a reasonable insurance premium to pay to avoid failure in a range-bound or bear market.

SR: If what you are describing is true, why shouldn't I just buy bonds?

VK: Again, approaching strategies on a "cost of being wrong" basis, the Active Value Investing strategy should outperform bonds in a bull market, in a range-bound market, and in a bear market caused by or coinciding with inflation. The only time bonds will do better than stocks is if the U.S. economy goes into a severe deflation-caused recession. And even in this case government default-free bonds should do comparatively well, whereas corporate bonds' performance would be questionable as their default rates are likely to skyrocket.

SR: Is this an academic book?

VK: No. I have little patience for academic investment books that are riddled with Greek symbols, heavy footnotes, and long formulas. This is not one of those books. Though we look at some formulas, I promise no Greek symbols, and the formulas will be simple enough for a seven-year-old to understand.

    I'll also be sensitive to the fact that finance talk can rival the dryness of the Sahara. I've learned in my years of teaching investments that when students start bringing six-packs of double-shot espresso to my lectures I am doing something wrong. I'll attempt to make the journey as concise and as interesting as possible, keeping humor to the maximum and interjecting as many real-life, practical examples as my editor allows me to keep.

SR: Looking at your bio, I cannot figure out who you are: teacher, writer, or investor. Pick one.

VK: If I had to pick just one, I'd say investor. I love investing. I love everything about it: the uncertainty of every decision. The intellectual exercise of putting different pieces of the puzzle together while never having enough information at your disposal. The constant battle with one's emotions—the hardest and the most important battle of all. The never-ending pursuit of perfection despite its unattainability, how just when you think you have figured it out, the market has a new lesson in store for you. The humbling aspect of the market—arguably the most humbling mechanism ever invented by humans. The people, the debate, the search for the truth. The fact that for every trade there are two opposing sides (buyer and seller), and time is the variable that separates them from discovering who was right and who was wrong. And finally, the hidden, rarely recognized, but fascinating impact that randomness plays in many outcomes.

    I discovered that I wanted to invest for a living when I was a sophomore in college, so both my undergraduate and graduate degrees were in finance. I topped them off with a Chartered Financial Analyst (CFA) designation. I invest for a living. It is my job, but actually more like a paid hobby. I've got the best job in the world!

If I did not miss my family and friends, I'd do it 24/7. (For my personal story of arrival to the United States, see pages 269–271.)

SR: But how does it tie in with teaching and writing?

VK: The university allowed me to create the curriculum for my class from scratch, so it is designed to be a practical and fun extension of my day job. Plus I have a captive audience.

SR: And writing?

VK: Several years after I started teaching, I discovered another passion — writing. I write only when I have an insight and interest in the topic, as a by-product of my investment process. I am a regular contributor to the *Financial Times* and Minyanville.com and have written articles for *Rocky Mountain News*, MarketWatch by Dow Jones, The Motley Fool, The Street.com, and RealMoney. This book, for example, is the result of my personal trifecta of investing, teaching, and writing — all focused around the same thing, really.

SR: How come there are few books that talk about the range-bound market idea? Actually, I don't see a single other one that talks about how to invest in range-bound markets!

VK: Investment books are usually written about investment strategies for bull markets. From a business perspective this makes sense. Books are published to sell, and interest in investing, and thus interest in buying books about investing, is highest when investors are making money — during a bull market. But this shortchanges you, my serious Skeptical Reader/Investor, as over long periods of time the stock market has spent as much time going nowhere as it has rising. Range-bound markets may not be as exciting or profitable to the average investor, but why be average? My hope is that you will find the fortitude to stay invested during this difficult market rather than running away to bonds or cash, and use the book as a resource to help you squeeze decent mileage out of a difficult market full of exhilarating highs and surprising lows.

What the Future Holds

CHAPTER 1

Introduction: Range-Bound Markets Happen

It is hard to make predictions, especially about the future.
—Attributed to Yogi Berra

FASTEN YOUR SEAT BELTS AND LOWER YOUR EXPECTATIONS

For the next dozen years or so the U.S. broad stock markets will be a wild roller-coaster ride. The Dow Jones Industrial Average and the S&P 500 index will go up and down (and in the process will set all-time highs and multiyear lows), stagnate, and trade in a tight range. They'll do all that, and at the end of this wild ride, when the excitement subsides and the dust settles, index investors and buy-and-hold stock collectors will find themselves not far from where they started in the first decade of this new century. And these at best minuscule returns are unacceptable!

The length, the angles, and the twists of the ride are yet to be written by history, but the ultimate long-term flat trajectory of the ride has been set by the 18-year bull market that ended in 2000. If history is any guide, until about 2020, give or take a few years, the U.S. stock market will continue to dance the range-bound foxtrot it has been dancing since the end of 2000. Welcome to the range-bound markets!

What a gloomy, unexciting way to start a book, you may say. But the cold shower of reality is needed to snap investors into a different mode of investing—not the mode that they have been conditioned to by the 1982–2000 bull market, but the state that we will discuss in depth throughout this book. I use the word *different* cautiously since it is a part of a dangerous phrase: "This time is different." This time is *not* different!

There has been nothing different taking place in the U.S. broad market indexes since 2000 (or is likely to be taking place for another good dozen years) from what took place in the past. One just has to look back far enough, past the last secular bull 1982–2000 market, to notice it, and we will do just that.

The performance of U.S. stocks during the twentieth century overwhelmingly supports this rather bold (at first look) prediction; as demonstrated in Exhibit 1.1, every long-lasting bull market in the twentieth century has led to a stagnating, long-lasting range-bound market (the Great Depression that followed a prolonged bull market was the only exception).

LET'S IDENTIFY THE ANIMAL

According to Wikipedia, "A bull [upward-sloped] market is a prolonged period of time when prices are rising in a financial market faster than their historical average, in contrast to a bear [downward-sloped] market, which is a prolonged period of time when prices are falling." What about markets that have a flat, horizontal trajectory? They are known to professionals as range-bound or trendless markets, and they look different from bear markets, although investors often lump them together. We'll talk about their differences in the next chapter.

Since investors are so used to associating animals with the slope of the market, I have some suggestions for range-bound market names—chicken, or sheep perhaps. Or my personal favorite, cowardly lion, whose bursts of occasional bravery lead to stock appreciation, but are ultimately overrun by fear that leads to a subsequent descent.

For those who are used to thinking of markets in the bull and bear terms and are indifferent to cowardly lions (amazingly, I've been told, some people are), may I suggest adding another type of species to their bear vocabulary—the range-bound market bear. Thus declining bear markets you may call the grizzly bear market, whereas the market that is more or less flat you may call a range-bound bear market.

SECULAR VERSUS CYCLICAL

Let's get some more definitions out of the way. We'll be using the terms *secular* and *cyclical* to describe market conditions. A secular market describes a long-lasting (more than five years) condition that takes place once in a generation or so. Cyclical conditions, in contrast, are significantly shorter market cycles that may last months or a few years.

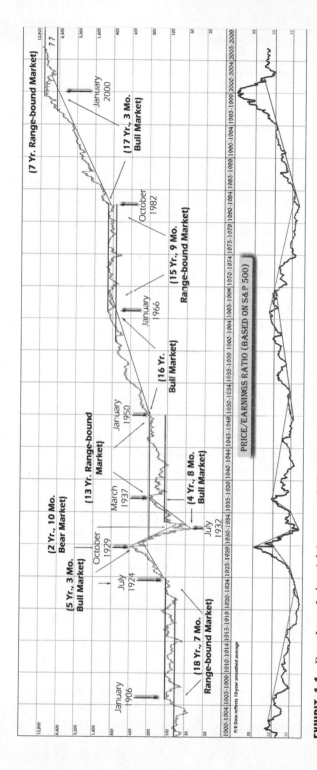

EXHIBIT 1.1 Dow Jones Industrial Average, 1900–2006

Copyright 2007, Kevin A. Tuttle, Tuttle Asset Management, LLC (www.tuttleassetmanagement.com). P/E data from Dr. Robert J. Shiller.

Investment is not an exact science like mathematics or physics, where definitions are precisely crafted. It is like economics (a dismal science) and thus definitions are often subjective and open to different interpretations. For instance, the market decline that was caused by (or some argue caused) the Great Depression, which precipitated one of the greatest drops in stock prices in U.S. history, doesn't qualify as a secular bear market according to the definition, as it lasted only two years and 10 months, less than five years as required. However, the Great Depression really was a secular bear market. (See Chapter 2 for additional information about the Great Depression.)

The long-lasting decline of the Japanese Nikkei fits well into the definition of a secular bear market, as it lasted for 13 years, starting in January 1990 and bottoming (or so it appears) in April 2003.

Since this book is focused on secular markets, when I discuss secular bull, bear, or range-bound markets, I'll refer to them just as bull, bear, and range-bound markets. I'll make sure to use the word *cyclical* when referencing cyclical markets.

DISTINCTION BETWEEN SECULAR BULL, BEAR, AND RANGE-BOUND MARKETS

Range-bound and bear markets are different in nature; the distinction is rarely made but important. Range-bound markets present unique investing opportunities and were a lot more common in the preceding century than bear markets, as Exhibit 1.1 clearly shows. Over the 100 years from 1900 to 2000, range-bound markets were occurring over half the time.

Range-bound markets are the bear markets of price-earnings (P/E) ratios (they decline), whereas bear markets are the bear markets of P/Es *and* earnings (they both decline).

Range-bound markets are so-called payback markets—investors are paying back in declining P/Es for the excess returns of the preceding bull market.

Bear markets, such as the one in Japan, are caused by a combination of excess valuation (a predominant feature of range-bound markets as well) and prolonged economic distress. High P/Es and economic distress at the same time are a lethal combination. High P/Es reflect high investor expectations from the economy. Economic blues (runaway inflation, severe deflation, subpar or negative economic or earnings growth) disappoint investors' optimistic expectations. They anticipate that the economy (and stocks) will keep performing far above average, but instead the performance is not average, but below average. The bear market has started.

Economic growth is the wild card that differentiates between range-bound and bear markets. But economic growth is not the vital factor in creating a bull or a range-bound market—market valuation is.

On a shorter-term basis, economic growth has its ups and downs during both bull and range-bound markets, adding to the intermediate volatility of stock prices, and is often responsible for relatively short-term (cyclical) bull, bear, and range-bound markets. However, long-term economic growth during both range-bound and bull markets is fairly stable.

As shown in Exhibit 1.1, the bull markets of the twentieth century started at the end of exhausting range-bound markets or sharp bear markets (the Great Depression). In all cases, they started when P/Es were much below average and economic growth was normal, not earth-shattering and not much better or worse than during range-bound markets.

IS 100 YEARS LONG ENOUGH?

In the first part of the book I'll be making a number of observations based on U.S. stock market data from the twentieth century. Is 100 years long enough? Can we arrive at a statistically significant result by looking at only three range-bound markets, one bear market, and three bull markets (counting the bull market started after 1929 crash)? No, we cannot.

So let's throw in another 100 years. In his book *Stock Cycles* (iUniverse, 2000), Michael A. Alexander analyzes stock market cycles from 1802 to 2000. Since I already showed performance of the stock market from 1900 to 2006 in Exhibit 1.1, in Exhibit 1.2 I show only real (after inflation) returns from U.S. stocks by market cycle from 1802 to 1906, using data compiled by Mr. Alexander. Now we have price data going back another

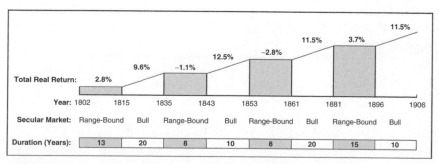

EXHIBIT 1.2 Stock Market Performance, 1802–1906
Data Source: Michael A. Alexander, *Stock Cycles* (iUniverse, 2000).

100 years. Again, bull markets are followed by range-bound (or bear) markets, time after time, in the nineteenth century as well.

One little technicality: Mr. Alexander did not differentiate in his book between range-bound and bear markets, but I'll stick to my range-bound definition, as none of the returns look drastically bear market–like (remember, they are real after-inflation returns).

Is a 200-year period long enough? It is better than 100 years, but again it is not long enough to be statistically significant. Academics would argue that we'd need thousands of years' worth of stock market data to come to a statistically significant conclusion—a luxury that we don't have. In this book I am not making a case that range-bound markets follow bull markets because of statistical significance—I simply don't have enough data to make this case.

However, no matter how much things change, they remain the same. Whether a trade is submitted through a Western Union telegram, as was often done at the turn of nineteenth century, or through the video game look-alike screen of an online broker, as often happens today, it still has a human originating it. And all humans come with standard emotional equipment that is, to some degree, predictable.

Human emotions and thus long-term market trends are here to stay. Over the years we've become more educated, with access to fancier, faster, and better financial tools. A myriad of information is accessible at our fingertips, with speed and abundance that just a decade ago were available to only a privileged few. But despite all that, we are no less human than we were 10, 20, 50, or 100 years ago. Unless technology and innovations strip away our emotions, we'll behave like humans no matter how sophisticated we become. Unless we completely outsource all of our investment decision making to computers, markets will still be impacted by human emotions. Emotions are the price—and joy—of being human.

STOCKS CARRIED THE TORCH IN THE LONG-RUN MARATHON

In the 100-year investment marathon that took place in the twentieth century, U.S. stocks came out as a clear winner, leaving the returns of gold and bonds in the dust. The race was not without obstacles. Stocks overcame World War I, a worldwide influenza epidemic that killed over half a million Americans and over 20 million people worldwide, the Great Depression, the shock of Pearl Harbor and subsequent U.S. involvement in World War II, the Korean War, the Cuban Missile Crisis (which brought the United States to the brink of nuclear war with Russia), the assassination of John

F. Kennedy, the Vietnam War, a presidential impeachment, an oil crisis, one Cold War, two Gulf Wars (okay, to be factually correct the second Gulf War took place starting in 2003—the twenty-first century), terrorist attacks, numerous natural disasters, and much more.

As shown in Exhibit 1.3, though stocks lost some sprints to gold and bonds, their long-term dominance over them is indisputable. $100 invested in stocks at the end of 1925 would turn into $328,450 by the end of 2006, far exceeding the $7,169 invested in Treasury bonds and the $3,078 resulting from investment in gold, which barely kept up with inflation as measured by the consumer price index (CPI) and with Treasury bills (T-bills).

Bonds, though left behind by a huge margin, were the runner-up to stocks. Unlike stocks, whose upside return potential is unlimited, bonds' cash flows, and to a large degree their upsides, are predetermined by contractual agreement and have a maximum monetary value. Unless a company defaults on interest and debt principal payments, cash flows from bonds don't vary with the company's profitability. A company's increased profitability may send the stock price to the stratosphere, but bondholders will receive the same return, regardless.

From a default risk perspective, bonds are less risky than stocks. Bondholders are first in line to receive disbursements of a company's assets

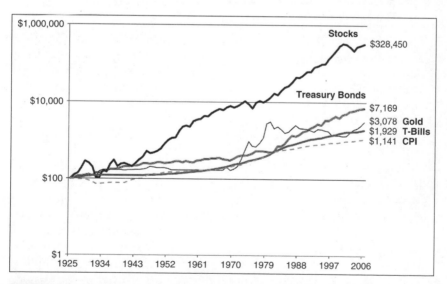

EXHIBIT 1.3   Total Return: Stocks, Bonds, Gold, Inflation, 1925–2006
Data Sources: Robert J. Shiller—Stocks (S&P 500), CPI; Ibbotson Associates—Treasury bonds and bills.

in case of bankruptcy, whereas stock investors may lose all their invested capital. Bond investors may recoup all or a portion of their investments, depending on the seniority (place in the bond line) of the bonds and the severity of the bankruptcy.

In his book *Stocks for the Long Run* Jeremy Siegel did a terrific job of examining the returns of stocks and bonds from 1802 to 2001, and he wrote the following:

> *In every 5-year period since 1802, ... the worst performance in stocks, at −11 percent a year, has been slightly worse than the worst performance in bonds or bills. Moreover, for 10-year holding periods, the worst stock performance actually has been better than that for bonds or bills. ... It is significant that stocks, in contrast to bonds or bills, have never offered investors a negative real holding period return yield over periods of 17 years or more. ... The safest long-term investment for the preservation of purchasing power clearly has been a diversified portfolio of equities. ... For 10-year horizons, stocks beat bonds and bills over 80 percent of the time; and for 30-year horizons, it is virtually 100 percent of the time.[1]*

INTERNATIONAL STOCKS WERE BRIGHT LIGHTS, TOO

Stocks' resilience and superior performance in the twentieth century were not limited to just the United States. The real returns for stocks from 1926 to 2001 compiled by Jeremy Siegel in *Stocks for the Long Run* were fairly consistent, ranging between 6 and 7 percent for the United States, the United Kingdom, and Germany. Stocks in other developed nations won their respective marathons, overcoming incredible obstacles in the process. German stocks suffered real declines of over 90 percent when World War II started; however, investors who held on to their stocks were made whole by 1958.

Germany's World War II ally Japan staged an incredible recovery as well. During and after the war, Japanese stocks lost 98 percent of real value. However, despite two of its major cities being obliterated by atomic bombs, and the hyperinflation that followed, Japanese stocks made a great recovery, approaching predecline levels by the early 1960s. Japan's real returns of 2.39 percent during the same time frame, expressed in U.S. dollars, were substantially understated, as the Japanese yen was in gradual decline against the U.S. dollar throughout the twentieth century. If the real stock returns were to be measured in yen, they would have exceeded the returns of U.S. stocks.[2]

Bond investors were not so lucky. According to Siegel, neither Japanese nor German bond investors recouped the real value of their original investments. German bonds didn't recover even a meaningful fraction of their real value lost to hyperinflation. The problems were initiated soon after World War I in 1919, when the Treaty of Versailles forced Germany to pay substantial reparations to the nations that won the war. The German economy was weak at the time: The country had no money. In order to pay for reparations and rebuild the economy, the German government printed money. However, the German public had no faith in this money, and hyperinflation began. Prices rose several million percent per month (prices doubled every 49 hours).[3]

Japanese inflation began in 1939, when the government, severed from its main sources of income in Japanese-occupied eastern China, printed more money to support the mounting costs of wartime operations. Japanese bond investors were luckier than their German counterparts, but not by much. They recovered some of the real bond value that was lost due to hyperinflation that started during World War II.[4]

Why did stocks outperform bonds? Will this outperformance continue into the future? The asymmetrical nature of the risk-return profile is likely to keep the marathon torch with stocks. The well-defined downside risk of stocks (investors can lose only 100 percent of their investment, similar to bonds and gold, assuming no leverage is used) and unlimited capital appreciation potential, mixed with human ingenuity and a healthy dose of greed, are likely to keep stocks dominating other asset classes in the twenty-first century as well. Remember what Gordon Gekko said in the movie *Wall Street*: "Greed is good."

WILL GOLD SHINE AGAIN?

Gold is an important but very different asset class that competes with stocks and bonds, and although it falls in the commodities asset class I'd like to briefly touch upon it in the following discussion. Unlike stocks and bonds, its main attractions are scarcity, durability, and resistance to oxidation—it simply never stops shining. In fact, most of the gold ever mined is still around today. It is exhibited in museums, worn as jewelry, and buried deep in the vaults of the central banks. Peter Bernstein, in his *The Power of Gold*, wrote the following:

> *Despite the complex obsession it created, gold is wonderfully simple in essence. Its chemical symbol AU derives from aurora, which means "shining dawn," but despite the glamorous suggestion of AU, gold is chemically inert. That explains why the radiance is forever. In Cairo, you'll find a tooth bridge made of gold for an*

Egyptian 4500 years ago; its condition is good enough to go into your mouth today.... Stubborn resistance to oxidation, unusual density, and ready malleability—these simple natural attributes explain all there is to the romance of gold.[5]

Despite its unique properties, gold has not been a good investment. Over the past 100 and 200 years its returns have barely kept up with inflation. Its value has a low correlation with stocks (prices of gold and stocks move independently of each other most of the time), which is a big positive from the portfolio construction perspective, as diversifying with gold can reduce a portfolio's fluctuations (volatility). However, the diversification benefit comes at a large cost: Once added to the portfolio, gold substantially reduces that portfolio's risk-adjusted returns—its dismal returns negate any benefit the portfolio receives from reduced volatility.[6]

One thing about gold, however—it is real! You can hold it and touch it, and see its shine. This tangibility makes it seem impervious to the whims of politics, nature, and time, as opposed to paper assets such as stocks and bonds. Gold's physical attributes attract investors during times of economic uncertainty, and so it serves a purpose in the markets and society—it is a stabilizing influence. It feels safe.

The thinking of the so-called gold bug (a believer in gold's supremacy, a gold aficionado) often takes on a variation of this form: While in the bunker (or any other variance of the "world falling apart" scenario), you cannot pay for food with paper—a stock or bond certificate (the overwhelming majority of the time they are actually electronic bytes and bits, anyway). You may do so with real tangible assets, however, such as gold. If this scenario played out (God forbid), it is conceivable that gold could become the de facto currency. In that event, you need to have real gold in a safe or buried in your backyard. The wise gold bug would have managed portfolio risk by also investing in a good arsenal of guns, as the demise of government bonds would likely lead to the end of the rule of law as well. Gold held by your broker or through ownership of gold stocks or exchange-traded funds (ETFs) will not come to the rescue; these bytes and bits are not superior to default-free bytes and bits (i.e., U.S. Treasuries). Canned food may actually be a better store of value in this "world coming to an end" scenario.

The ever-increasing complexity and globalization of the financial system, rapid spread of international trade, and the availability of risk-free investment instruments that were not available to investors in previous economic crises may have changed investor behavior during economic doomsday times. Financial instruments such as Federal Deposit Insurance Corporation (FDIC)-insured checking and savings accounts, U.S. Treasury bills, and Treasury inflation-protected securities (TIPS) may challenge gold's status as the safest haven in times of inflationary crisis.

GOLD'S RECENTLY EMERGED COMPETITION

TIPS may turn out to be the key challenger to gold's store-of-value supremacy status in the future. Aside from being issued by the U.S. Treasury and therefore backed by the full faith of the U.S. government, they also protect investors from inflation—one of gold's most valued qualities. TIPS' principal is tied to the CPI: The principal value increases with inflation and falls with deflation. When the security matures, the original or adjusted principal is repaid, whichever is greater.

Though TIPS appear to have superior financial properties to gold, they still lack one of gold's main attractions—tangibility. After all, they are still just bytes and bits on a brokerage firm's or bank's mainframe, or pieces of flammable paper stored in a safe. In addition, the inflation component that goes into TIPS pricing is calculated based on the CPI, which is calculated by the U.S. government. Many investors argue that the CPI calculation is outdated and that it chronically understates inflation.

Any cash-flow-generating asset, like a stock or a bond, can be valued on the future cash flows that it is expected to generate. Predicting gold prices is extremely difficult, as gold is not a cash-generating asset. In fact, it is important to note that gold actually has a negative yield (cost of carry). Gold is a cash-consuming asset (its safekeeping and transportation cost money), whereas TIPS as well as any bonds and dividend-paying stocks have a positive yield—they pay investors for holding them.

Gold is also considered a good currency hedge, especially for the U.S. investors who are concerned about the declining dollar. Again, our financial ingenuity is stealing gold's long-held exclusivity on that trade, providing options that were not available a few decades ago. To protect themselves against the declining dollar, U.S. investors can use currency futures and options, foreign-currency-denominated mutual funds, and certificates of deposit (CDs); they can buy foreign stocks on foreign exchanges or through American depositary receipts (ADRs); and of course there is a most recent development—currency exchange-traded funds (ETFs).

In both the long run and the short run, gold prices are driven by fear of the world coming to an end and investors' expectations of future infla-tion. Although gold has some industrial applications (in jewelry, dentistry, computers, jet engines, electronics, as a superconductor, etc.), linking its intrinsic value directly to its price is difficult. Perception of its ability to store and preserve real value (especially in an inflationary environment) is the key driver of gold's price. As long as investors perceive gold to be a refuge in times of uncertainty, gold will act as such.

It is important to note that gold's monopoly as an instrument of choice at the time of fear and uncertainty has been undermined by other very capable and often superior financial instruments.

THE DECEPTION OF THE LONG RUN (MARATHON)

> *Soar into space, and the earth loses its distinctive features: the Himalayas flatten; the Grand Canyon appears no deeper than a ditch.... [The view from space] gives few, if any, clues to the harsh geographical and financial realities that you should face walking across the earth's surface.... If you take a long-term view on the stock market, perhaps fifty or seventy-five years, it becomes a beautiful blue chip market. But the long-term rise in the market obscures the realities that affect almost every investor.*
> —Ed Easterling, *Unexpected Returns* (Cypress House, 2005)

Looking at stocks' phenomenal performance in the twentieth century, it is hard not to get a warm and fuzzy sense of security over their future long-term performance. They were clearly the champions of the twentieth-century marathon. However, akin to looking at Earth from space, looking at history only over the long run may inadvertently distort one's perspective, sending you onto the wrong investment path, as the often harsh realities of stock investing appear smoothed and distorted.

In the nineteenth and twentieth centuries, average real (after inflation) stock returns were consistently at about 7 percent, with about 3 to 4 percent inflation (nominal returns, including inflation, were about 10 to 11 percent a year). Investors have been trained by finance textbooks, Ivy League and not so Ivy League college professors, and a parade of investment experts to expect the long-term average return from any market, at any valuation, over any investment time horizon, and at any time. As we are about to discover, it is not that simple.

The U.S. economy may (or may not) be facing the golden years of prosperity. However, investors expecting the average returns observed over the past century are likely to be disappointed, as average happens a lot less frequently than we've been told. And contrary to common perception, strong economic growth doesn't always lead to positive stock market returns.

Stock market returns to a significant degree are a function of starting valuation (P/E) at the time of investing.

Protracted periods of above-average returns—bull markets—are usually followed by below-average returns—range-bound markets—of similar duration. This is how the average is created.

This is important to understand because if you are planning for the future using God-given (or so you've been told by experts) 7 percent real or 10 to 11 percent nominal long-term rates of return for your passive buy-and-hold stock portfolio, you may be disappointed by the cold reality of range-bound markets.

Let's take a peek at the four market cycles that took place from 1937 to 2000: two bull markets and two range-bound markets. We will exclude the time period surrounding the Great Depression, as it had a tremendous impact on the investment habits of the generation that lived through it—a psyche of a small minority of investors in today's market. The average range-bound market lasted about 15 years and brought total annual nominal and total real returns of 5.5 percent and 0.6 percent, respectively. The average bull market lasted a bit longer—about 17 years—and brought astounding total nominal and total real returns for faithful investors of 16.3 percent and 13.8 percent, respectively.

As shown in Exhibit 1.4, if the average of what happened from 1937 to 2000 (two range-bound and two bull markets) played out in the future, the investor faithfully buying an equity index fund or holding a broad market portfolio of stocks from the beginning of the average secular range-bound market would have to wait 32 years to receive a long-term average real return. If the same investor had a shorter time horizon, say 15 or 20 years, the cumulative annual rate of return would fall below the average expectation dramatically, producing 0.6 percent and 3.75 percent total real returns, respectively.

A similar pattern took place during the 1966–2000 full market cycle (see Exhibit 1.5), which comprised a 1966–1982 range-bound market and a 1982–2000 bull market. However, there was a lot more volatility in the interim than in the average (Exhibit 1.4) example. Investors who bought the Dow Jones Industrial Average in 1966 expecting to receive the long-term average returns during this period over 15- or even 20-year time horizons would have been disappointed, as real returns turned out to be far below the expected long-term average returns. In fact, a broad market portfolio invested in 1966 would have received no real returns for 16 years, until the start of the bull market in late 1982 and early 1983. It took 34 years (the full market cycle) for investors who bought a broad market index in 1966 to receive a 6.8 percent annual real rate of return.

RANGE-BOUND MARKETS ERODE BULL MARKET RETURNS

Above-average returns from the bull markets gradually were eroded by the meager returns of the secular range-bound markets that followed. If the

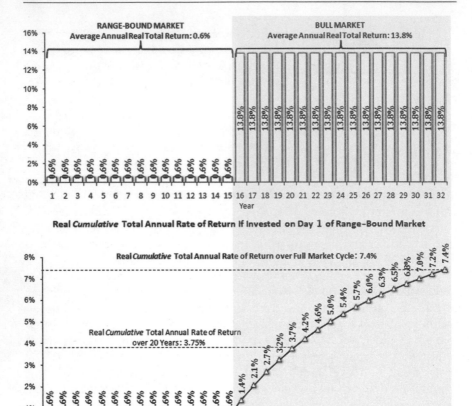

EXHIBIT 1.4 Total Annual Real Rate of Return from Average Range-Bound to Average Bull Market

average of what took place from 1937 to 2000 plays out in the future as demonstrated in Exhibit 1.6, investors holding a broad market index at the end of the bull market (as investors did in 2000) will painfully watch their returns from the bull market era be eroded by the range-bound market's below-average returns.

Let's take a look at the last full bull range-bound market cycle of 1950 to 1982. As shown in Exhibit 1.7, in 1966, at the end of the 1950–1966 bull market, investors' total real rate of return stood at an impressive 14 percent. If, by inertia, investors stayed the course with a buy-and-hold strategy (which worked well in the preceding 16 years), the annual real rate

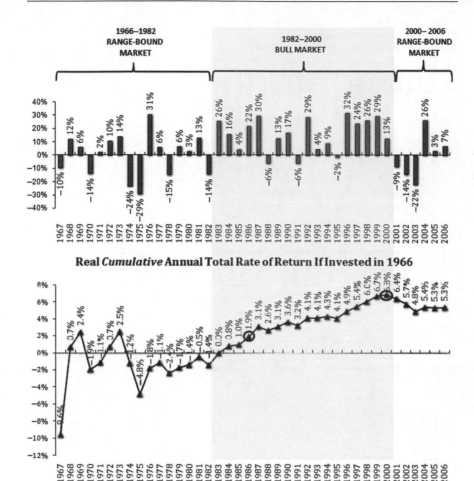

EXHIBIT 1.5 How Investors Fared in the 1966–2000 Full Market Cycle and Since (January 1967–January 2006)

of return of their portfolios would have declined to 6.5 percent over next 16 years, the end of the 1966–1982 range-bound market.

THE LONG RUN FOR US MAY BE SHORTER
THAN WE THINK

Few of us have the luxury of a 50- or 75-year long-run investment horizon. A 30-year time horizon is trying for many. Investors need to pay for cars,

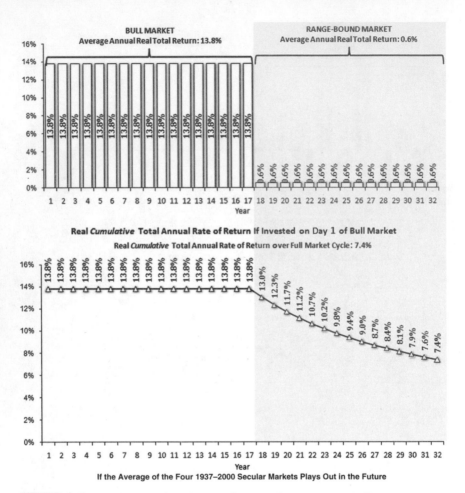

EXHIBIT 1.6   Total Annual Real Rate of Return from Average Bull to Average
Range-Bound Market

homes, second homes, kids' college tuition, weddings (cannot forget those),
and finally retirement.

Furthermore, even those who have 30 years to wait to receive average
returns find that it is extremely difficult to remain committed to an asset
class for a long period of time, while receiving plenty of volatility and
meager or no real returns in return for their loyalty.

Few of us have the patience to wait a couple of months to save money
for the latest and greatest gadget; we just charge it to our credit card. We
want instant gratification. Our behavior is not that much different when it

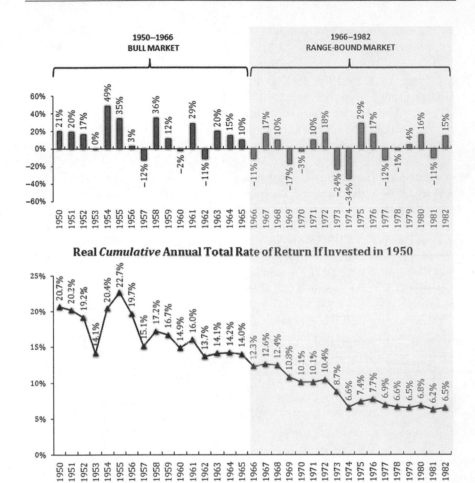

EXHIBIT 1.7 How Investors Fared in the 1950–1982 Full Market Cycle (December 1950–December 1982)

comes to investing. According to Dalbar, Inc., a research and ratings firm, a study covering 1984 to 2002 showed that:

> *Motivated by fear and greed, investors pour money into equity funds on market upswings and are quick to sell on downturns. The average equity [mutual fund] investor earned a paltry 2.57% annually, compared to inflation of 3.14% and the 12.22% the S&P 500 index earned annually for the last 19 years. The average fixed*

income investor earned 4.24% annually, compared to the long-term government bond index of 11.70%.[7]

From January 1984 to December 2002, the time period used in the Dalbar study, investors *substantially* underperformed the broad market indexes. The average mutual fund, after fees and expenses, lagged the performance of the S&P 500 by almost 2 percent if measured by the Lipper 1000 index (capturing the performance of the 1,000 largest equity funds in the United States), which was up 10.6 percent during that time frame. What is shocking is that equity mutual fund investors (not the mutual funds they invested in—an important distinction) even lagged returns of T-bills, which earned investors 5.5 percent during the same time frame.

As shown in Exhibit 1.8, from January 1984 to December 2002 an investor who put $100 in the S&P 500, an equity mutual fund (tracked by the Lipper 1000 index), or even T-bills on December 31, 1983, would have had $906, $672, or $276, respectively, on December 31, 2002, compared to only $155 if the same $100 were placed by an average equity mutual fund investor.

Impatience and the insatiable desire for instant gratification resulted in this substantial underperformance against market indexes and the mutual

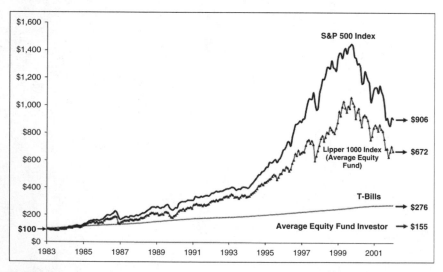

EXHIBIT 1.8 Performance of Average Equity Fund Investor, 1984–2002, versus S&P 500 versus Average Equity Fund versus T-Bills
Data Sources: Lipper 1000 Index—Lipper Inc.; Stocks (S&P 500)—Robert J. Shiller; Average Equity Fund Investor—Dalbar; Treasury bills—Ibbotson Associates.

funds they invested in. Amazingly, this study covered one of the greatest secular bull markets in the twentieth century. Investors' returns are likely to be a lot worse during a secular range-bound market, as these markets have a flat trajectory and high volatility that is evenly distributed to the upside and downside (described in the next chapter).

Even if investors have very long-term time horizons, most don't have the patience to match those time horizons. Investors, on average, need to see consistent returns from their portfolios to stay the course over the long term, and this is what we'll try to help you accomplish in this book.

CHAPTER 2

Emotions of Secular Bull, Bear, and Range-Bound Markets

After several months of despair, Livermore finally summoned up the courage to analyze his behavior and to isolate what he'd done wrong. He finally had to confront the human side of his personality, his emotions and his feelings. . . . Why had he thrown all his market principles, his trading theories, his hard-earned laws to the wind? His wild behavior had crashed him financially and spiritually. Why had he done it? He finally realized it was his vanity, his ego. . . . The outstanding success of making more than $1 million in one day had shaken him to his foundations. It was not that he could not deal with failure—he had been dealing with failure all his life—what he could not deal with was success.
—Richard Smitten, *Jesse Livermore*

In this chapter we explore the emotions that dominate bull, bear, and range-bound markets. Investors' emotional state is important, as we discussed in Chapter 1, because I believe emotions are responsible for the formation of the long-term cycle.

BULL MARKET EUPHORIA

In the bull market, rising prices intensify emotions such as optimism and euphoria, pushing market valuations to uncharted territories and defying logic (for example, at the height of the late 1990s bubble, America Online was trading at a valuation that priced every person on earth and some from remote parts of the galaxy as potential customers).

The more persistent and longer-lasting the ascent, the more certain and confident investors become in their abilities; this in turn feeds expectations of higher and higher returns. Investing in the early stages of a bull market is just something investors do with their retirement assets; however, later in the cycle it turns into a sport, which for some then turns into a full-time occupation. Although investors' true risk tolerance (the level of uncertainty of returns or losses one can handle) doesn't change, their perception of risk gets duller as investment success continues, turning even the most risk-averse investors into risk seekers. As the old saying goes, everyone looks brilliant in a bull market.

By the end of a bull market, investors have started to perceive stocks to be riskless, as memory of losses has been wiped out by a prolonged string of spectacular returns. (Where is the risk if stock prices keep rising?) This so-called risk amnesia at the late stages of a bull market is not just common to stocks. It has happened time and again with other asset classes: tulips in the 1630s in the Netherlands (yes, tulips—have you never thought of a flower as an asset class?), the Florida swampland boom of the 1920s, oil and gold bullion in 1970s, junk bonds in the 1980s, another real estate bubble in the 2000s, and the commodity rise in 2006.

A "this time is different" attitude becomes pronounced in the late stages of a stock bubble. We still remember the "eyeballs" models touted by newly emerged dot-com gurus in the late 1990s bubble: that conventional valuation tools could not capture the true value of the new virtual companies. Cash flow and earnings per share valuation techniques were tossed aside for "eyeballs" and "clicks" and other nonrevenue, nonprofitability measurements. Just about everyone knows how that ended. It turned out that cash flow and profitability do matter after all. And these same sorts of measurements matter in almost all asset classes. But time and again, a "this time is different" mentality comes back into vogue. You would think that we would learn.[1]

It is painfully obvious that bull markets leave investors with a lot of overvalued stocks, and several bubbly sectors that trade at astronomical valuations, some requiring a Hubble telescope (another new metric to value stocks?) to explain their valuations. And, finally, there is a perception that double-digit stock returns are a birthright, setting up investors for a painful disappointment.

Let's take Kenny (not his real name), for example. Kenny is an honest carpet layer and he is good at what he does. He has his own business, works hard, and saves every penny. I met him in late 1999 while visiting at a friend's house. Kenny was putting the finishing touches on my friend's new carpet. Once he found out that "I do stocks for a living" (his words), he told me that he was looking to retire in the not-so-distant future. "I am a millionaire," he stated, explaining that he and his wife had a couple of hundred thousand dollars stashed away. Her individual retirement account (IRA) was in a mutual fund that had produced a return of over 20 percent in the past five years, and his IRA was invested in five stocks: Oracle, Cisco Systems, Sun Microsystems, Microsoft, and Intel—the fantastic five. His broker friend told him that these were the stocks he must own (the key word here is *must*). In his conservative estimates he expected it to be at about a million in a few years (he was assuming that both accounts would keep growing at the "conservative" rate they had grown at for the prior five years).

"I am a long-term investor. I just keep buying them [the fantastic five] every month. If they decline, I buy more of them as if they were on sale." Kenny asked my opinion, but he did not really want to hear it, as he'd already committed himself to this investment strategy. He owned the best stocks, the ones that everybody raved about, and nothing else mattered. He did not want to hear that stocks were overpriced—they were the best companies and were on the cover of every other business magazine. What did I know? The distinction between good companies and good stocks (something we'll discuss in Chapter 8) fell on deaf ears. He did not want to hear that he and his wife were not diversified—a mutual fund and a large portion of their wealth in five fantastically overvalued technology stocks was hardly a model for a diversified portfolio. He did not want to hear that his expectations for the future returns of their investments were unrealistic. Kenny was confident in what he was doing, and he had every right to be confident in his strategy, as it had worked flawlessly to that point.

Kenny's behavior was typical investor behavior at the pinnacle of a bull market. Kenny was not alone. The market was (and still is) comprised of millions of Kennys who became overconfident because of persistently rising prices. *Return* is the word that dominates the vocabulary of the bull market investors, while *risk* is an obscure four-letter word, the meaning of which many have forgotten. But that's what bear and range-bound markets are for.

BEAR MARKET DOLDRUMS

In a bear market the inverse takes place. The optimism from a bull market turns into pessimism, euphoria into anguish. Investors were trained by the bull market to buy on dips. Initially driven by inertia, they keep buying on declines; however, the number of purchase decisions is (in most cases) directly correlated with negative confirmations (as most of purchase decisions lead to more losses) and thus pain. Declines that were supposed to be dips end up being staging points for further market declines and thus even more pain.

Risk tolerance doesn't change, but the risk senses sharpen. Even a benign, low-probability risk that previously would go unnoticed is magnified from the size of a fly into that of an elephant in investors' minds. A lot of wealth and self-confidence is destroyed by declining bear markets, at the end of which investors either liquidate most of their stock positions at substantial losses or let them drift. Unopened monthly investment statements from mutual funds or brokers go directly from mailbox to trash as, unable to bear reminders of the carnage, it becomes too painful for people to look. The bottom has been formed.

Bear markets instill fear and impact the investing psyche of generations that follow, changing forever their attitude toward stocks. We still hear anecdotes of people who lived through the Great Depression and refuse to own stocks, keeping their entire savings in Treasury bills, gold, or cash buried in the backyard (or hidden under the mattress). It took investors who bought stocks in August 1929, 25 years to break even on their purchases, not counting the dividends.

All secular bear markets in the twentieth century that took place in the United States, except the crash of 1929, were actually range-bound markets (a common confusion).

Although, as we briefly discussed in Chapter 1, the 1929 crash doesn't fit into the secular definition of a bear market as it lasted less than three years, I'd put it into a secular category anyway. The 1929 crash, depicted in Exhibit 2.1, was a true bear market, as over two years and 10 months prices dropped by 89 percent. Nothing even remotely of this magnitude has ever again been observed in the United States. The crash was preceded by a spectacular five-year ascent; the market raced at an 18.5 percent annual rate over the preceding five years. What started as an abrupt but normal price correction to an overextended market was driven into a crash by inadequate (to say the least) Federal Reserve policies. "In effect, the Fed continued to treat the American economy for the fever of inflation long after the patient had begun to freeze to death in the greatest deflation in the country's history."[2]

Both higher than expected inflation and the slightest signs of deflation are unwelcome headwinds for the stock market. The Federal Reserve is a great deal more effective at fighting inflation than deflation, as it has a greater variety of monetary tools at its disposal to fight inflation than to counteract deflation. Thus, since the Great Depression, the Federal Reserve has always taken a proactive stance in fighting even the slightest signs of deflation, always willing to err on the side of inflation by flooding the market with liquidity.

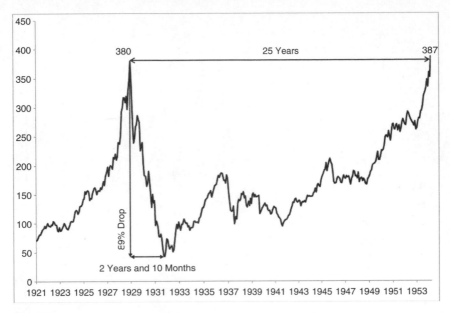

EXHIBIT 2.1   Dow Jones Industrial Average—1929 Crash

Japanese "By the Book" Secular Bear Market

Across the world, we see a similar picture with Japan. The Japanese 13-year-long bear market (shown in Exhibit 2.2) is sad testament of the central bank's inability to effectively fight deflation. Japan's Nikkei 225 stock prices declined over 80 percent from their 1989–1991 highs until they bottomed in 2003 (the market seems to be coming back now). For more than a decade the country struggled with deflation caused by its banking system coming to a near halt on the heels of a collapsing of real estate market and the bad loans that came with it.

In the second half of the 1980s, the Japanese economy was steadily expanding, inflation was low, and an expansionary monetary policy was driving the money supply higher. Banks were entering into a renaissance era as a strong, low-inflation economy was accompanied by steady growth in deposits. Based on expectations that the economic prosperity would continue, banks grew their loan portfolios using real estate as their collateral of choice. A strong economy and easy financing drove real estate prices higher and higher, allowing real estate developers to use their properties as collateral to get even more loans from banks, which were delighted to oblige.[3]

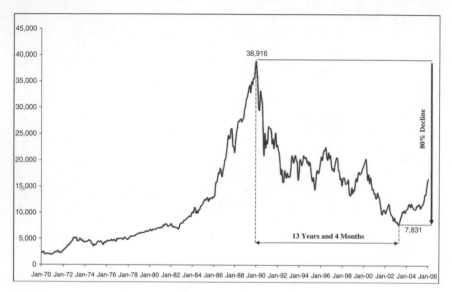

EXHIBIT 2.2   Japanese Nikkei Secular Bear Market

Then, in the 1990s, the Japanese real estate bubble burst, and real estate prices declined. Highly indebted companies could not repay their loans due to substantial declines in the value of their collateral, and nonperforming loans ballooned. Banks' asset bases started to shrink, forcing them to call in more loans and sell stocks—which in turn drove asset values even lower. This was a gradual process, with the rate of growth slowing in the 1990s and eventually going negative.

When prices started to drop, banks had to sell the collateral (stocks and real estate), which drove their prices even lower. The collateral was not enough to repay the loans, which led to widespread insolvency.

Fear about the future, the instability of the economy, and the uncertain job market led to a dramatic increase in saving—people stopped spending money and bought a load of U.S. Treasuries and gold. Even interest rates that were brought down to nothing by the Japanese central bank did not entice consumer and business spending. Many would argue that inadequate regulation of the Japanese banking system was at least in part responsible for the severity of the recession.

A unique aspect that contributed to the severity and longevity of Japanese deflation was a cultural issue: The Japanese government intervened and did not allow structurally defunct companies to go bankrupt, thus tampering with the nucleus of capitalism (and Darwinism as well)—creative destruction. This unwillingess to swallow bitter medicine resulted in a prolonged zombielike economy, where semidead companies, artificially sustained on life support, were competing with healthy ones, preventing the strong from succeeding and reaping the rewards of their success.

Nevertheless, although we may see sharply declining markets in the future, it is unlikely that declines will be of the magnitude observed during the Great Depression or in Japan. The Federal Reserve will use every weapon it has in its arsenal to fight deflation, and is unlikely to repeat the previous mistakes. But then again, long ago I learned the hard way to never say never!

WHAT DOES A SECULAR RANGE-BOUND MARKET FEEL LIKE?

The emotional state of a range-bound market is more complex than the clear highs and lows of bull and bear markets. A range-bound market is composed of cycles that include bullish periods, bearish periods, and trendless times. Where the long-term direction of the range-bound market is more or less flat, the shorter-term slope can point up, down, or sideways.

Similar to Chinese water torture in which the victim is slowly driven insane, the investor's confidence is gradually chipped away as the majority of investment decisions over an extended period of time result in poor returns. After years of diminutive returns, investors lose interest in the stock market and either start looking for other asset classes or abandon the markets altogether. For example, after the burst of the late 1990s bubble and volatile range-bound markets that followed, many stock investors found refuge in the real estate market or went to cash altogether with whatever they had left.

We can easily observe the migration from stocks into real estate by taking a look at Exhibit 2.3, which compares median home price appreciation in the United States to the performance of the S&P 500 index over three five-year periods. Through the 1990s, when the S&P 500 was more or less doubling every five years, the median home price was rising just several percentage points a year. However, from 2000 to 2005, the S&P 500 declined 5.5 percent (in the interim, the index dropped by over 35 percent from December 2000 to March 2003 but recovered most of its losses by the end of 2005), and investors, dissatisfied with subpar returns, shifted their money from stocks into real estate. This shift, along with multidecade low interest rates, drove median housing prices up by 54 percent over the aforementioned time period.

During secular range-bound markets, every bull market becomes nothing more than a short-lived cyclical bull market that lasts a couple of years at the most (sometimes only months), followed by a declining cyclical

EXHIBIT 2.3   S&P 500 Performance versus Median Home Price Appreciation

	S&P 500 Index	Median Home Price
12/31/1990–12/31/1995	86.5%	13.2%
12/31/1995–12/31/2000	114.4%	28.3%
12/31/2000–12/31/2005	−5.5%	54.0%

Data Sources: S&P 500—Standard & Poor's Compustat©; Median Home Price—The Bureau of the Census.

bear market, which in turn may be interrupted by a cyclical range-bound market (as if things were not confusing enough). This cycle has been replayed in different variations over and over again. Exhibit 2.4 shows the 1966–1982 range-bound market (a typical range-bound market) that consisted of a handful of cyclical bull and cyclical bear markets and a cyclical range-bound market.

During a range-bound market, every attempt to establish a long-lasting and definite direction, up or down, fails (as it failed every time through the 1966–1982 range-bound market). As time goes by and hopes for returns

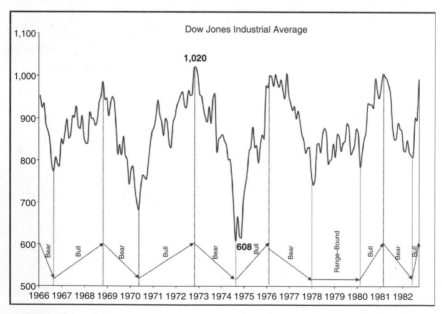

EXHIBIT 2.4   1966–1982 Secular Range-Bound Market

get shattered, investors become indifferent to the markets, which induces further P/E contraction and in turn leads to greater nonperformance and more indifference—the start of a vicious circle. A question that comes to mind: How do you know when the range-bound market is over? I'll try to answer that question in Chapter 3.

VOLATILITY OF BULL AND RANGE-BOUND MARKETS

Stock returns have fluctuated during range-bound markets almost as much as during bull markets. The positive slope of bull markets tilts most of the return fluctuations (volatility) to the upside, as evident in the bull market exhibits shown here. However, this is not the case with range-bound markets. Range-bound markets' returns to a large degree are direction neutral. Though volatile, as you can see in the range-bound market exhibits, the year-over-year stock returns in range-bound markets have gone up about as much as they have gone down.

In Exhibits 2.5 through 2.10, I segment volatility into three groups: significant upside volatility—year-over-year returns that exceeded 10 percent; significant downside volatility—returns that fell below −10 percent; and midrange volatility—returns that were between +10 percent and

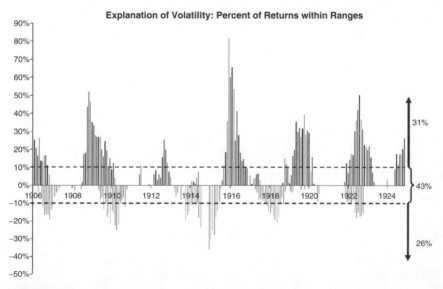

EXHIBIT 2.5 1906–1924 Range-Bound Market Volatility

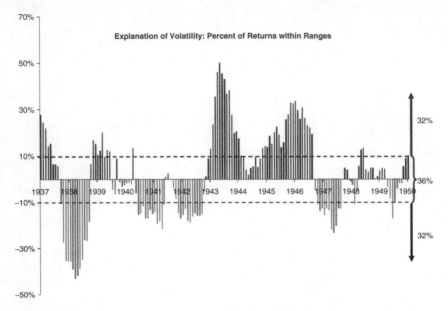

EXHIBIT 2.6   1937–1950 Range-Bound Market Volatility

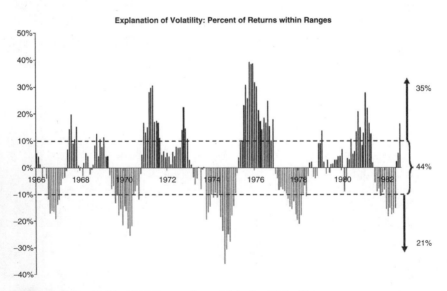

EXHIBIT 2.7   1966–1982 Range-Bound Market Volatility

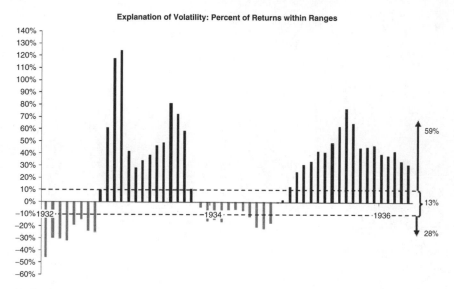

EXHIBIT 2.8   1932–1937 Bull Market Volatility

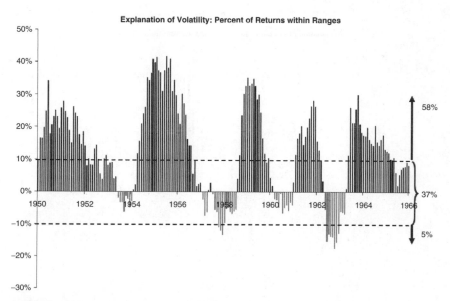

EXHIBIT 2.9   1950–1966 Bull Market Volatility

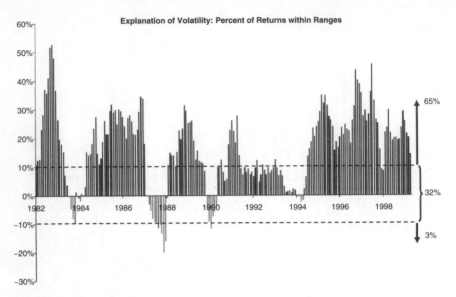

EXHIBIT 2.10   1982–2000 Bull Market Volatility

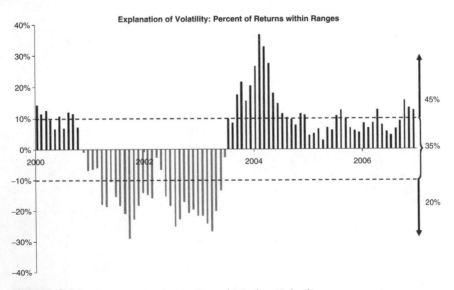

EXHIBIT 2.11   2000–2006 Range-Bound Market Volatility

−10 percent. I computed 12 month trailing returns for the S&P 500 and plotted them on a monthly basis, and then I identified the percentage of time the returns fell into each group.

Let's take the 1966–1982 secular range-bound market volatility shown in Exhibit 2.7. Midrange volatility took place only 44 percent of the time. Markets had a similar bias to significant upside gains as to downside losses, which took place 35 percent and 21 percent of the time, respectively. Similar volatility was observed in other range-bound markets that took place during the twentieth century, as shown in Exhibits 2.5 and 2.6.

By contrast, let's take the 1982–2000 bull market volatility shown in Exhibit 2.10. This time midrange volatility took place only 32 percent of the time; significant downside volatility was minor, as it took place only 3 percent of the time; and significant upside volatility was a predominant feature, as it happened 65 percent of the time. As you can see in Exhibit 2.8 and Exhibit 2.9, similar patterns have been observed in other secular bull markets.

Looking at the volatility of returns from 2000 to 2006 shown in Exhibit 2.11, we can see that they resemble the volatility of returns observed during preceding secular range-bound markets shown in Exhibit 2.5, Exhibit 2.6, and Exhibit 2.7. Stocks went sideways for six years with significant downside and upside volatility in the process.

CHAPTER 3

Stock Market Math

Get your facts first, and then you can distort them as much as you please.

—Mark Twain

Even if you are reading this book years after publication (my greatest hope), unless the market indexes are trading at far below average valuations, all the concepts discussed in this chapter are still relevant. How low should the market valuations be for the message of this chapter still to be relevant? Well, I guess this is a chicken-or-egg type of problem: You need to keep reading to find out if you still need to keep reading.

In this chapter we examine sources of stocks' total return. From a pure arithmetic perspective, as shown in Exhibit 3.1, stock investors receive

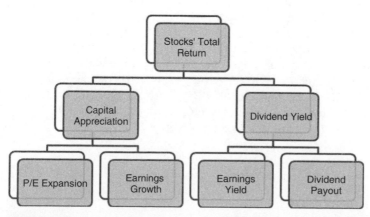

EXHIBIT 3.1   Stock Market Math

returns from two sources: capital (stock) appreciation and dividends. Capital appreciation is comprised of price-earnings (P/E) ratio expansion and earnings growth, where dividend yield is a function of earnings yield (earnings divided by price) and dividend payout (dividend divided by earnings).

Exhibit 3.2 illustrates the sources of the returns for different types of secular markets. We will refer to this table often throughout the chapter.

SOURCES OF CAPITAL APPRECIATION: EARNINGS GROWTH

I am putting the finishing touches on this book in early 2007. For your benefit, all necessary stock and index price data when applicable goes through December 31, 2006. However, not all economic or earnings data is available at this time; some of the fourth quarter 2006 economic and earnings data has not been released or reported yet. To have the most complete and up-to-date picture possible, I'll use estimates for the fourth quarter 2006 numbers that are still missing.

It Is Not the Economy, Stupid

Are bull markets driven by superfast economic growth? Are range-bound markets caused by subpar economic growth? The answers are no and definitely not, respectively.

Though it is hard to observe it in the everyday noise of the stock market, in the long run, stock prices are driven by two factors: earnings growth (or decline) and/or price-to-earnings expansion (or contraction).

In Exhibit 3.3, we see that it is difficult to establish a connection between stock performance and economic (e.g., gross domestic product [GDP], revenues of the economy) and corporate earnings growth. In the 1940s, nominal GDP grew at 11.2 percent and S&P 500 earnings per share (EPS) at 7.7 percent; however, stocks went up only 2.9 percent (corporate earnings are nominal, before inflation, earnings, and that is why we compare them with nominal, as opposed to real, GDP. During the 1950s, both GDP and S&P 500 earnings grew at slower rates, 6.3 percent and 5.4 percent respectively, but stock prices rose by an impressive 13.6 percent.

Could the subpar market performance be related to high or low inflation? Maybe the returns of the 1950s were driven by superlow 2.1 percent inflation. However, low inflation doesn't seem to be answer: In the 1960s inflation fell even lower, to 1.9 percent, whereas stocks went up at only

EXHIBIT 3.3 Composition of Annualized Market Returns

	Bear Market	Range-Bound Markets				Bull Markets		
	1929–1932	1906–1924	1937–1950	1966–1982	Average	1950–1966	1982–2000	Average
Earnings Growth	−28.1%	2.5%	7.6%	6.6%	5.6%	4.7%	6.5%	5.6%
+/− P/E Growth	−12.5	−2.2	−7.4	−4.2	−4.6	6.3	7.7	7.0
= Stock Return	−37.1	0.2	−0.3	2.1	0.7	11.3	14.7	13.0
+ Dividend Yield	7.1	5.9	5.7	4.1	5.3	4.3	3.0	3.7
Total Return	**−32.6**	**6.1**	**5.4**	**6.3**	**5.9**	**16.0**	**18.2**	**17.1**
Inflation/Deflation	−8.4	3.8	4.0	7.0	4.9	1.9	3.2	2.5
Total Real Return	**−26.4**	**2.2**	**1.3**	**−0.6**	**1.0**	**13.9**	**14.6**	**14.2**

EXHIBIT 3.3 Returns One Decade at a Time

Decade	Nominal Gross Domestic Product	Real Gross Domestic Product	S&P 500 EPS	Inflation/ Deflation	S&P 500	
					Stock-Only Return	Total Return
1930–1940	−1.4%	0.5%	−5.0%	−1.9%	−5.3%	0.0%
1940–1950	11.2	5.9	7.7	5.0	2.9	8.9
1950–1960	6.3	3.8	5.4	2.1	13.6	19.3
1960–1970	6.6	4.5	5.6	1.9	4.4	7.8
1970–1980	9.7	3.2	7.9	6.3	1.7	5.8
1980–1990	8.3	3.1	5.5	6.3	12.5	17.3
1990–2000	5.6	3.0	7.1	3.4	15.1	18.0
1930–2000	6.7	3.5	5.2	3.3	6.5	11.0
Bull Markets	**4.8**	**3.7**	**5.0**	**0.8**	**12.6**	**17.4**
Range-Bound Markets	**9.3**	**4.0**	**7.0**	**5.5**	**2.2**	**7.3**

a 4.4 percent annual rate during that time period. High inflation did not answer investors' prayers, either, as in the 1970s inflation skyrocketed to 6.3 percent, but stocks went up a meager 1.7 percent. Throughout the 1980s inflation remained at 6.3 percent, but stocks rose 12.5 percent.

From the data shown in Exhibit 3.3 it is difficult to see a link between the rate of economic growth and the animal (bull, bear, or cowardly lion) in the driver's seat of the stock market. Undoubtedly the connection does exist, but periods of disconnect appear to last for decades at a time.

Let's see if by looking at economic statistics you can identify the animal in the driver's seat of the secular market. Exhibit 3.4 shows nominal and real GDP growth, S&P 500 earnings growth, and inflation for the last five secular markets that have taken place in the United States (from 1930 to 2000), grouping them by the headings "Alpha" and "Beta." Try to guess which were the secular range-bound markets and which were secular bull markets.

EXHIBIT 3.4 Guess the Animal

	"Alpha" Market			
Decade	Nominal Gross Domestic Product	Real Gross Domestic Product	S&P 500 EPS	Inflation/ Deflation
First Instance	9.4%	5.3%	7.9%	3.9%
Second Instance	9.3%	2.7%	6.1%	7.0%
"Alpha" Market Average	9.3%	4.0%	7.0%	5.5%

	"Beta" Market			
Decade	Nominal Gross Domestic Product	Real Gross Domestic Product	S&P 500 EPS	Inflation/ Deflation
First Instance	1.8%	3.2%	2.7%	−2.8%
Second Instance	6.4%	4.1%	4.8%	1.9%
Third Instance	6.3%	3.7%	7.5%	3.3%
"Beta" Market Average	4.8%	3.7%	5.0%	0.8%

Have you made your guess? As you can see, it is difficult to find a significant difference between the economic performance of range-bound and bull markets. Alpha were the range-bound markets and Beta were the bull markets.

As it is clear from Exhibits 3.3 and 3.4, real GDP growth has remained consistent during the past three bull markets and the past two range-bound markets. The U.S. economy in real terms (excluding inflation) has grown at a consistent rate over the past 70 or so years, measured in decades (see Exhibit 3.3) and throughout secular market cycles (see Exhibit 3.5). Interestingly, the S&P earnings growth was actually higher during the range-bound markets. However, if we exclude the 1932–1936 bull market, earnings growth of 7 percent during the range-bound markets was just a bit higher than the 6.1 percent earnings growth during the last two bull markets shown in the chart.

The rate of economic growth (as long as it was positive) had little impact on the long-term returns from stocks and the slope of the stock market. Although in the short run the rate of GDP and the rate of earnings growth were responsible for relatively short-term (cyclical) swings in the market, in the long run, as long as the rate of growth was positive, the chance of a secular bull market or a range-bound market unfolding were about the same. Therefore, we can conclude that earnings growth and economic vitality were not responsible for creating bull and range-bound markets.

But what about interest rates?, you may ask. A great question. Exhibit 3.6 shows earnings yields for the S&P 500 (based on one-year trailing earnings) and yield of long-term bonds. The Fed Model, a model used by economists to explain high valuations of the stock market, suggests a tight relationship between long-term Treasury bonds and the returns on stocks (expressed as earnings yield, earnings divided by price). Though the name of the model implies that it is endorsed by the Federal Reserve, it is not. It was created by Ed Yardeni when he was a strategist at Prudential Securities.[1]

By taking a look at the last full 1966–2000 range-bound/bull market cycle (see Exhibit 3.6), we can see that the Fed Model perfectly predicted the direction of equities in relation to interest rates (okay, assuming you could predict interest rates). Long-term interest rates were rising from 1966 to 1982 and the year's yield was rising (P/Es were falling), whereas from 1982 to 2000 interest rates were dropping and yields were dropping (P/Es were rising). Intellectually that makes sense, because stocks and bonds compete for investors' capital and thus higher interest rates make equities less attractive and vice versa. However, the relationship between earnings yield and interest rates is not conclusive if we look at other secular markets.

EXHIBIT 3.5 Returns One Market at a Time

Secular Trend	Years	Nominal Gross Domestic Product	Real Gross Domestic Product	S&P 500 EPS	Inflation/ Deflation	S&P 500	
						Stock-Only Return	Total Return
Bull	1932–1937	1.8%	3.2%	2.7%	−2.8%	15.1%	21.8%
Range-Bound	1937–1950	9.4	5.3	7.9	3.9	1.1	6.9
Bull	1950–1966	6.4	4.1	4.8	1.9	9.2	13.7
Range-Bound	1966–1982	9.3	2.7	6.1	7.0	3.4	7.7
Bull	1982–2000	6.3	3.7	7.5	3.3	13.4	16.7
Bull Market Average		4.8	3.7	5.0	0.8	12.6	17.4
Range-Bound Market Average		9.3	4.0	7.0	5.5	2.2	7.3

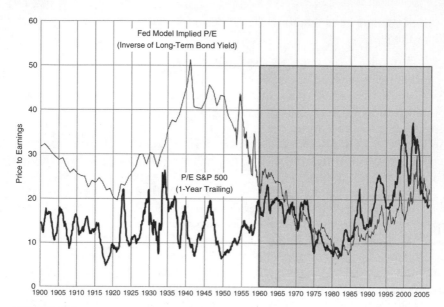

EXHIBIT 3.6 Does the Fed Model Work? Interest Rates versus S&P 500 Earnings Yield

During the 1906–1924 range-bound market, interest rates went from 3.4 percent to 3.9 percent—not a significant move by any stretch of the imagination. Over the next range-bound market (1937–1950) they dropped from 2.7 percent to 2.3 percent—again, not a significant move. Rates also dropped during the 1929–1932 bear market; that makes sense, as it was a deflationary environment. Interest rates have consistently gone down during the 1924–1929, 1932–1937, and 1982–2000 bull markets, but went up from 2.3 percent to 4.6 percent during the 1950–1966 bull market.

With the exception of the 1966–2000 periods, it is hard to find a significant relationship between interest rates and the animal with its name on the secular market.

If earnings growth remains consistent with the past, P/E is the wild card that is responsible for future returns. Though continued economic growth appears to be an unreasonable assumption, it is not. With the exception of the Great Depression (see Exhibits 3.3, 3.4, and 3.5), economic growth was fairly stable throughout the twentieth century. Earnings, though more volatile than real GDP, grew consistently decade after decade, paying no attention to the animal (bull, bear, or cowardly lion) lending its name to the stock market.

Myth: Earnings have Consistently Grown at a Faster Pace than GDP

Corporate earnings lost the race to GDP. Contrary to common perception, corporate earnings have not grown faster than nominal GDP in the twentieth century. In fact, when comparing GDP and earnings growth side by side, decade by decade (see Exhibit 3.3), S&P earnings growth has outpaced GDP growth only once—in the 1990s, when nominal GDP grew at 5.6 percent and S&P 500 earnings rose at 7.1 percent! This, coupled with the superhigh earnings growth in the mid-2000s, has led many investors to believe that earnings growth in the future is likely to exceed nominal GDP growth.

After a major earnings decline in 2001, S&P 500 earnings grew at a fast pace, far exceeding GDP growth of 5.4 percent, from 2002 to 2005. Many investors were caught off guard by the surprising earnings growth.

As you can see in Exhibit 3.7, earnings of S&P 500 companies grew more than 20 percent during 2004 and 2005, and climbed another 6 percent in 2006. This astonishing growth has exceeded the GDP, which topped out at 7 percent in 2004 and has grown at a slower rate in 2005 and 2006.

There were two reasons for supernormal, above-GDP earnings growth rate after 2002:

1. In the 2001 recession, S&P 500 earnings were halved. The growth of earnings that followed came from a depressed based (see Exhibit 3.7).
2. After 2003, growth came from the corporate margin expanding into above-average territory (see Exhibit 3.8)—as we are about to learn, a finite type of growth.

The Profit Margin Paradigm

> *Profit margins are probably the most mean-reverting series in finance, and if profit margins do not mean-revert, then something has gone badly wrong with capitalism. If high profits do not attract competition, there is something wrong with the system and it is not functioning properly.*
>
> —Jeremy Grantham, *Barron's*

Maybe we are in a new era of faster than GDP earnings growth. Profit margin is a link between GDP and earnings growth. It appears (see Exhibit 3.8) that the source of this abnormal earnings growth is profit margin expansion (here we define profit margins as corporate profits divided by GDP), from 7.0 percent at the end of the third quarter of 2001 to a

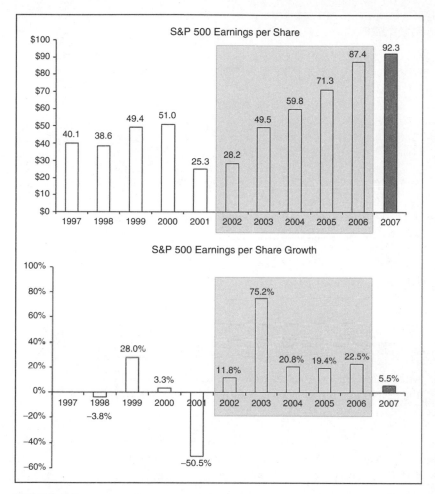

EXHIBIT 3.7 S&P 500 Earnings Growth
Data Source: Standard & Poor's Compustat (2006 and 2007 EPS are estimated).

whopping 12.4 percent in the third quarter of 2006. As profit margins rise, corporations get to keep more of their sales revenue, leading to improved profitability. To put things in perspective, the average profit margin for corporate America from 1981 to 2006 was approximately 8.8 percent, 3.6 percent less than it is at the end of 2006.

Are the billions of dollars dedicated to productivity enhancements between the 1990s and the 2000s finally paying off? Has the new era of technology-induced corporate efficiency descended upon us? Are we in a

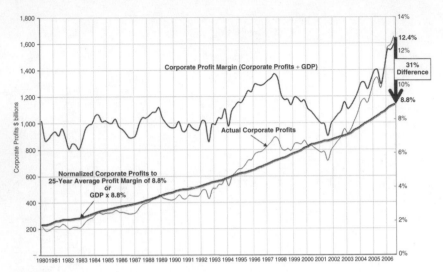

EXHIBIT 3.8   The Future of Corporate Profits: The "E" in the P/E Equation
Data Source: U.S. Bureau of Economic Analysis (www.bea.gov).

new economy, a higher profit margin paradigm? The answer to all questions is no.

The Fallacy of Composition

Corporate America's enormous investment in technology did not go to waste. It made companies more efficient, helping them to produce more with less—the definition of productivity. That's the good news. The bad news is that technology improvements have been available to everyone. Oracle will sell its software to any company that can spell "Oracle" on a multimillion-dollar check. This is where the economic concept fallacy of composition (what is true for a part may not be true for the whole) kicks into high gear. Though technological investment may help the first adapter to cut costs and get a leg up on the competition, competitors won't watch their economic pie being eaten by a more efficient company. Those who sit still will be driven out of business. The others will adapt by writing a big fat check to Oracle or Microsoft, eventually catching up and competing the higher margins away. Thus, what was true for one company is not true for the industry.

As much as we would love to believe that productivity improvements brought to us by technological innovations will transform into corporate profitability, historically that has not been the case. Wal-Mart, for example, has changed the retail landscape by installing the most (at the time) revolutionary inventory management and distribution systems, passing on the cost savings to the consumer, and driving less efficient competitors out of business.

However, Wal-Mart-like technology is available off the shelf to any retailer aspiring to coexist in today's competitive landscape. Even companies like Dollar General, with stores the size of several Wal-Mart bathrooms put together, wrote sizable checks to Manhattan Associates and installed perpetual inventory and automatic reordering systems. This investment will keep Dollar General in the game by helping it survive in the new competitive environment, but is unlikely to send its margins much higher than today's level.

In short, we have likely maxed out on profit growth, at least from new technologies that companies implemented in the past 10 years. There may be newer technological breakthroughs to come that will lead to further improvements in profits, but this scenario will take decades to play out and provide only a temporary (key word: *temporary*) shot in the arm for corporate profit margins.

Should All-Time-High Corporate Margins Worry Investors?

Exhibit 3.8 also shows where corporate profits would have been historically if the profit margins were always at average—normalized profits. I took 8.8 percent (the average profit margin over the past 25 years) and multiplied it by the corresponding GDP. As we can see, every time corporate profits (profit margins) have risen above normalized territory they have reverted back. As is also apparent from Exhibit 3.8, at the beginning of 2007 corporate profit margins are still hovering at levels much above average; if they come back and stop at their average, corporate profits would decline by 31 percent.

Going into 2007, stock market valuation is higher than it may appear. At some point margins will revert to the historical average and corporate earnings growth will either decelerate—disappointing Wall Street expectations—or decline, driving earnings, the "E" in the P/E equation, down. The broad market index fund investor may be in a pickle when a cheap market suddenly becomes more expensive. If corporate profitability reverts toward the mean profit margins observed over the past 25 years, corporate profits will decline. (A side note: This may be the cause of the next cyclical bear market; investors got used to double-digit profit growth, but they'll get declining or stagnating earnings growth instead.)

Putting macro-shmacro stuff aside, why does this all matter to investors holding individual stocks? Companies that don't have a sustainable competitive advantage (a metaphorical moat around their business, as Warren Buffett puts it) will not get to keep the benefits of increased productivity. These benefits will get competed away, and their margins will decline. Do you own one of those companies? I strongly recommend you take a look at the companies whose margins are hitting all-time highs, and examine their competitive landscape and their business for sustainable competitive advantage.[2]

Growth of GDP will likely outpace earnings growth over the next several years as corporate profit margins embark on a mean reversion voyage, dragging earnings growth with them.

Reversion to the Mean Fallacy

The concept of mean reversion is often misunderstood. The mean is the center point number between a series of low and high numbers—no surprise there. The confusion usually arises in application of reversion to the mean concept. Profit margins are some of the most mean-reverting ratios in finance. Investors often assume when the mean reversion takes place that these ratios settle at the mean; this is incorrect.

Although profit margins may settle at the mean, that is not what the concept of mean reversion implies; it implies *direction* of the movement. Assuming the center point of a given ratio is still the center point, the ratio should revisit the other extreme while going through the mean. If profit margins are in the area above the mean, they at some point should revisit the area below the mean, and vice versa. The same logic applies to other mean-reverting measures (e.g., return on capital, P/Es, etc.).

Maybe if the mean reversion concept were given a different name—for instance, "reversion toward and beyond the mean"—nobody would expect P/Es and profit margins to automatically settle at the mean.

SOURCES OF CAPITAL APPRECIATION: PRICE TO EARNINGS

Elements of P/E

To understand valuation, we have to look at the elements that comprise it. In this section we get into the brass tacks of valuation, and we'll need to use jargon. If you know what all the terms mean, skip ahead. Otherwise, I get to be your terminology teacher.

Take the phrase "P/E based on 12-month (or 1-year, 3-year, 5-year, 10-year) trailing earnings." Some may think I speak like this so I sound smarter. I do! There are many different ways to calculate a ratio as an "any price to anything" ratio (price to cash flows, price to book, price to sales, price to square feet, etc.).

First, we need to understand what price-earnings (P/E) ratio means. The "P" is typically the price of a stock or an index on the date of the reference. "P" or price is usually consistent. The only exception being Robert Shiller's data (Dow Jones, S&P, price, earnings, dividends, CPI) from his web site (http://www.econ.yale.edu/~shiller/), which I frequently used throughout the book. Shiller doesn't use a closing price for the month in reference. Rather, he averages the prices for the month. His argument is that investors buy stocks throughout the month, not on the last closing day of the month; thus average monthly price is a more appropriate measure of index performance.

In the ratio of price to anything, most of the change takes place in the denominator. In the P/E ratio, the "E" could reference a wide variety of time periods—trailing earnings trail the stock price by a certain declared period of time. Five-year trailing earnings are an average of earnings over the past five years. The same logic applies to any number that exceeds 12 months.

Why would anybody use 10-, 5-, and 3-year earnings averages to calculate P/E? To smooth out short-term noise. One-year data has a lot of volatility that comes with the natural cyclicality of the economy. Corporate profit margins may be hitting all-time highs or lows, and one-year look-back earnings may understate or overstate the true economic earning power of a stock or an index. Taking an average of earnings over a longer period often solves that problem, as a span of several years typically is enough to cover at least part of an economic cycle, reducing the noise in the data.

The Price to Earnings Acrobatics or Reversion Beyond the Mean

Where are we? I hate to be the one delivering bad news in the beginning of 2007, but long after the last leg of the 1982–2000 bull market ended, the valuations are still high.

Some may argue that using the "E"—earnings in the P/E ratio— calculated for just one time period (e.g., latest trailing 12 months) may be incomplete and misleading, as it could be easily distorted by one-time events, and I agree. So to put any concerns to rest I've calculated in Exhibits 3.9, 3.10, 3.11, and 3.12 P/Es based on "E" covering diverse time spans, 1-, 3-, 5-, and 10-year average earnings.

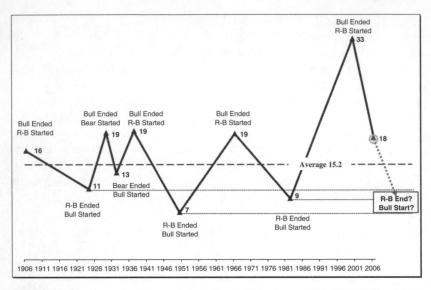

EXHIBIT 3.9 Reversion Beyond the Mean: Beginning and Ending 1-Year Trailing P/Es for S&P 500

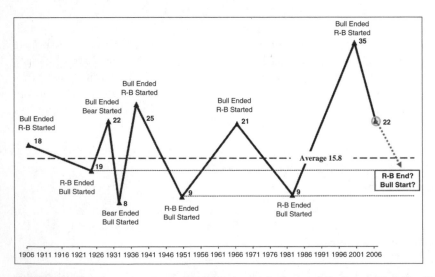

EXHIBIT 3.10 Reversion Beyond the Mean: Beginning and Ending 3-Year Trailing P/Es for S&P 500

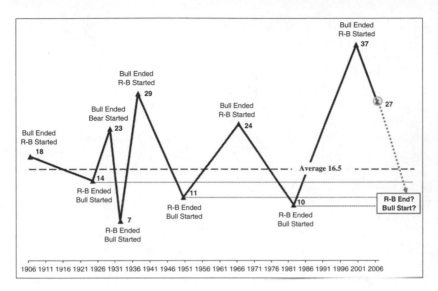

EXHIBIT 3.11 Reversion Beyond the Mean: Beginning and Ending 5-Year Trailing P/Es for S&P 500

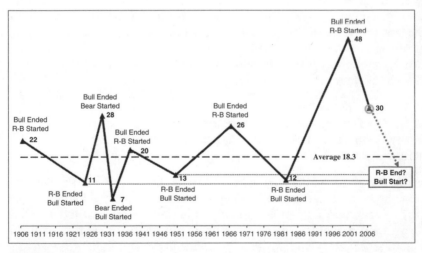

EXHIBIT 3.12 Reversion Beyond the Mean: Beginning and Ending 10-Year Trailing P/Es for S&P 500

The secular bull market of 1982–2000 ended (and the 2000–2020 or so range-bound market started) at the highest P/E of any bull market in the twentieth century. The highest! In 2000, the S&P 500's P/E was at 33 times 1-year earnings, 35 times average 3-year earnings, 37 times average 5-year earnings, and 48 times average 10-year earnings.

The higher the valuations of stocks are at the beginning of the range-bound market, the more likely that the range-bound market will last longer. It takes more time to gradually deflate a higher starting P/E to the below-average one, assuming economic growth doesn't change much from the past (we will discuss this in greater detail in just a couple of pages).

Even at the end of 2006, after investors had already received close to six years of little or no returns from the broad market indexes, S&P 500 P/E ratios (computed on 1-, 3-, 5-, and 10-year trailing earnings) still were close to the levels where previous range-bound markets have started. Therefore, even though the range-bound markets in the twentieth century lasted from 13 to 18 years, the current range-bound market has all the markers in place to indicate that it will last longer than the ones that took place in the twentieth century.

Finally, as Exhibit 3.8 showed, P/E calculated based on 1-year trailing earnings appears to be understated (as "E" in the P/E ratio is overstated), considering that corporate profit margins are hovering at all-time highs and are likely to revert toward and even beyond the mean (i.e., go lower), leading to a lower "E" in the P/E equation.

Stocks are unlikely to settle at their fair valuation—they never have, at least in the twentieth century. Negative emotions that accumulate in the market since the prior bull market are apt to drive stock prices far below their intrinsic value, as has occurred every time in the past century. At the end of each of the range-bound markets that took place in the twentieth century, as is apparent from Exhibits 3.9, 3.10, 3.11, and 3.12, P/Es fell far below the average.

It Is Not the Economy, It Is Not Earnings, It Is Not Inflation. What Is It? Valuation! Starting Valuation Matters—A Lot

We just discussed that at the end of 2006 the U.S. stock market was still trading at high valuations. Why does it matter? Starting valuation is one of the most important factors in determining future returns. Exhibit 3.13 clearly supports that statement. I computed a median annual rate of return for both stocks only and stocks plus dividends over 5- and 10-year time periods, as if an investor bought the S&P 500 index, breaking down the returns based on the P/E at the time of purchase. This study covered the 1900–2005 time period. One doesn't have to be a statistician to observe a clear correlation between the P/E at the time of the investment and the returns (stocks only and/or total returns) that an investor receives in 5 or 10 years.

Lower P/Es lead to higher returns, and higher P/Es lead to lower returns. The conclusion is consistent when "E" in the P/E equation is computed on 12-month, 3-year, and 5-year trailing earnings. If stocks are bought when

EXHIBIT 3.13   Starting P/E Matters!

Median Returns from S&P 500 Stocks, 1900–2005

| | P/E Based on 1-Year Trailing Earnings | | | |
| | Stocks Only | | Total Return | |
Returns in:	5 Years	10 Years	5 Years	10 Years
P/E Less Than 10	10.5%	10.8%	16.6%	16.1%
P/E Between 10 and 12	8.2	6.8	13.5	12.6
P/E Between 12 and 16	3.8	3.2	8.9	9.0
P/E Between 16 and 20	3.0	2.3	7.3	7.1
P/E Greater Than 20	4.3	4.3	7.9	8.2

| | P/E Based on 3-Year Average Earnings | | | |
| | Stocks Only | | Total Return | |
Returns in:	5 Years	10 Years	5 Years	10 Years
P/E Less Than 10	11.7%	11.1%	17.3%	16.2%
P/E Between 10 and 12	7.6	8.4	12.8	14.1
P/E Between 12 and 16	3.3	2.4	8.8	8.3
P/E Between 16 and 20	4.2	3.3	8.6	7.8
P/E Greater Than 20	2.1	3.3	5.6	7.5

| | P/E Based on 5-Year Average Earnings | | | |
| | Stocks Only | | Total Return | |
Returns in:	5 Years	10 Years	5 Years	10 Years
P/E Less Than 10	11.5%	10.2%	17.3%	16.2%
P/E Between 10 and 12	11.1	10.1	16.4	14.7
P/E Between 12 and 16	3.3	2.9	8.7	9.0
P/E Between 16 and 20	4.5	4.5	9.3	8.6
P/E Greater Than 20	2.8	2.2	6.1	6.8

the P/E is below average (less than 12), P/E is the investors' best friend, as its expansion turns into a source of returns (adding to earnings growth and dividend yield). However, if stocks are purchased when the P/E is above average (greater than 16), the P/E turns into a foe, as its compression diminishes returns.

Still not convinced? In Exhibit 3.14, I dissect the source of stock appreciation/declines for every secular market that took place during the twentieth century.

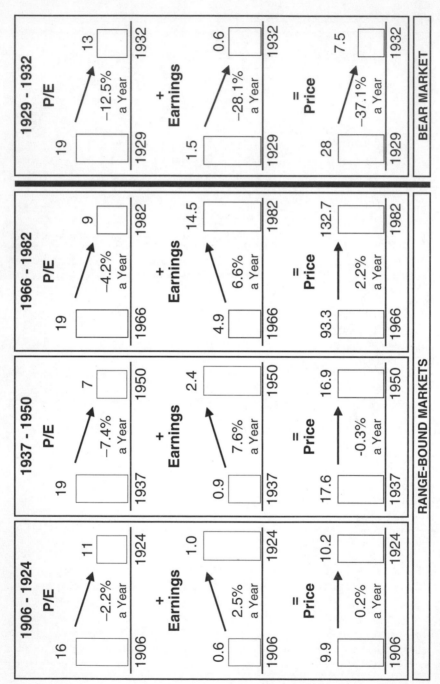

EXHIBIT 3.14 Sources of Capital Appreciation

1906 – 1924

P/E
16 → 11
−2.2% a Year
1906 — 1924

+

Earnings
0.6 → 1.0
2.5% a Year
1906 — 1924

=

Price
9.9 → 10.2
0.2% a Year
1906 — 1924

1937 – 1950

P/E
19 → 7
−7.4% a Year
1937 — 1950

+

Earnings
0.9 → 2.4
7.6% a Year
1937 — 1950

=

Price
17.6 → 16.9
-0.3% a Year
1937 — 1950

1966 – 1982

P/E
19 → 9
−4.2% a Year
1966 — 1982

+

Earnings
4.9 → 14.5
6.6% a Year
1966 — 1982

=

Price
93.3 → 132.7
2.2% a Year
1966 — 1982

RANGE-BOUND MARKETS

1929 – 1932

P/E
19 → 13
−12.5% a Year
1929 — 1932

+

Earnings
1.5 → 0.6
−28.1% a Year
1929 — 1932

=

Price
28 → 7.5
−37.1% a Year
1929 — 1932

BEAR MARKET

54

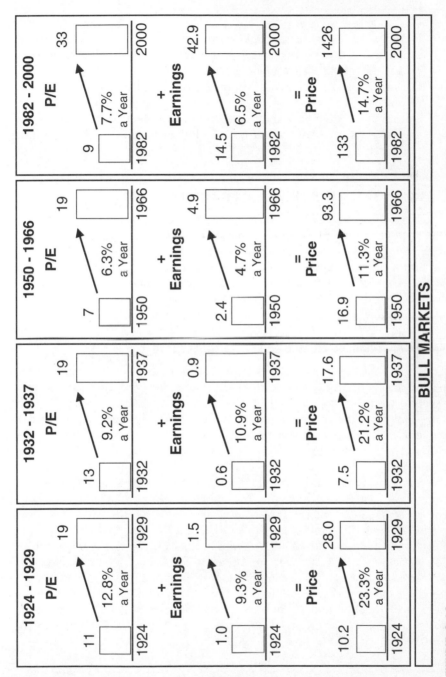

BULL MARKETS

EXHIBIT 3.14 *(Continued)*

It is evident that:

- P/E expansion was the source of returns, the tailwind in the sails of the bull market boosting stock returns. It was solely responsible for sending returns for stocks into double-digit territory.
- P/E turned into a headwind in range-bound and bear markets, solely responsible for paltry returns of stocks in range-bound markets. P/E contraction during bear and range-bound markets was the payback for excessive returns that came from the P/E expansion of the preceding bull market.

P/E Expansion Is a Finite Source of Stock Appreciation

The P/E may expand for a long period of time, as happened in every secular bull market during the twentieth century. However, P/E expansion is finite. Although there is no arithmetical limit to how much the market P/E could expand, P/Es have never touched the stars (though some may argue that in the late 1990s they came close); P/Es always found their limits. Stocks compete with other asset classes, and as P/Es rise investors pay more for the same earnings, making stocks less attractive than alternatives.

The Market Spends Little Time in a Rational State

The stock market is a strange fellow: It has multiple personalities. One personality is in an extreme state of happiness, but the other suffers from severe depression. Rarely do the two come to the surface at once. Usually one dominates the other for long periods of time. In the long run these personalities cancel each other out, so on average the stock market is a rational fellow. But rarely does the stock market behave in an average manner.

The extremities of human emotion prevent the market from spending much time in a rational state—at fair valuation. In Exhibit 3.15 I compute the percentage of time the three-year trailing P/E for the S&P 500 spent within different P/E ranges (14–16, 13–17, and 11–19). As we can see from Exhibit 3.10, during the twentieth century stocks traded on average at 15.8 times earnings, the perceived fair valuation level. But Exhibit 3.15 shows that stocks spent only 13 percent of the time between P/Es of 14 and 16, 27 percent of the time between P/Es of 13 and 17, and only about half the time between P/Es of 11 and 19. In the majority of cases the market reached its fair valuation (P/E of around 15) in passing from one irrational extreme to another (see Exhibit 1.1).

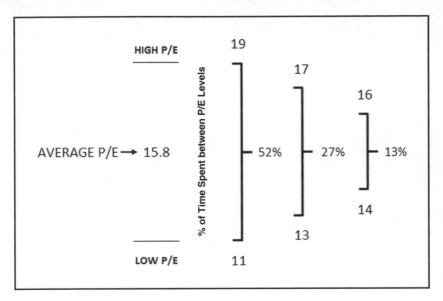

EXHIBIT 3.15 Time Spent within Ranges of P/Es for S&P 500 Stocks, 1900–2006 (Based on Three-Year Trailing Earnings)

At what P/E will the market settle this time? Mark Twain said: "History doesn't repeat itself—but it rhymes." One outcome appears to be likely: The market will bottom at a rhyming P/E that will fall significantly below the historical average P/E of 15—it has every single time at the end of each range-bound market in the twentieth century.

The 1982–2000 bull market ended at a P/E much above those of the preceding bull markets. The current range-bound market has all the predispositions (particularly high valuation) to last longer than the ones that came before it.

SOURCES OF DIVIDEND YIELD

Earnings Yield

A double shot of espresso may be required to prevent you from falling asleep while we take a stroll down dividend yield lane. Conversations about dividend yield are as exciting as the volatility of returns from money market funds or Treasury bills. Suddenly I feel like that anthropologist making jokes about dinosaur reproduction and being the only one to understand the humor and laugh at the jokes. However, as unexciting as dividends are, Exhibit 3.16, in which I dissect sources of returns in different secular markets, shows that dividends contributed the bulk of the returns to previous range-bound markets. In fact, of the 5.9 percent average total return investors received in the range-bound markets of the twentieth century, 5.3 percent came from dividends; dividends contributed more than 90 percent of total return!

The current secular range-bound market started (or the secular 1982–2000 bull market ended) with a 1.2 percent dividend yield—historically the lowest by far in relation to yield at the start of previous range-bound markets. At the end of 2006, six years into a range-bound market, the dividend yield was nothing to be excited about; it has increased since 2000, but as is apparent from Exhibit 3.17, it is still low.

EXHIBIT 3.16   Sources of Total Return for S&P 500

	Twentieth Century
Source of Return	1/31/1900– 12/31/2000
Price	4.6%
Dividends	5.5%
Total Return	10.4%
% of Total Return from Dividends	45%

	Range-Bound Markets			
Source of Return	1/31/1906– 12/31/1924	1/31/1937– 1/31/1950	1/31/1966– 10/31/1982	Average
Price	0.2%	−0.3%	2.1%	0.7%
Dividends	5.9%	5.7%	4.1%	5.3%
Total Return	6.1%	5.4%	6.3%	5.9%
% of Total Return from Dividends	97%	106%	65%	90%

	Bull Markets			
Source of Return	12/31/1924– 10/31/1929	8/31/1932– 1/31/1937	1/31/1950– 1/31/1966	10/31/1982– 1/31/2000	Average
Price	23.3%	21.2%	11.3%	14.7%	17.6%
Dividends	4.7%	4.8%	4.3%	3.0%	4.2%
Total Return	29.1%	27.0%	16.0%	18.2%	22.6%
% of Total Return from Dividends	16%	18%	27%	17%	19%

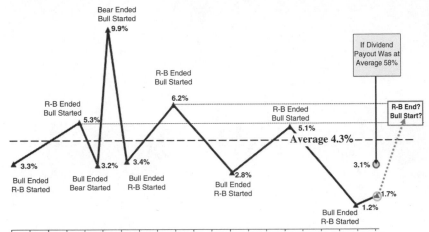

EXHIBIT 3.17 Dividend Yield Ups and Downs (Based on One-Year Trailing Dividends and Earnings of S&P 500)
Data Sources: Robert J. Shiller; Standard & Poor's Compustat.

Return received from dividends is expressed in dividend yield—dollar dividend per share divided by stock price. Or it can be expressed:

$$\text{Dividend Yield} = \frac{\text{Dividend per Share}}{\text{Price}} = \frac{\text{Earnings per Share}}{\text{Price}}$$
$$\times \frac{\text{Dividend}}{\text{Earnings per Share}}$$

Or:

$$\text{Dividend Yield} = \text{Earnings Yield} \times \text{Dividend Payout}$$

The higher the P/E ratio, the lower the earnings yield. The dividend yield at the end of 2006 is low, just as market valuation (P/E) is high, as Exhibits 3.9, 3.10, 3.11, and 3.12 indicate. Yes, it is that simple.

Dividend Payout

High valuation is only part of the reason why the dividend yield at the end of 2006 was so low; the dividend payout is at one of the lowest levels ever.

As is apparent from Exhibit 3.18, the dividend payout at the end of 2006 was about 32 percent. If the dividend payout was at the average level, based on earnings at the end of 2006, dividend yield would have translated

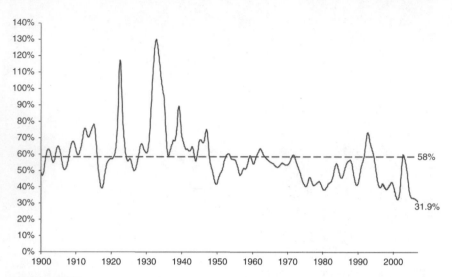

EXHIBIT 3.18   Dividend Payout Is Close to All-Time Low (Computed Based on S&P 500 One-Year Trailing Dividends and Earnings)

into about 3.1 percent. This is close to yields exhibited at the beginning of preceding range-bound markets, but still substantially below the levels occurring when the range-bound markets ended and bulls markets started (see Exhibit 3.17).

A note of warning about judging dividend payouts: Remember that the dividend payout is the dividend divided by earnings. There is some natural cyclical volatility to earnings: During the economic expansion cycle earnings (profit margins) are higher, and during economic contractions earnings (profit margins) are lower than the full economic cycle average. Dividend payments, in contrast, are less volatile time series. During an economic recession companies usually maintain their dividends despite lower earnings; this leads to a higher dividend payout. During an economic expansion phase, growths of dividend payments lag earnings growth, resulting in a lower dividend payout ratio.

Throughout the 1990s, corporate America used an "unfavorable tax treatment" excuse to explain relatively low dividend payout ratios and a preoccupation with stock buybacks. This is because dividends were taxed at the ordinary income tax rate—usually higher than the capital gains tax rate at the time of 20 percent. Companies argued that investors could create a "homegrown" dividend by selling a portion of appreciated stock to create the desired dividend and pay lower taxes on the capital gain in comparison to the tax on a dividend payment. However, the tax cuts of 2002 took that excuse away, and long-term capital gains and dividend payments became taxed at the same rate.

In time, investors, disappointed with subpar stock performance and meager dividend yields on the majority of U.S. stocks, will force companies (by shareholder activism and by favoring companies with higher dividend yields) to raise dividend payouts at the expense of share buybacks. Therefore, the dividend growth of the overall market is likely to outpace earnings growth over the next decade.

WHY RANGE-BOUND MARKETS FOLLOW BULL MARKETS

There is one constant in the world, and that is human emotions. Range-bound markets follow bull markets not because the investment gods want to play a practical joke on gullible humans, who have become accustomed to receiving above-average returns during prolonged bull markets. Nor is it because there is some kind of hidden order (the conspiracy theorist's dream), or a subliminal pattern, or a multilegged wave buried in the deep psyche of the stock market. They follow because excess optimism feeds on itself and drives stock market valuation to one extreme, and then unmet expectations turn into disappointment, driving stock valuations to the opposite extreme. Long excesses require lengthy corrections.

During the 1990s bull market, investors became accustomed to receiving bull market returns that were supersized by significant P/E expansion. As the bull market ends at valuations far above average, P/Es go from expansion into a contraction phase (reversion toward the mean); therefore, stocks start bringing returns to investors that are not average but far below, shattering linear expectations of an above-average (bull market) paradise with a cold shower of reality that is constantly getting even colder.

It takes a long time for an emotional cycle to reach its climax, and thus it takes a similar time to reverse that cycle and drive valuations to the other extreme. This is why in the twentieth century every protracted secular bull market (which all ran about 17 years, give or take a few) was followed by a similar length range-bound market. For the next sustained bull market to start, a strong thrust of P/E expansion is needed, and therefore the market has to revisit a below-average P/E environment first.

IT IS NOT OVER UNTIL IT IS OVER

In Chapter 1, I made a claim that if history is any guide the current range-bound market will last until 2020 or so. How do I know that? I don't. I guesstimated based on the framework I am about to discuss.

I like simple things, and this framework is fairly simple and straightforward. We only need to take a stab at several wildly unpredictable variables and voilà, we have ourselves an answer. We need to forecast inflation, real earnings growth, the P/E level at which the stock market will settle at the end of the range-bound market, and, finally, whether the slope of the market will be completely flat, or slightly tilted upward or downward. And did I mention we are making these forecasts for a long-term time period, 10 to 20 years out?

As I'll mention many times throughout the book, paraphrasing John Maynard Keynes, I am just trying to be vaguely right, not precisely wrong. Don't let the precision of the calculations in this chapter deceive you; I am about to use a precision of math just to illustrate a point—that we are still years away from the end of this range-bound market.

I have no illusions about my forecasting crystal ball. It is as helpful as the snow globes I buy at the airport gift shops for my kids after every business trip. And these snow globes tell me that it snows in all major cities of the United States all the time and any time of the year; so they are not very predictive, though still right on occasion. But understanding the inputs that create a range-bound market's longevity is even more important than guessing when it will end. So let's dive in.

- *Real economic growth*. As we discussed in this chapter, the real GDP growth was consistent through the twentieth century, hovering around 3.5 percent. We also discussed that the profit margin is a link between GDP (the sales) and earnings growth. So if history keeps repeating itself and real GDP growth keeps going at 3.5 percent, we only have to focus on the profit margins. Given that the profit margins are at above-average levels, I am inclined to forecast earnings growth to be lower than GDP growth. By how much? Be my guest. I picked annual real earnings growth to be a nice round number of 3 percent. With this assumption I am basically ignoring short-term ups and downs, focusing on the long term.
- *Inflation*. As we can see from Exhibit 3.3, inflation averaged a bit higher than 3 percent during the twentieth century. Some may argue that with globalization upon us, the inflation rate is likely to decline. I say all right, how about using inflation of 2.5 percent?
- *Nominal earnings growth*. Now that with scientific certainty (not!) we picked real annual earnings growth rate of 3 percent and inflation of

2.5 percent, we can agree that nominal annual earnings growth will be around 5.5 percent a year.

- *Net earnings growth.* If market prices are at exactly the same level at the end of the range-bound market as they are while reading this, then net earnings growth and nominal earnings growth would be the same thing. However, cyclical markets may drive the market price significantly up or down. As you can see from Exhibit 3.14, in the first two range-bound markets (1906–1924 and 1937–1950) the prices of the S&P 500 index did not go up or down much from where those respective range-bound markets started. However, during the third (1966–1982) range-bound market, the prices of the S&P 500 actually went up at a 2.2 percent annual rate.

  If you forecast that stock prices may appreciate over the full duration of the secular range-bound market, that appreciation should be subtracted from nominal earnings growth, as it slows down the approach to the final P/E. If you forecast a decline in stock prices, that earnings growth in price should be added to the nominal earnings growth, as it accelerates the approach to the final P/E. Let's take the 1966–1982 range-bound market. The net earnings growth was about 4.4 percent (6.6 percent nominal annual earnings growth less annual price appreciation of 2.2 percent). My crystal ball is mute on whether, in the long run, price appreciation will be positive or negative, so I'll assume that the prices will not change much and the price level will stay where it is as of this writing.

  Also, please realize we are not talking about significant long-term appreciation or decline; otherwise we'd be staring into a bull or bear market. Unless the economic picture deteriorates substantially in the long run, the bear market is an unlikely scenario (using history as a guide), and for a bull market to start we'd need to see the other side, below-average P/E.

- *The final P/E.* Depending on whether you choose to use 1-, 3-, 5-, or 10-year P/E, average earnings will differ. I like the 5-year P/E number because it filters out a lot of noise that comes from volatility of profit margins, and still covers a relevant time period. Again, in the twentieth century, range-bound markets ended when the 5-year trailing P/E was between 10 and 14. Since we are coming off one of the U.S.'s greatest bull markets, using "the higher they come up the harder (lower) they'll fall" logic, my instinct would be to use the lower P/E. But out of curiosity I'll guesstimate the longevity of the range-bound market using 10 (low), 12 (average), and 14 (high) ending P/E ratios.

- *A starting P/E.* Since I am using 5-year trailing earnings, I'll use 5-year starting P/E as well, which at this writing stood at 27 times (see Exhibit 3.11).

EXHIBIT 3.19 Years to Bull Market? Earnings Growth 5.5 Percent

Starting Price to Earnings

Ending Price to Earnings	37	36	35	34	33	32	31	30	29	28	27	26	25	24	23	22	21	20	19
18	13.5	12.9	12.4	11.9	11.3	10.7	10.2	9.5	8.9	8.3	7.6	6.9	6.1	5.4	4.6	3.7	2.9	2.0	1.0
17	14.5	14.0	13.5	12.9	12.4	11.8	11.2	10.6	10.0	9.3	8.6	7.9	7.2	6.4	5.6	4.8	3.9	3.0	2.1
16	15.7	15.1	14.6	14.1	13.5	12.9	12.4	11.7	11.1	10.5	9.8	9.1	8.3	7.6	6.8	5.9	5.1	4.2	3.2
15	16.9	16.4	15.8	15.3	14.7	14.2	13.6	12.9	12.3	11.7	11.0	10.3	9.5	8.8	8.0	7.2	6.3	5.4	4.4
14	18.2	17.6	17.1	16.6	16.0	15.4	14.8	14.2	13.6	12.9	12.3	11.6	10.8	10.1	9.3	8.4	7.6	6.7	5.7
13	19.5	19.0	18.5	18.0	17.4	16.8	16.2	15.6	15.0	14.3	13.7	12.9	12.2	11.5	10.7	9.8	9.0	8.0	7.1
12	21.0	20.5	20.0	19.5	18.9	18.3	17.7	17.1	16.5	15.8	15.1	14.4	13.7	12.9	12.2	11.3	10.5	9.5	8.6
11	22.7	22.1	21.6	21.1	20.5	19.9	19.4	18.7	18.1	17.5	16.8	16.1	15.3	14.6	13.8	12.9	12.1	11.2	10.2
10	24.4	23.9	23.4	22.9	22.3	21.7	21.1	20.5	19.9	19.2	18.6	17.8	17.1	16.4	15.6	14.7	13.9	12.9	12.0
9	26.4	25.9	25.4	24.8	24.3	23.7	23.1	22.5	21.9	21.2	20.5	19.8	19.1	18.3	17.5	16.7	15.8	14.9	14.0
8	28.6	28.1	27.6	27.0	26.5	25.9	25.3	24.7	24.1	23.4	22.7	22.0	21.3	20.5	19.7	18.9	18.0	17.1	16.2

The model is simple. We have a starting point (starting P/E) and ending point (final P/E). We have the net earnings growth rate (the metaphorical train that left the high P/E station and is cruising toward the low P/E station at a constant rate). All we need to do is figure out how much time it would take for the market (the train) to get to the final destination before it changes its direction and turns into a bull market.

I created several simple tables differentiated by the net earnings growth. Exhibit 3.19 is included in this chapter, and the rest are waiting for you in the Appendix. You need to pick starting points—the beginning P/Es—and a final destination—the final P/E—and thus figure out how much time it would take to get to the final destination. Let's take Exhibit 3.19, for example: If net earnings growth is 5.5 percent and the final P/E is 14, it would take a secular range-bound market about 12.3 years to reach its final destination—the assumption I used to arrive at my 2020 estimate of the run for the current range-bound market. If the net earnings growth rate remained at 5.5 percent and final P/E were 10 or 11, it would take the market 18.6 or 16.8 years to reach the final destination, respectively.

CHAPTER 4

Bonds: A Viable Alternative?

*Stocks usually yield a higher average rate of return than bonds,
since stocks have a variable rate of return (including, sometimes,
no return at all), while bonds have a guaranteed fixed rate of
return. It is not the moral principle that makes it happen. It
happens because people will not take the risk of buying stocks
unless they can expect a higher average rate of return than they get
in bonds.*

—Thomas Sowell, *Basic Economics*

WHY NOT BONDS?

In this chapter we briefly examine the performance of stocks and bonds in
various markets. Why not just buy bonds and forget about stocks? That
sounds like a worry-free plan, doesn't it? Especially considering that returns
from stocks in range-bound markets are nothing to brag about.

Unfortunately, in the past two range-bound markets returns from
bonds have not been home runs, either. As is apparent from Exhibits 4.1
and 4.2, during the 1937–1950 and 1966–1982 range-bound markets, U.S.
Treasury bond returns actually lagged the returns from stocks, but not on a
consistent basis.

As we can see in Exhibits 4.1 and 4.2, U.S. Treasury bills significantly underperformed both stocks and U.S. Treasury bonds during the
1937–1950 range-bound market, but they outperformed both U.S. Treasury bonds and stocks in the 1966–1982 range-bound market; this makes
sense, as the latter time period was characterized by high inflation. Treasury
bills are short-term instruments; they mature in less than a year and as soon
as 30 days. At the time of maturation/reissuance, investors may demand
higher yield from fixed income instruments. Since U.S. Treasury bills are

EXHIBIT 4.1   Real Returns of Stocks versus Fixed Income Instruments, Range-Bound Market of 1966–1982

Data Sources: Treasury bonds and bills—Ibbotson; Stocks (S&P 500) and CPI—Robert J. Shiller (12/31/1965–10/30/1982).

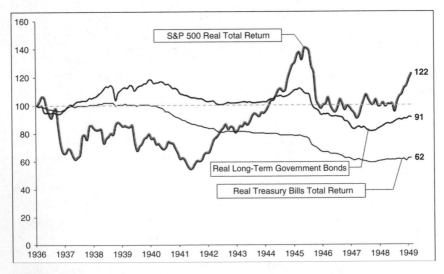

EXHIBIT 4.2   Real Returns of Stocks versus Fixed Income Instruments, Range-Bound Market of 1937–1950

Data Sources: Treasury bonds and bills—Ibbotson; Stocks (S&P 500) and CPI—Robert J. Shiller (12/31/1936–1/31/1950).

reissued more often than Treasury bonds, which by definition take at least 10 years to mature, U.S. Treasury bill yields adjust more quickly to an environment of higher inflation.

However, looking at real stock and bond performance, one cannot dismiss the fact that stocks have outperformed both U.S. Treasury bonds and U.S. Treasury bills on a marginal basis—although, again, not all the time. In fact, bonds dominated returns of stocks for a good two-thirds of the 1937–1950 range-bound market. Treasury bills actually outperformed stocks, albeit by a small margin, in the 1966–1982 range-bound market.

Taking a quick glance at real stock, Treasury bond, and Treasury bill returns in bull markets (see Exhibits 4.3 and 4.4), it is evident that stocks have beaten their counterparts with their eyes closed—no surprise there. Dominance of either buy-and-hold or passive investment strategies is not, however, as clear and persistent during range-bound markets.

ASSET ALLOCATION ROLE IS DIMINISHED IN RANGE-BOUND MARKETS

Ninety percent of returns comes from asset allocation, says an old Wall Street adage, implying that it is more important to pick the right asset class than to pick individual securities in each corresponding asset class. Is this adage true for all markets?

Exhibits 4.5 and 4.6 depict the performance of stocks, U.S. Treasury bonds, and U.S. Treasury bills during the 1982–2000 bull market and the 1966–1982 range-bound market, respectively. I've computed five-year annual rates of return for these asset classes from the beginning to the end of those markets on a continuous monthly basis. I used five-year time periods to eliminate short-term noise from the returns. Then, I separated these annual rates of returns into four quartiles and computed an average return for each quartile.

As shown in Exhibit 4.5, in the 1982–2000 period stock returns dominated U.S. Treasury bonds and U.S. Treasury bills hands down. Even at their worst performance (bottom quartile) stocks outperformed the first three quartiles of U.S. Treasury bonds and all four quartiles of U.S. Treasury bills. Thus, during a bull market asset allocation (being in stocks versus fixed income instruments) accounts for the majority of returns. Even if an investor had owned U.S. Treasury bills at their best performance stretch between 1982 and 2000, their returns would still have lagged the returns of stocks at their worst performance stretch.

It is apparent that even if an investor assembles a diversified portfolio of so-so stocks, does little reshuffling of the portfolio, and stays fully invested

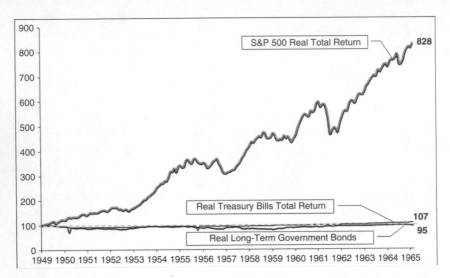

EXHIBIT 4.3 Real Returns of Stocks versus Fixed Income Instruments, Bull Market of 1950–1966
Data Sources: Treasury bills and bonds—Ibbotson; CPI and Stocks (S&P 500)—Robert J. Shiller.

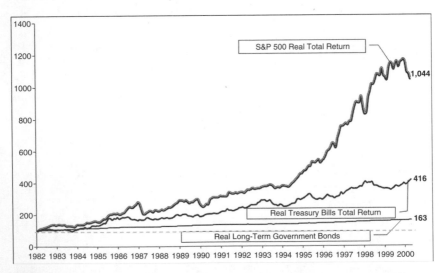

EXHIBIT 4.4 Real Returns of Stocks versus Fixed Income Instruments, Bull Market of 1982–2000
Data Sources: Treasury bills and bonds—Ibbotson; CPI and Stocks (S&P 500)—Robert J. Shiller.

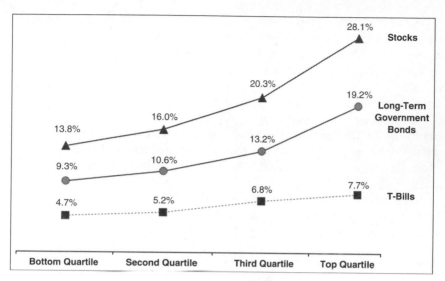

EXHIBIT 4.5   Annual Returns during 1982–2000 Bull Market
Data Sources: Treasury bills and bonds—Ibbotson Associates; Stocks (S&P 500)—
Robert J. Shiller.

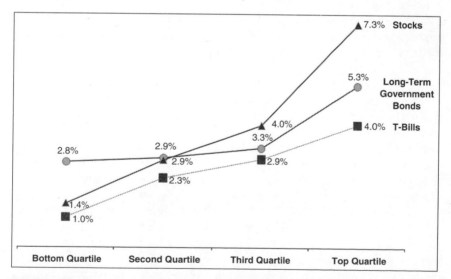

EXHIBIT 4.6   Annual Returns during 1966–1982 Range-Bound Market
Data Sources: Treasury bills and bonds—Ibbotson Associates; Stocks (S&P 500)—
Robert J. Shiller.

(maintains as little as possible in cash or bonds), the portfolio would outperform even the best-of-breed short-term fixed income instruments or crème de la crème bonds. A rising tide really does lift even so-so boats in bull markets, and the difference of returns between stocks and fixed income instruments is tremendous. Asset allocation is responsible for a significant portion of the returns during the secular bull markets.

The same cannot be said about performance of these asset classes during the 1966–1982 range-bound market, as shown in the Exhibit 4.6. At a time when U.S. Treasury bills were in their best performance stretch, they beat stocks in the lower two quartiles and matched their performance in the third. Also at their best, U.S. Treasury bills outperformed the top three quartiles of bond returns. And although stocks outperformed U.S. Treasury bills in all four quartiles, their dominance over bonds was marginal at best. In fact, bond returns in the lower two quartiles exceeded or matched the returns of stocks in the same quartiles. In the top two quartiles, when stocks managed to outperform bonds the outperformance was achieved by a small margin of 0.7 percent to 2 percent.

The "90 percent of the returns comes from asset allocation" adage doesn't hold water in range-bound markets. Asset allocation plays a less significant role in range-bound markets as the tailwind of a secular bull market turns into a headwind (P/E compression). The difference in returns between stocks and fixed income instruments is not nearly as significant in secular range-bound markets as it is in bull markets. Stock selection plays a more important role during range-bound markets, and asset allocation—the trade-off among bonds, stocks, and short-term securities—is not as important as it is during secular bull markets.

The right stocks still rule the range-bound markets! In bull markets, all stocks dominate bonds. Owning a broad market index—a passive buy-and-hold strategy—does wonders. During range-bound markets, *all* stocks don't dominate fixed income instruments; only the right stocks do. Thus a finely tuned, actively managed portfolio still has the best shot at outperforming bonds and short-term securities over the course of a range-bound market. Rigorous stock selection and a disciplined buy-and-sell strategy must be employed to achieve the desired results.

However, the opportunity cost of being invested in fixed income instruments as opposed to average quality stocks is much lower in a range-bound market than in a bull market. Don't own stocks just to be invested. In the absence of attractive equity investments—right stocks—fixed income instruments (or cash) are viable alternatives to a marginal stock.

What is the right stock? The next part of the book is about to tell you just that!

PART TWO

Active Value Investing

Analytics

Introduction to Analytics: The Quality, Valuation, and Growth Framework

As was discussed in Part I, stock returns during range-bound markets are pitiful, not due to lack of earnings growth, but because earnings growth is eaten away by declining P/Es—a staple characteristic of range-bound markets. Thus, to achieve superior returns in the range-bound market, you need to lose as little as possible to P/E corrosion by heightening the total return requirements in the portfolio. This is accomplished by adjustments in the three cornerstones of the analytical process:

1. Increasing the required margin of safety.*
2. Increasing earnings (cash flows) growth rates.
3. Increasing dividend yield requirements for stocks in the portfolio.

---

*Margin of safety (a concept popularized by Benjamin Graham, the "grandfather" of value investing) is the discount that results when a stock is purchased for less than its perceived intrinsic value. For instance, buying a stock that is believed to be worth $100 for $70 results in a $30, or 30 percent, margin of safety.

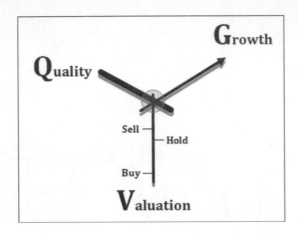

In a perfect, black-and-white world, we'd easily assemble a portfolio of stocks at the top of the scale on each of the Quality, Valuation, and Growth dimensions (see above). They would have a Microsoft-like monopolistic competitive advantage, and would bring along a cash-rich balance sheet and return on capital for the rest of the capitalistic world to envy, Google-like revenue and earnings growth, and finally a General Motors–like single-digit P/E valuation (assuming the "E" is still there when this book goes to print).

But as Yogi Berra said: "If the world were perfect, it wouldn't be." Rarely is the world perfect, nor is investing black and white. The investment process is usually filled with varying shades of gray. The Quality, Valuation, and Growth framework adds a much-needed contrast to this gray world of investing. This contrast will aid you in assembling a portfolio of stocks that thoughtfully encompass the three cornerstones of the analytical process.

Having discussed the stock market from 30,000 feet, let's get down in the trenches, roll up our sleeves, and jump into action.

CHAPTER 5

The "Q" — Quality

The definition of a great company is one that will be great for 25 or 30 years.

—Warren Buffett

One of your main objectives in the range-bound market should be to lose as little money as possible, as it is much more difficult to make the losses back. Companies don't operate in a competitive vacuum. Independent of the market, even the most successful company will stumble at some point. Whereas the strong (quality) get up and regroup to move forward, weaker ones may not. This is why it's imperative to own high-quality companies in the range-bound market. The word *quality* is a subjective term; however, in this chapter I'll try to clarify it.

COMPETITIVE ADVANTAGE

Sustainable competitive advantage—a deep defensive moat around the business (barbed wire if you like dramatics), often created by strong brands, high barriers to entry, patent protection, and other factors that allow a company to have a leg up against competitive threats—is a key characteristic of the quality company.

The value of any asset is the present value of its future cash flows. The further investors can look into the future and estimate with confidence a company's cash flows, the more valuable the company is. A *sustainable* competitive advantage builds a protective barrier around those cash flows, protecting them from inroads by competition and providing a higher confidence level with which to more accurately estimate future cash flows, thus making the company more valuable.

A company that is earning above-average returns on capital (the best kind) will attract new competition. Competitors will look at the above-average returns the same way bees look at sugar water—they'll want some of that. Unless the company possesses a strong competitive advantage, competitors will march in and, depending on the nature of the product or service that the company provides, force it to either lower prices, give up some of the volume, or invest heavily in differentiating—or do a combination of all these things. After the dust settles, the company's return on capital will decline toward the mean.

Competitive advantages that can prevail come in many different flavors: strong brands, patents, unique know-how, regulated monopolies, unique preferential access to natural resources, and so on. Michael Porter created a competitive structure framework in the 1980s that is widely used now in business schools and throughout corporate America. In *Competitive Strategy: Techniques for Analyzing Industries and Competitors* (Free Press, 1998), he describes forces that shape the industry structure: threat of entrants and substitutes, bargaining power of suppliers and buyers, and finally, rivalry among existing competitors. This industry structure is ultimately responsible for a company's profitability in the long run.

Competitive advantage is not a gift from the economic gods that lasts forever. Change is the only constant in the business world, just as it is in the rest of life, and the velocity of change has increased with the progression of the information age and gradual flattening of the world. The Internet made prices more transparent and also has widened the range of available competition. Now a multinational corporation doesn't compete just with other multinationals but with little Joe Schmoes around the world who have access to outsourced manufacturing, off-the-shelf state-of-the-art software systems (that used to be available to just a few large corporations), and advanced logistical networks that are gladly provided by the likes of FedEx and UPS.

A company without a competitive advantage may survive in the environment where the market it serves is growing rapidly, as competitors are satisfied with growing sales in tandem with the market. However, once market growth decelerates, competition intensifies and a company without a competitive advantage will be crushed by competitors that put further downward pressure on pricing and profits when they fight for their own growth.

Warren Buffett, when asked what he looks for in a quality company, answered without hesitation: sustainable competitive advantage. I agree that this should be the one criterion that investors should not be willing to compromise on.

Strong Brands: Not All Brands Are Created Equal

Strong brands often serve as great moats around a business to deter new entrants from stepping into the marketplace and to keep the existing competition at bay, often resulting in higher margins and stable, predictable cash flows. For example, customers ordering a soft drink at a restaurant ask for Coke or Pepsi expecting a certain familiar taste from the drink. Both of these brands became ubiquitous as cola products. Over the past 50 years both Coca-Cola and PepsiCo have spent billions of dollars on marketing and raising consumer awareness of these brands. A competitor choosing to compete in this segment would have to overcome incredible brand awareness and consumer attachment to the unique tastes of these products.

However, not all brands are created equal. In some industries brands provide a right to compete but not the right to charge premium pricing. Take Sara Lee, for example. It produces Sara Lee, Jimmy Dean, Hillshire Farm, Ball Park, L'eggs, Hanes (spun off to shareholders in 2006), and many other respectable brands. Strong brands are supposed to command higher pricing and should have lower price elasticity (price increases should not have a substantial impact on product demand).

Interestingly, that has not been the case with Sara Lee. In 2004, every time the company tried to charge a premium price for its brands (often as a result of passing higher commodity prices on to the consumer), demand dropped substantially. Consumers did not stop eating hot dogs and sausages, or wearing underwear, or eating pies. When Sara Lee raised prices, consumers switched to other well-known brands. Segments where Sara Lee competes are saturated by well-known brands. A strong, well-known consumer brand doesn't always guarantee a higher selling price/higher margin, but does guarantee shelf space and a price higher than that of a generic store brand. In the case of Sara Lee, its strong brands may prevent new entrants from barging into the industry, but its brand strength doesn't protect it from the incumbent "high-branded" competitors undermining its profit margins.

Consumers are overwhelmed by an abundance of brands in retail channels. Any innovation by one strong brand company is quickly copied by another company with a similarly strong brand identity. Thus, in some industries brand is becoming a necessity to participate in the game (compete), but it doesn't guarantee premium pricing—not anymore.

I am not dismissing the importance of brands, but rather issuing a warning: Just because a company has a well-known, respected brand, you cannot assume that the brand will bring a sustainable competitive advantage to the table; it may or may not be the case.

MANAGEMENT

Management should be analyzed and evaluated as meticulously as a company's balance sheet. Its comments should be filtered through our internal common sense filter, no matter how successful management's track record is. Management's pay and incentives are tied to company stock performance, creating enormous pressure to maintain a perpetually rising stock price.

Management is responsible for creating and executing a company's strategy, but (most importantly) its primary goal should be to enhance the company's long-term sustainable competitive advantage; increasing shareholder value will follow.

CASE STUDY: Dell versus Gateway *or* Management versus Management?

It is easy to become mesmerized by earnings per share, the hits and misses of quarterly reports, and various financial ratios and forget that companies are run by people—management. They may make more money, live in bigger houses, and drive fancier cars than most of us, all the while exerting the confidence of business gods, but they are not any more or less human than we are and thus are susceptible to the same human frailties as the rest of us.

It is difficult to find a better example of the drastic difference in the performance of two close competitors driven solely by the quality of the management team than Dell and Gateway. What is striking about these two companies is that in 1992 they were both similar in size and had the same chance of succeeding.

Dell and Gateway were founded about the same time: Dell in 1984 and Gateway in 1985. As you can see in Exhibit 5.1, by 1992 Gateway had a return on assets three and a half times greater than Dell's. Dell's sales were almost twice those of Gateway, but the companies' net incomes were about the same. Gateway was the pioneer in the direct-to-consumer model. It started selling its personal computers through advertisements in magazines and catalogs (remember, those were the dark ages, before the Internet became as ubiquitous as electricity). Dell tried selling through warehouse clubs and computer stores, with limited success. In the mid-1990s, Dell abandoned its retail strategy and began focusing solely on the direct-to-customer strategy. At the time, neither company had a unique competitive advantage over the other. They were similar, with the exception of one little detail—different management teams—and thus different competitive paths were chosen.

Let's fast-forward to 2005. A lot happened in the intervening years. Dell became the largest computer maker in the world, whereas Gateway is struggling to stay alive. What is shocking is that Dell's success was not achieved through making acquisitions or through elaborate financial engineering. All of its revenue growth was organic. Dell simply kept selling more and more computers to businesses and consumers hungry for high-quality computers at low prices.

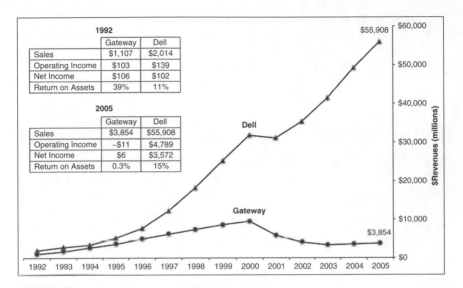

EXHIBIT 5.1   Gateway versus Dell, 1992–2005

Data Source: Standard & Poor's Compustat® (sales, operating income, and net income are in millions).

Initially, Dell's enormous success was not achieved at Gateway's expense. From the mid- to late 1990s the computer industry was growing at a rate several times higher than GDP, and Dell was taking market share from the big boys (at least at the time), IBM and Packard Bell.

In the mid-1990s, Gateway gave up its cost advantage by opening Gateway Country stores; it was not a pure direct seller anymore. The direct sales model has a significant competitive cost advantage over more traditional distribution models, as it bypasses distributors and retailers and leads to higher margins and much lower inventory levels.

In 2001, computer industry growth had come to a screaming halt. Dell started a price war in an attempt to grow sales through capturing market share. Dell succeeded! It had a competitive advantage that Gateway gave up—the lowest cost structure. Being a low-cost producer became increasingly important, as consumers perceived computers produced by top-tier manufacturers (i.e., Dell, Gateway, IBM, Hewlett-Packard, Compaq, etc.) to be of the same quality. The basic specifications, such as processor speed, memory, and hard drive size, were easily standardized, and computers became commodities; price became the most important differentiating factor.

Gateway was stuck in the middle (it was not a low-cost producer, nor did it have a vast distribution system of traditional computer manufacturers), and it paid for it dearly; as you can see from Exhibit 5.1, its sales declined whereas Dell's almost doubled.

Gateway and Dell are not soulless entities, either; they are run by people as well. Though they had the best intentions, Gateway's management made a series of decisions that put Gateway on a wrong track that stripped away its competitive advantage.

In any market, we want to own successful companies, not endangered ones. The goal is to avoid the likes of Gateway and find as many Dell-like companies as possible. The dichotomy in performance between Dell and Gateway highlights the importance of having the right management running the company—one that will cultivate and strengthen a company's competitive advantage.

Arm Yourself with a Healthy Dose of Skepticism

Paul Krugman of the *New York Times* pulled together some comments that Toll Brothers' chairman and founder, Robert Toll, made over the years (before and after the real estate market decline).[1] What really struck me is Robert Toll's denial of what took place in the housing industry leading up to 2006.

Here are a few samples of his comments from 2005, before real estate started to decline substantially: "We've got the supply, and the market has got the demand. So it's a match made in heaven." "Why can't real estate just have a boom like every other industry? . . . Why do we have to have a bubble and then a pop?"

And more in the second half of 2006, after the market turned ugly: "[This] is unlike anything I've seen: Sales are slumping despite the absence of any 'macroeconomic nasty condition' taking housing down along with the rest of the economy." He also claimed that "unease about the direction of the country and the war in Iraq is undermining confidence. All I have to say is: pop!"

Mr. Toll is a smart person. He has built a multibillion-dollar company, one of the largest homebuilders in the country; clearly he is no dummy. But he simply had a bias. He had so much personal wealth at stake (close to $1 billion, according to the company's proxy filed in February 2007) that he convinced himself that the housing market was going through a normal boom and rejected clear arguments that almost any other rational person would see without a magnifying glass. And thus he may have truly believed in his "no bubble" argument.

Also, his whole sales organization's job is to convince potential buyers to buy bigger, better houses. Toll Brothers salespeople had to answer the "Are we in a housing bubble?" question from potential buyers constantly. You don't sell houses by telling buyers that they are purchasing a bubbly asset. Even if his salespeople never read his comments, these comments for sure would send the stock down and thus his net worth.

It is impossible to know what Mr. Toll was actually thinking, but while he was making cheerleading comments about the housing industry, he was selling Toll Brothers stock (several hundred million dollars' worth, according to Securities and Exchange Commission filings) as if it was going out of fashion.

The car salesman may be telling you the truth about the car, but you still don't take him at his word, as he has an inherent bias to sell you a car. He is not a bad person, but he may have a family to support. What would you expect? We are more inclined to believe the corporate executive than the car salesman, but that doesn't mean that corporate executives are more truthful than car salespeople.

Mr. Toll's comments before and after the housing bubble burst illustrate an important lesson: Management's comments always have to be looked at with a healthy dose of skepticism and have to be filtered through their biases and our common sense.[2]

We need to slightly recalibrate our common sense filters so we don't get swayed by the personality delivering the message. Executives are usually well-spoken and confident individuals—qualities required to run a company. But these qualities can overwhelm us. We need to humanize the speaker, stripping away the success, fancy title, and confidence, and removing the appearance of infallibility. Try to imagine the executive wearing a clown suit or whatever else will do the trick of removing the superhuman aura. Once we humanize the executive, our common sense filters are more likely to recognize the bias and adjust for it.

Is the Right Management Team Running the Company?

It is hard to generalize about management. What makes a good or a bad manager? You want a manager to be down to earth, rational, smart, and humble (doesn't have an ego the size of Texas, though that quality is hard to come by); they should be in love with what they do, care deeply about the business, and "have skin in the game" (own the stock)—all those things and more.

The two qualities that I would like to emphasize are integrity and a focus on long-term shareholder value creation, even if it means displeasing the Street in the short run.

How do we judge the management team? Listen to conference calls, read press releases and annual reports, talk to them, and get a sense of whether they are honest with shareholders and with themselves. Why themselves? To recognize a problem, one needs to be willing to admit to oneself that there is a problem.

As for integrity, every manager will make a mistake at some point; they are human, after all. But the ability to admit to and own your mistakes is often what separates a good manager from a not so good one. I wrote the following comments in December 2004 for TheStreet.com, after listening to a Dollar General conference call. (My firm owned the stock at the time of the conference call.)

> *I think the numbers are even worse than they appear on the surface. Sales grew 11.5 percent—not a spectacular number and below my long-term expectations. But it seems this is the least of Dollar General's problems. Cost of goods sold [as percent of revenues] went up 1.2 percent—a huge increase considering the razor-thin margins in retail. If you think problems could not get any worse—well, they do. Sales, general, and administrative expenses [as percent of revenues] went up 0.54 percent; . . . inventory turnover was down and operating cash flows were almost wiped out by a huge increase in inventory.*
>
> *It feels like there is a disconnect between Dollar General management, the stock market, analysts that were on the call, and reality. Management was talking about the great improvements it is making as if the company did not have one of the worst quarters ever. Analysts are completely ignoring the issue of rising inventory and the collapse of profit margins. . . . Although management has been talking about improvements that it has made over last 10 months, all I wanted to do was yell: "Show me the money!" They bragged that they have improved apparel merchandise and that sales of jerseys were very good, but then they said that overall apparel sales were disappointing. I am getting tired of hearing about the great improvements that management is boasting about quarter after quarter and not seeing the results.*

We sold our position in Dollar General for about $20 immediately after that conference call. Several weeks later S&P Equity Research upgraded the stock, citing the quarter's strong results, driving the stock to $22. It would have been tempting to think that I had made a mistake, but I stuck by my analysis. I don't know if Dollar General's management was biased, deluded, or incompetent, but what was apparent to me from looking at their performance was that they had too many stores; at that time they had over 7,000 stores, and were still opening about 700 stores a year (that is two stores a day). It appeared that management was ignoring the "location, location, location" mantra by opening stores anywhere, and they were having a hard time finding qualified people to run them.

Perhaps management was sugar-coating the truth that was so apparent if one just looked at the variables that have the most impact on a company's valuation—value creators/destroyers. Maybe they were aware of the problems and were not able to fix them, and chose to spin their situation to investors. In either case, whether unaware or dishonest, I did not want to stick around this company to find out. A good management team should admit to themselves and to shareholders that mistakes have been made and try to fix them.

As of the third quarter of 2006, Dollar General reported disappointing quarter-after-quarter performance, and was trading at around $12.

This underlines several important points:

- Do your own research; be aware of Wall Street analysts' opinions, but don't be blindly driven by them. Even analysts working for reputable firms such as Standard & Poor's are wrong at times—they are human, after all.
- Listen to what management is saying and compare it to reality. What does common sense tell you?
- When management either is deluded or doesn't recognize a problem that is staring it in the face, run for your life!

P.S. Six months after I wrote this, in March 2007, Kohlberg Kravis Roberts (a private equity firm) announced their intention to take Dollar General private at $22 a share. Was I wrong about selling Dollar General several years earlier? Not at all.

Importance of Long-Term Value Creation

Though wise short-term and long-term decisions are not mutually exclusive, to grow a tree (a long-term investment) seeds have to be planted (immediate expense). Management faces these decisions on a daily basis and unfortunately often destroys long-term value to please the short-term junkies—Wall Street.

I was shocked to hear the following response by Costco's CEO to an analyst question on the company's conference call. He was asked what he loses sleep over.

> *What I lose sleep over, and not a lot frankly, is more as it relates to the short-term stock price movements, because short-term stock price movement is impacted by expectations and the fact that at some point, and perhaps this quarter is a good example that we just announced, if you look at quarters two, three, and four last year we beat those by a little bit.*[3]

Costco is run by one of the best management teams in the country, one that created tremendous value for its shareholders by constantly focusing on improving its sustainable competitive advantage. They have built a highly profitable company, the biggest discount warehouse company in the United States, despite facing fierce competition from the 800-pound gorilla, Wal-Mart. But the pressure of the stock's short-term performance even weighs on Costco's CEO.

Even if the best in the business feel the pressure to perform in the short term—beating (analysts' quarterly forecasts) by a little bit—what will happen to second and third best? On a daily basis, corporate management makes decisions that aim to benefit corporate performance in the short term versus the long term.

Several years ago I had an informal breakfast meeting with the management of a wholesale club (not Costco). I asked why they did not open more pharmacies at their existing clubs, as the company had plenty of free cash flow and opening pharmacies seemed to improve traffic.

The response was: "Yes, pharmacies are a good investment, but it takes a while for them to reach profitability; thus we'd be taking a short-term hit on earnings. Therefore, we are stretching the openings out."

Management of that wholesale club was sacrificing a good investment opportunity for fear of not feeding the short-term appetite of Wall Street.

Management should not get all the blame for their focus on short-term performance. One disadvantage of being a public company is its master—the shareholder (Wall Street). Wall Street is short-term oriented, and it has an insatiable need for constantly growing short-term returns.

In another example, I was surprised to hear this answer to an analyst's question from Lionsgate Entertainment (an independent movie studio) on the company's conference call in 2006 (first quarter of the 2007 fiscal year):

> **Analyst:** There does appear to be a move toward really squeezing those windows closer together [time between when a movie comes out in the theater and in DVD]. I am wondering what the pros and cons of that are.
>
> **Jon Feltheimer (CEO):** We think 16 weeks is still about the right amount between windows. I do not think we see really compressing them much more than that. I think there are times, particularly as a public company, when you are trying to get certain revenues within your fiscal year, and you move a movie a couple of weeks, so maybe the window changes a little.[4]

In a rational, long-term value creation world, the movie or DVD release to the public would have nothing to do with when its release falls within a quarter; it would be based on when people (not Wall Street) would likely want to see it and when the company would make the most money.

Over time the Street's obsession with short-term goals has shifted management focus from creating long-term value for shareholders to becoming Wall Street's lap dog trying to jump to the next level every quarter as the bar is inexorably raised by its masters.

What should you do? Look for a management team that has the guts and the confidence to keep a long-term focus and to make fewer cowardly, compromising decisions that hinder a company's long-term sustainable competitive advantage merely to serve a short-term hungry master.

PREDICTABLE EARNINGS

Before Enron entered our vocabulary as a five-letter word for financial disaster, investors were proud to own companies that delivered rulerlike earnings (going up consistently year after year). As investors painfully discovered, the source of those earnings was often the result of accounting manipulations, not business proficiency.

The list of consistent growers that delivered performance through earnings manipulations is long and includes the who's who of corporate America: Bristol-Myers Squibb was caught stuffing distribution channels with drugs to recognize sales prematurely. MCI WorldCom (and Enron) delivered consistency by making up numbers through lies or shenanigans. Even General Electric, the bluest of the blue-chip club, has tinkered with its insurance reserves to deliver its expected growth to Wall Street.

To find truly predictable earnings, you will need to dig deeper, below the surface of the reported numbers, and look at the actual business to identify the qualities that make companies' earnings predictable.

Companies that have high recurring revenue components usually exhibit lower sales volatility and greater predictability of their earnings and cash flows, thus exhibiting less operational risk.

Recurrence of revenues is the number-one source of predictability. Companies whose customers need to buy their products or services on a consistent basis usually exhibit less earnings volatility and thus less risk than companies whose customers don't. For instance, insurance brokerage firms are hired by companies (from mom-and-pops to Fortune 500 companies) to find appropriate insurance coverage at the best price. A large portion of their business comes from recurring revenues, as they receive commissions as long as an insurance policy stays in place—and policies stay in place for a long time. The typical insurance broker sees attrition of only about 8 percent in lost clients a year. In other words, 92 percent of its revenues are recurring. For the insurance broker to grow revenues 10 percent a year, it has to increase new sales by about 18 percent, as it has to replace the 8 percent lost due to attrition.

For a computer manufacturer, in contrast, to grow revenues 10 percent, it has to generate 110 percent of new sales. It has to sell as many computers as it sold last year (probably more due to constant price deflation in this business) plus 10 percent in new computers.

A high level of recurring revenues creates higher predictability and sustainability, and this reduces risk for investors. It also removes a lot of strain from growth, since a company with high recurring revenues has to put forth a lot less effort to grow revenues.

Revenue predictability is complemented by product disposability. Let's contrast two very different companies: a home builder (pick one: Toll Brothers or MDC Holdings) and a medical instrument company (let's go with Becton Dickenson, maker of disposable needles and syringes). Home builders have absolutely no recurrence of revenues in their business. None! They buy land, build a house, sell a house, and move on to the next new house. Becton Dickenson, in contrast, has incredible recurring revenues—you use a needle and/or a syringe once and throw it away. Before you know it you need another.

Continuous demand for needles and syringes depletes the supply in the market. Home builders are quite the opposite. Once a house is built and purchased, it ultimately increases a future supply—new homes compete with existing homes. To increase sales, a home builder has to sell as many homes as it did the previous year, similar to a computer manufacturer (assuming prices stay constant), plus some. Becton Dickenson doesn't compete with its past, as the needles and syringes it sold last year are already thrown away. The only thing it competes for is space in the dumpster. The past may haunt home builders for a long time, as homes are a long-term asset. People who want to buy a home will have plenty of choices available from the houses that were built in preceding years, and looking at the rise of the construction industry over the past decade, there'll be a lot of those.

What does it all mean? Should you forever avoid investing in home builders? No, there have been ample opportunities to make money in home building stocks, and there is an appropriate time to own them (usually not right after a significant supply has flooded the market). Timing is extremely important when buying companies that produce highly durable products that have a very long useful life (houses, capital equipment, cars, etc.).

These companies compete against external competitive threats and their own past sales. You should also be aware of the increased risk that comes with their earnings, and for that matter the earnings of any company that doesn't have high recurring revenues. The risk of earnings volatility should be compensated by the strength of the company's balance sheet (which will be discussed next) and/or increased margin of safety (which I'll address in Chapter 7 on valuation).

STRONG BALANCE SHEET

Debt Is Good Except When It Is Not

Often companies that could afford to use debt don't, and the ones that shouldn't do. High return on capital and significant free cash flows usually lead investors to companies that underutilize debt.

Two industries that should not use debt but use it excessively are the U.S. auto manufacturers (General Motors and Ford) and airlines (most U.S. airlines with the exception of Southwest and a few others). They have high fixed costs—planes and factories are expensive and, to a large degree, their expense is independent of the level of sales generated, a classic definition of operational leverage. They are highly unionized, and therefore it is difficult to lay off employees—their employees are a fixed cost as well. Their businesses are extremely sensitive to economic growth (cyclicality), as cars and air travel (vacation and business travel) are mostly big ticket discretionary items and the first to get cut when economic growth slows.

This high degree of total leverage (a combination of high operational and high financial leverages) mixed with volatile sales is a recipe for disaster. Costs do not decline with sales, leading to significant losses.

To make things even worse, a significant portion of costs is driven by unpredictable commodity prices—fuel costs for airlines and raw materials (iron, oil, aluminum, etc.) for auto companies—adding another layer of risk to their cash flows.

Companies that have little debt have more room to make mistakes. Debt is good when it is judiciously used by a company with stable and predictable cash flows. However, a company that has volatile cash flows and a high degree of operational leverage (fixed assets) should use debt with great caution.

Stock Buybacks Distort Balance Sheet

In a world where corporate America has fallen in love with stock buybacks, analyzing a company's debt level by looking at debt-to-assets or debt-to-equity ratios is often a misleading exercise. Stock buybacks inadvertently distort the appearance of the balance sheet when market-value transactions such as this are mixed with historical entries on the balance sheet, such as issuance of common stock and retained earnings. In the frequent case where the market value of equity substantially exceeds its book value, share repurchases may actually lead to negative equity (at least on the balance sheet).

To gauge a company's true indebtedness and the risk that comes with it, you should utilize debt and interest coverage ratios in relation to net income; earnings before interest, taxes, depreciation, and amortization (EBITDA); operating cash flows; and/or free cash flows. These ratios tell a more accurate story about the balance sheet (debt) risk and are not distorted by share buy-backs. Here are some examples of these ratios: debt/EBITDA; debt/operating cash flows; EBITDA/interest expense; operating cash flows/interest expense; and many others).

CASE STUDY: Colgate-Palmolive's Capital Structure

If you solely used debt-to-assets or equity-to-debt to analyze Colgate-Palmolive Company's indebtness from 1999 to 2002, you would come to the wrong conclusion on the company's financial risk. As shown in Exhibit 5.2, over that four-year period the company repurchased over $3 billion of its common stock, reducing its common equity on balance from $1.816 billion to $0.367 billion (part of the buyback was offset by the company increasing retained earnings by more than $1.5 billion).

However, as you can see in Exhibit 5.3, from 1999 to 2002, Colgate-Palmolive's equity as a percent of assets shrank from about 24 percent to 5 percent and debt as a percent of assets went from less than 38 percent to almost 51 percent, all due to aggressive share buybacks. On the surface, significant changes in capital structure appeared to be a sign of deep trouble.

Debt and interest coverage ratios in Exhibit 5.4 show a different, clearer, and more accurate picture as the company's financials have strengthened over the aforementioned time period. The free cash flow interest coverage ratio, for instance, went from 4.1 times in 1999 to 8 times—a sign of significant improvement in the company's financial health. Also,

EXHIBIT 5.2 Snapshot of Colgate-Palmolive's Balance Sheet ($ Millions)

	Dec02	Dec01	Dec00	Dec99
Retained Earnings	4,653	4,148	3,624	3,076
Common Stock	1,867	1,902	1,878	1,796
Less: Treasury Stock	6,152	5,204	4,043	3,056
Total Equity	367	851	1,458	1,816
Total Interest-Bearing Debt	3,604	3,239	2,978	2,790
Total Assets	7,087	6,985	7,252	7,423

Data Source: Standard & Poor's Compustat.

EXHIBIT 5.3 Colgate-Palmolive's Traditional Capital Structure Ratios ($ Millions)

	Dec02	Dec01	Dec00	Dec99
Total Equity	367	851	1,458	1,816
	÷	÷	÷	÷
Total Assets	7,087	6,985	7,252	7,423
Total Equity to Total Assets	**5.2%**	**12.2%**	**20.1%**	**24.5%**
Interest-Bearing Debt	3,604	3,239	2,978	2,790
	÷	÷	÷	÷
Total Assets	7,087	6,985	7,252	7,423
Total Debt to Total Assets	**50.9%**	**46.4%**	**41.1%**	**37.6%**

Data Source: Standard & Poor's Compustat.

EXHIBIT 5.4 Colgate-Palmolive's Debt and Interest Coverage ($ Millions)

	Dec02	Dec01	Dec00	Dec99
Operating Cash Flow	1,611	1,600	1,536	1,293
	÷	÷	÷	÷
Interest Expense	158	192	204	224
Operating Cash Flows Interest Coverage*	**10.2**	**8.3**	**7.5**	**5.8**
Free Cash Flows	1,268	1,259	1,170	920
	÷	÷	÷	÷
Interest Expense	158	192	204	224
Free Cash Flows Interest Coverage (Times)*	**8.0**	**6.5**	**5.7**	**4.1**
Total Interest-Bearing Debt	3,604	3,239	2,978	2,790
	÷	÷	÷	÷
Operating Cash Flow	1,611	1,600	1,536	1,293
Debt Payoff from Operating Cash Flows†	**2.2**	**2.0**	**1.9**	**2.2**
Earnings Before Interest and Taxes (EBIT)	2,024	1,861	1,721	1,564
	÷	÷	÷	÷
Interest Expense	158	192	204	224
EBIT Interest Coverage*	**16.3**	**17.5**	**16.2**	**12.8**
Total Interest-Bearing Debt	3,604	3,239	2,978	2,790
	÷	÷	÷	÷
Free Cash Flows	1,268	1,259	1,170	920
Debt Payoff from Free Cash Flows†	**2.8**	**2.6**	**2.5**	**3.0**

Data Source: Standard & Poor's Compustat.
*Times covered.
†Years to payoff.

it is apparent from Exhibit 5.3 that, despite increased debt levels, debt payoff ratios have not changed much. For instance, Colgate-Palmolive could still pay off all of its debt in less than three years (if it decides to do so) from its free cash flows. Note that interest expense declined despite an increase in interest-bearing debt. This happened because a large portion of Colgate's debt matured from 1999 to 2002 and was refinanced at much lower interest rates.

I am not applauding Colgate's share buyback. Not at all; as I'll discuss in the next chapter, it was done when the stock was overvalued. I am just using Colgate to illustrate the impact that share buybacks may have on the balance sheet and the false tale that the traditional capital structure ratios may tell unsuspecting investors. Share buyback was especially distortional to Colgate's balance sheet, as the company's stock traded at a substantial premium to its book value.

Off Balance Sheet

I'd love to say that one's analysis of debt is completed just by looking at debt ratios, but it isn't. It is a start but by no means the end to the liability analysis.

Underfunded defined-benefit plans, operational leases—all are neatly tucked away off balance sheet, and should be carefully analyzed. Close attention needs to be paid to the assumptions management uses in estimating the assets and liabilities of its defined-benefit plan. For instance, a company has to estimate the expected return it will receive on its plan assets. If this assumption is too high, the estimated value of the plan's assets is overstated, which can create an unfunded liability that can be crippling when it catches up on the books.

General Motors, for example, expects its pension plan's assets to appreciate at 9 percent a year. Is it achievable, considering the age of General Motors retirees? This is open for discussion. However, if the company and/or its auditors (and actuaries) decide that the assumptions for its long-term rate of return are too aggressive, its assets will shrink and the plan will be underfunded; that is a significant risk.

Michelle Leder, in her book *Financial Fine Print: Uncovering a Company's True Value* (John Wiley & Sons, 2003), made an interesting observation: The conservativeness of pension assumptions (discount rate, compensation increase, long-term rate of return) is a good and easily identified indicator of how conservative a company is with its accounting policies. For instance, if a company uses a high rate of return on its plan assets (an indication of accounting aggressiveness), you should take out a larger magnifying glass when examining the company's financial statements and footnotes.

Off balance sheet leases should be put back on the balance sheet. Let's take a retailer, for instance. It has a choice between buying a store outright, financing it with debt or equity (simultaneously creating an asset and a liability), or entering into a lease. In the last case, it is still responsible for making lease payments for a store, even when the store is closed (unless it is subleased). Credit agencies put operational leases back on the balance sheet as assets with corresponding liabilities (debt). So should you.

An Underleveraged Company Is Likelier to Be Acquired

I find there is another hidden benefit for companies with a stellar balance sheet—they make great acquisition targets. Acquisition means that a premium will be paid for an acquired stock by an acquirer, as the acquirer can then leverage the target's balance sheet to finance the purchase—making such companies better investments!

For instance, this happened when Lincoln Financial, a life insurance company, purchased another life insurer, Jefferson Pilot. At the time, Jefferson Pilot had a stellar AA-rated balance sheet—among the highest in the industry and far superior to Lincoln Financial's (still respectable) A– rating. Lincoln Financial announced that after the acquisition closed, Jefferson Pilot would take out several hundred million dollars in debt to bring its rating down to Lincoln Financial's level. The net effect was that, by leveraging Jefferson Pilot's relatively unrevealed balance sheet, Lincoln Financial made Jefferson Pilot pay in part for its own acquisition.

SIGNIFICANCE OF FREE CASH FLOWS

One way to define free cash flows is as the cash flows left after a company pays for all its ongoing needs such as salaries, taxes, inventory, interest expense, management's country club memberships, various other yearly expenses, and all other expenses required for future growth, such as investment in fixed assets (capital expenditures for factories, equipment, and the like)—basically, operating cash flows less capital expenditures. Another way to define free cash flows is reconciliation of net income to the cash changes in the balance sheet less investments made into fixed assets for future growth.

Companies that generate significant free cash flows and are managed by smart, shareholder-oriented management will be able to take advantage of volatility of range-bound markets and thus create additional shareholder value through appropriate stock buybacks (at a time when the company's stock is significantly undervalued or—simply put—cheap).

Significant reduction of share count results in higher earnings and dividends per share, thus acting as a flotation buoy under the stock.

For instance, in 2004 and 2005 when Nokia's stock had been scraping through multiyear lows, trading as low as 12 times free cash flows, the company was generating over $5 billion of free cash flows a year and had about $15 billion in cash and virtually no debt. Nokia management took advantage of this opportunity and bought approximately 11 percent of its common shares back, creating substantial shareholder value. This example also speaks to the benefits of having a strong balance sheet.

There are some additional benefits of high free cash flows:

- Companies that generate significant free cash flows are not capital intensive due to low capital expenditures (they don't require large investments into property, plant, and equipment), which often leads to a higher return on capital and higher earnings growth.
- Significant free cash flows lower the risk of the business, as the company is not as dependent on outside financing; it can finance its operations internally through free cash flows. As poet Robert Frost said: "A bank is a place where they lend you an umbrella in fair weather and ask for it back when it begins to rain." At a time when companies are swimming in liquidity (they can easily issue stock or borrow money by issuing bonds or taking out bank loans), self-reliance on internal financing may go unnoticed. During the tough times, however, free cash flows separate the survivors from the rest of the pack.
- In times of economic difficulties or crises, the buying power of cash increases exponentially. Warren Buffett's Berkshire Hathaway was swimming in liquidity during the 2002 recession. The companies it owns spit out significant free cash flows, and Berkshire Hathaway had billions of dollars of cash on its balance sheet. Buffett was able to buy energy pipelines from distressed utilities (Williams and Dynegy) at bargain basement prices. He was able to negotiate the terms of those transactions from a position of strength, as utilities at the time were in desperate need of liquidity and he was able to provide it.

Not All Capital Expenditures Are Created Equal

It is important to understand the nature of capital expenditures. In the free cash flow definition there is almost no quarrel over what constitutes operating cash flow: It is net income adjusted for all noncash (mainly depreciation and amortization) and operation-related balance sheet items. However, capital expenditure levels may understate or overstate company free cash flows, as not all capital expenditures are created equal.

An important distinction between investment in future growth and maintenance capital expenditures often goes unnoticed. The differences in these capital expenditures play a crucial role in value creation when a company's sales growth slows down.

- *Maintenance*—investments into fixed assets that are required for a company to maintain its current sales level. A semiconductor company, for instance, has to constantly upgrade its factory just to maintain current sales, as technology and manufacturing processes are constantly evolving. Oil companies, too, have to spend billions of dollars every year just to replenish depleting wells (reserves). To identify maintenance capital expenditures, ask yourself a question: What would happen to the subject company's sales if it stopped investing in fixed assets? If its sales would be expected to decline over time, as would happen to semiconductor and oil companies, all other things being equal, then you have uncovered maintenance capital expenditures.
- *Future-growth capital expenditures*—investments that are necessary for a company to grow its sales, such as a retailer building new stores, a shipbuilder expanding its shipyard, or a software company expanding its office space. If a company stopped making growth capital expenditures, all other things being equal, its sales growth would decelerate but sales would not decline.

Why is this distinction important? We live in a finite world where infinite supernormal (a fancy word for above-average) growth of earnings (and cash flows) is not possible. At some point even the most successful company will reach a size at which a supernormal growth rate is not possible—a company growing at a rate substantially above industry growth at some point will become the industry, and then the entire economy.

The large numbers (not to be confused with the statistical law of large numbers) applies as well: The larger a company becomes, the more difficult it is to grow at the same high rate. It's as inevitable as gravity, setting in slowly but surely.

Let's take one of the most successful companies as an example—Microsoft. As shown in Exhibit 5.5, throughout the 1980s its sales grew at over 50 percent a year, reaching almost $1.2 billion in 1990. Its growth eventually slowed down to just (most companies would kill for that "just") over 30 percent a year, reaching $23 billion in the sunset of the twentieth century, and they have been growing a little bit over 10 percent since. If Microsoft continued to grow sales at its 1980s pace, its sales would have reached $700 billion by 2005, and by today's profit margins its net income would have accounted for one-sixth of total corporate profitability of the

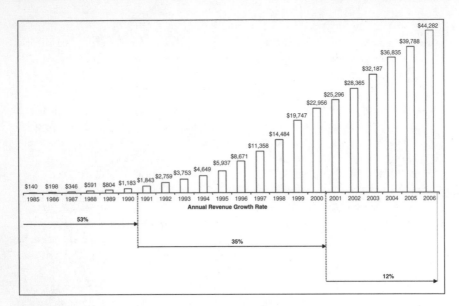

EXHIBIT 5.5 Microsoft Revenues, 1985–2006 ($ Millions)
Data Source: Standard & Poor's Compustat.

United States. A couple more years of that kind of growth and its sales would have exceeded California's GDP (fifth largest world economy with a GDP around $1.5 trillion).

Many companies defy the law of large numbers by constantly going after new markets or branching out into new industries. However, the inevitable can be postponed but not escaped. The faster the growth and the longer it lasts, the more difficult it is to repeat—Microsoft's past and recent performance is a testament of that.

However, when inevitability encroaches on a company that has a high level of maintenance capital expenditures, it is unlikely to generate higher free cash flows—even after it stops growing sales—as it will keep pouring money (albeit lower amounts) into fixed assets to keep existing sales from declining (oil companies come to mind here; if they stop looking for new oil, over time they'll deplete their reserves and will be out of business).

A company with low maintenance capital expenditures will see a substantial increase in free cash flows once it stops growing sales (investing for growth), as its capital expenditures will decline and free cash flows and income will rise. Its stock price is likely to suffer less relative to the company with high maintenance capital expenditures, as it will face a lower P/E contraction (that inevitably comes with slower growth) and be able to boost dividends and buy back stock. In addition, an increase in earnings and free cash flows due to lower capital expenditures may also soften the decline from the P/E contraction.

Wal-Mart, for example, spent over $14.5 billion on capital expenditures in 2005, amounting to over 80 percent of its operating cash flows. The majority of these capital expenditures were for future growth that went with opening new stores and building new distribution centers. If Wal-Mart decided that it had captured all the market it could possibly capture, its capital expenditures would decline substantially. The company might still spend a couple of billion dollars here or there to renovate existing stores to maintain sales (what's a couple of billion dollars among friends?). At the same time, Wal-Mart's free cash flows would go through the roof by a dozen billion or so. It would buy back stock, at least in part to help earnings per share growth and raise a dividend; both actions would increase shareholder return.

The Wal-Mart P/E would decline as investor expectations for higher future earnings growth did not materialize. However, some of the P/E decrease would be offset by higher earnings (due to lower depreciation— though not right away, as it would take time for depreciation expense to decline as Wal-Mart continued to depreciate investments in fixed assets made in the past) and much higher free cash flows (right away, as capital expenditure would immediately decline).

Volatility of Free Cash Flows

Free cash flow volatility is usually higher than volatility of net income. This is true for several reasons: Income statements are constructed based on accruals (matching sales with costs associated with sales), whereas operating cash flows are constructed based on actual (more volatile) operating cash inflows and outflows. Thus, unless a company's operating efficiency (how it deals with working capital) is improving or deteriorating, a significantly increased or decreased working capital balance (inventory, accounts receivable, and accounts payable) in one year is likely to revert the next year.

Also, whereas depreciation (an allocation of historical cost of fixed assets) is a stable expense on the income statement, there is nothing smooth about actual outlays for fixed assets (capital expenditures), as they are lumpy in nature.

Annual volatility of free cash flows may send you down the wrong track. One year free cash flow may be positive, only to go negative the next year. The best way to deal with free cash flow volatility is to either average or compute cumulative operating cash flows over a several-year span, and then reduce them to the average or cumulative capital expenditures over a similar time period. Depreciation expense is usually a good proxy for capital expenditures for capital-intensive businesses:

- In its high-growth stage, a company's capital expenditures exceed depreciation.
- Approaching maturity, capital expenditures should be close to depreciation.
- Finally, during the mature stage, depreciation expense exceeds capital expenditures.

Pay Attention to What a Company Plans to Do with Its Free Cash Flows

Free cash flows can destroy value if not used properly. There are several things a company can do with its free cash flows: pay down debt, buy back stock, increase or start paying a dividend, or make an acquisition; or it can do nothing. It is important to understand what a company plans to do with its free cash flows; these uses may provide an insight into corporate strategy.

Often management leverages abundant free cash flows to make acquisitions. Although some acquisitions create shareholder value, many are done to boost management's ego in their pursuit of building bigger (not better) corporate empires. AT&T is one of the infamous acquirers: It purchased NCR Corporation in 1992 just to sell it later at a fraction of its purchase price. It then spent billions in the late 1990s for TCI Inc., at the time touting it as a must-do acquisition, only to sell it to Comcast in 2002 at a loss.

CASE STUDY: IMS Health–VNU Merger

The IMS Health–VNU merger is a perfect example of one company trying to acquire another for empire-building purposes that would have destroyed shareholder value. In July 2005, Dutch company VNU Inc. announced that it would buy IMS Health for $6.9 billion (claiming to shareholders that the acquisition would really be a merger, despite a premium paid for IMS Health). This development took many investors in IMS Health (including me) by surprise.

IMS Health was spun off from Cognizant, which had been spun off from Dun & Bradstreet in 1996. At the time of spin-off, IMS was bundled with a collection of loosely related businesses, and since then has desperately tried to simplify and restructure by shedding these businesses. It took years of seemingly endless spin-offs and financial engineering to make progress on simplifying the businesses and create a simple, easy-to-analyze, transparent company. Finally, the company had a clean slate, but then the VNU acquisition was dumped on IMS Health shareholders' shoulders. Both VNU and IMS Health management teams sounded optimistic in the joint conference call, giving the usual synergy, cost-cutting, and *Star Trek*-ish "go where nobody has gone before" talk.

I have a theory that there is a *Mergers and Acquisitions for Dummies* handbook secretly floating in corporate hallways, as all merger/acquisition conference calls sound identical. Both companies are excited, and praises are sung about the quality of the opposing management team. Words like *synergy* (used seven times in the IMS Health/VNU conference call) are superseded only by *opportunity* (used 14 times in that conference call). Management usually makes sure to insert at least one of them in nearly every sentence. Since it is assumed that employees from the combined companies are listening, layoffs are downplayed and no specifics are given.

Few large mergers work out. In fact, most mergers fail miserably as egos, incompatibility of corporate cultures, and premiums paid make it difficult for the new entity to emerge successfully. This one looked no different.

Ironically, the two largest operating units of VNU (ACNielsen and Nielsen Media) and IMS Health used to be part of the same company—Dun & Bradstreet. At the time (in 1996) Dun & Bradstreet thought IMS Health and the Nielsons should not be together; thus they were spun off separately. Both companies now claimed that times have changed—they always do. But have they changed enough for two companies with little overlap in business to merge?

In my conversation with IMS Health management I brought up the idea of a joint venture. I was told such joint ventures are difficult, as the negotiation of structure often results in decision paralysis. Though there is some truth to that argument, the cost of a failed merger is a lot higher than the cost of a failed joint venture. Failure of a joint venture leads to an easy dating-like separation, but failure of a merger brings the companies to a Hollywood-like divorce. (I have another theory: Could the so-called failure of joint ventures be a myth that is spread by investment bankers, who get no fees for joint ventures but huge fees and bonuses for acquisitions/mergers?)

After seeing enough of these mergers and demergers take place, it was easy to picture a demerger conference call where, with a more somber tone, a CEO or president of the combined entity (the other CEO who was going to stay on to help run the combined entity had already taken a hefty severance package, cashed out his stock options, and left for personal reasons, as if anybody ever leaves for "impersonal" reasons) explains that the synergies were not as great as the company estimated, the company is too complex to analyze and thus investors did not grant the combined entity a fair P/E, and so on. It is easy to become a cynic when it comes to mergers. A working large merger is usually the exception, not the rule.

Luckily, shareholders of both companies did not share management's ambitions to own a larger, possibly less profitable, riskier, and more complex company. The merger plan fell apart several months after the announcement. Consequently, VNU's CEO was fired and the company was to be purchased by a consortium of hedge funds.

David Packard, the founder of Hewlett-Packard said, "More companies die of indigestion than starvation," thus unless a company has a long and flawless acquisition and integration record, every significant acquisition should be looked upon as a failure in the making unless and until proven otherwise.

HIGH RETURN ON CAPITAL

Return on capital shows how well invested capital is working for the shareholders. Return on capital that is far exceeding the cost of capital is a great indicator of how much a company can increase shareholder value.

Return on capital is one of two main ingredients in the earnings growth formula: ability to grow consists of high return on capital and having opportunities to grow. The higher the return on invested capital, the less equity or debt a company must issue to grow.

Assuming a company has growth opportunities—the second main ingredient in the growth formula—a company with high return on capital is able to grow based on internally generated capital, producing higher earnings growth for shareholders with less risk. Issuance of new stock dilutes returns, and issuance of debt adds another expense line on the income statement and increases the company's risk.

In addition, consistent high return on capital is a good indication of the presence of a strong competitive advantage. As we discussed, in the absence of a competitive advantage, high return on capital would attract new competitors; increased competition would bring down prices, in turn lowering a company's profit margins and sales or requiring larger reinvestments, subsequently leading to lower return on capital. Companies that have a history of producing a high return on capital have (in most cases) a competitive advantage that allows them to maintain that high return on capital. If the competitive advantage is still intact, then high return on capital is likely to persist going forward.

CONCLUSION

Sustainable competitive advantage, high-quality management, predictable earnings, significant free cash flows, strong balance sheet, and high return on capital are the wish list of a quality company. Some of these metrics, like sustainable competitive advantage and good management, should not be compromised on—period. However, some are interchangeable (weakness in one could be offset by strength in another); for instance, strong balance sheet requirements could be eased if a company has predictable earnings and cash flows. Or lack of significant free cash flows could be overlooked if a very large portion of capital expenditures goes for growth. But I'd recommend making as few sacrifices on quality as possible for the reason I mentioned in the beginning of the chapter—it is very hard to make up for losses in the range-bound market.

CHAPTER 6

The "G"—Growth

If a business does well, the stock eventually follows.
—Warren Buffett

SOURCES OF GROWTH: EARNINGS GROWTH AND DIVIDENDS

To effectively converse about the Valuation dimension of the QVG framework, we need to have a clear understanding of what goes into the Quality and Growth dimensions. Thus, despite Valuation being second in the QVG framework, we'll talk about the Growth dimension before we dive into a discussion of Valuation.

Buying out-of-favor stocks for which the market's love affair was put on temporary hold is a strategy of choice in the range-bound market (and any other market, actually), as it allows an investor to buy shares in a high-quality company and a growing company at an attractive valuation.

However, this strategy brings another risk: that the supposedly temporary breakup becomes a longer separation, turning the stock into dead money—staying undervalued and not going anywhere for a long time. This is where growth comes in handy. A company that is growing earnings and paying a dividend is compensating for the wait, substantially reducing the dead-money risk.

The Growth dimension encompasses both growth of profitability (expressed as earnings or cash flows growth) and dividends (expressed as dividend yield).

Dividends are real-time compensation for the wait for growth. Growing earnings are compressing the valuation spring (the P/E) under the stock. For instance, if you purchase a $15 stock that produces $1 of earnings per share (EPS) today, it is trading at 15 times earnings. If the company's earnings are growing 15 percent a year, its earnings will double in five years to $2 a share. Thus even if the stock never comes back to the purchased P/E of 15 and settles at 12 times earnings or $24 (12 × $2), you still make a decent 10 percent a year return. Thus, when the love affair with the stock resumes, P/E will be expanding on top of higher earnings, rewarding your patience. Even if you have slightly overpaid for the stock, the growth will heal this problem in time. Time is your best friend when a company's earnings are rising and dividends are constantly deposited in a brokerage account, but it turns into an enemy when that is not the case.

It is important to know the sources (the engines) of a company's profitability growth. The per share profitability growth could be illustrated as a pyramid flipped upside down (see Exhibit 6.1), where revenue growth is at the wider top of the pyramid and net income, free cash flows, earnings per share, and free cash flow per share flow to the narrower bottom.

If costs are growing at a slower rate than revenues, net margin will expand and net income growth will outpace revenue growth. If during the observed period a company buys back stock, share count will decline (net income will be divided by a smaller share count), which will lead earnings per share growth to outpace net income growth. And finally, if a company is able to manage its fixed and operating assets (working capital: accounts receivable, inventory, accounts payable) efficiently, free cash flow per share growth will outpace growth of earnings per share.

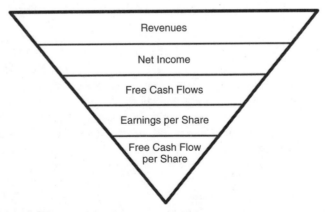

EXHIBIT 6.1   Flipped Growth Pyramid

In this example, shareholder value is created on many levels of the company's operating pyramid. In the analysis, each level of the growth pyramid needs to be examined to see if it will be creating or destroying value.

Most of the things in life are finite, but each is finite to a different degree. Sources of growth are much the same: Although all face finality, it impacts them differently. Whereas some parts of the pyramid may have driven a company's growth in the past, these growth drivers may be approaching the last inning. You should revisit each growth driver regularly, with an expectation of how much each driver should contribute to a company's future growth against which to compare the actual growth.

Revenue Growth

Revenue growth is the most natural way for a company to grow (other than by acquisition). There are several organic (nonacquisition) strategies for a company to grow revenues:

- *Selling more products and services to existing and/or new customers*—one of the commonly followed strategies by corporate America and companies around the world.
- *Expanding to new markets, domestic or international*—a lot of companies have found a second life expanding to growing international markets.

   Microsoft's success led to the company becoming de facto the entire market in the operation system, server, and information worker (office) segments of the software industry, leaving little room for growth. To keep growing revenues, Microsoft expanded into new software segments such as video gaming with its Xbox gaming console, web search (MSN), and operating systems for mobile phones and cable boxes.

   Dell found that its efficient low-cost distribution system and manufacturing expertise provided it with an opportunity to expand beyond computers to printers and television sets. Dell stepped out from the market where it had already achieved a high market share to brand new markets where it had no presence, thus extending the life span of its growth opportunity.
- *Raising prices*—a tricky strategy, and its success depends on elasticity of demand (impact of higher prices on customers' willingness to buy the product).

   Raising prices is a finite strategy, as higher prices increase the attractiveness of the industry to new entrants. Depending on barriers to entry, these new competitors may attempt to capture market share by lowering prices. Or even worse, customers may just get frustrated with higher prices and switch to substitutes or competing products.

■ *Lowering prices*—not the strategy that usually comes to mind, but it works if increase in demand offsets the decline in price and lowers costs. Lower prices did wonders for the wireless industry, as lower prices stimulated cell phone use and allowed wireless companies to spread fixed costs (the networks and customer service) among larger subscriber bases.

Of course there is also growth by acquisition strategy, though usually more expensive, but a way to grow the business. Some companies have done a terrific job growing by acquisition: General Electric, PepsiCo, and many large banks come to mind. But as we discussed in the Quality chapter, there are many external risks that come with acquisitions.

Growth from Margin Improvements

Margin improvements may come from different sources, such as operating efficiency and economy of scale.

Operating Efficiency   Improvements in operating efficiency have been the most common source of margin expansion for most U.S. companies in recent years as technological innovations have helped companies to become more efficient.

As we discussed in Chapter 3, as time goes on, technology that made one company more efficient will be available to other industry participants. Those who adapt it will have a similar operating structure to the early adapter, while those who don't will be marginalized.

As cost cutting (improved efficiency) becomes ubiquitous among the players, the cost structure among the competitors will become similar. The competition is likely to drive prices and companies' margins lower, and customers will be the final benefactors of lowered operating costs as they receive the fruits of improved efficiency in lower prices. Therefore, it is difficult for a company to keep the benefits from superior operating efficiency in the long run. Depending on the industry structure, sustainability, and degree of a given company's competitive advantage, some will be able to keep the benefits and some won't.

Cost cutting has a defined upper limit, as getting rid of all costs is a natural impossibility. A company may be successful at cost cutting for a while, but much sooner than later it will hit its limit. Colgate's management has done a terrific job cutting costs, bringing margins from low single digits in the late 1980s and early 1990s to as high as 14.4 percent in 2003. This margin improvement has created incredible shareholder value. However, it appears that in late 2003 the company hit an upper limit for margin growth, as it has not reached that level since.

It is important to make sure that cost cutting is not taking place at the expense of future growth. In the late 1990s, Becton Dickenson (a manufacturer of needles and syringes) was bringing to the market a safety needle-syringe system. The company invested tens, if not hundreds, of millions of dollars developing the technology for this needle. A nurse drawing blood from an HIV patient, for instance, could not get infected using the new system. The Food and Drug Administration was about to require hospitals to use the new safety needle-syringe system. Analyzing the company at the time, I asked management about the competition and was told there was none. The only meaningful competitor was U.S. Surgical, which was purchased by Tyco.

Tyco, a serial acquirer at the time, slashed U.S. Surgical's research and development (R&D) significantly, to boost (short-term) cash flows and show off to result-hungry Wall Street. Thus Becton Dickenson was coming to the market with a revolutionary syringe and U.S. Surgical had ... well, nothing.

Economies of Scale Economies of scale are a more sustainable source of margin expansion. Two things have to be present for economies of scale to materialize: sales growth and large fixed costs (i.e., software development costs, factory costs, etc.). As sales increase, costs don't rise as fast (since a large portion of them are fixed), leading to margin expansion. Similar to operating efficiency improvements, depending on the industry structure at least some of the margin expansion will spill over to customers, as competitors may be enjoying similar benefits from growing sales and a higher proportion of fixed costs.

I cannot overemphasize the importance of industry structure when it comes to economies of scale. If a company's competitors outsource manufacturing while the company keeps manufacturing in house, that company's economies of scale increase with the rise of volume, whereas competitors may not benefit to the same degree, since a lower portion of their costs is fixed.

Economies of scale are virtually unlimited in the software industry. It costs tens of millions of dollars to develop the first copy of a software program, whereas the cost of a second copy (the CD it is sold on) may cost pennies or be virtually free (if downloaded from the Internet).

A company that is taking market share from its competitors may benefit from economies of scale while at the same time its competitors will be hurt by diseconomies of scale, as their sales may be facing a decline. Food distributor Sysco is one of the pronounced beneficiaries of margin expansion from rising sales. Sysco distributes food to restaurants and hotels. It has grown organically and through acquisitions. Larger scale allowed it to spread distribution and warehousing costs among greater sales, resulting in profit growth outpacing sales. From 2000 to 2005, its sales increased at a 9.2 percent annual pace and net margin rose from 2.4 percent to 3.2 percent, driving annual earnings growth by an additional 6 percent a year, leading to about 15 percent net income growth.

Stock Buyback

Stock buybacks (if done at appropriate valuations) and nice, fat dividends create shareholder value. Often overlooked, they reduce the risk a company has to take to produce a total return for shareholders as it accelerates earnings per share and dividend growth. In other words, absent a dividend or share buyback, to achieve 12 percent total return (assuming P/E doesn't change) EPS needs to increase 12 percent. However, if the company paid a 3 percent dividend and bought back 2 percent of its shares, it would only have to grow earnings at 7 percent (the first 5 percent coming from dividend and share buyback) to achieve the same 12 percent total return. Usually a company has to take less risk to grow earnings 7 percent versus 12 percent. Share buybacks are not a substitute for organic growth, but are often an underappreciated bonus.

A note of clarification: The preceding statement is imprecise, as it ignores the power of compounding. For clarity I am using simple addition and subtraction, as opposed to doing the precise thing by multiplying and dividing. In future chapters, to simplify the illustration of concepts, I'll continue to be imprecise with my formulas for the sake of clarity by ignoring compounding.

This point ties into the other two dimensions of the QVG framework, Quality and Valuation. A company that is able to buy back a meaningful amount of its stock and pay a fat dividend while growing earnings needs to have significant free cash flows (not be in a capital-intensive business) and/or generate high return on capital—the elements of the Quality dimension. It also needs to trade at an attractive valuation, as dividend yield and the amount needed to buy back stock are also influenced by the stock's valuation.

Stock buybacks can create shareholder value if the stock is purchased cheaply, but they often destroy value when management overpays for the stock. Stock buybacks raise two questions:

1. Is management a good investor?
2. Is the stock purchased to make the numbers (to meet or beat Wall Street's expectations of earnings per share)?

More often than not, management isn't a good investor. Management has a bias—it is usually in love with its company. It spends an enormous amount of time to increase the company's profitability, to build a stronger franchise. This investment of time creates an attachment to the company, leading to a loss of objectivity. In the same way that parents lose objectivity concerning their children's drawing skills (I believe everything my six-year-old son draws is a masterpiece—it really is), management believes that its company is extra special, thus usually overestimating its value and overpaying for the stock.

(If you are analyzing a company in your portfolio and come to the conclusion that the company should not buy back stock at today's valuation, ask yourself a question: If I don't want the company to buy its fairly valued or overvalued stock, should I still own it?)

Management will often do anything to stimulate a company's EPS growth, even it means destroying shareholder wealth through stock buybacks. Colgate, for instance, was buying back stock when it traded at over 30 times earnings, arguably destroying hundreds of millions of dollars of shareholder wealth in the process. Stock buybacks when a stock is undervalued make sense as it is a value investor–like decision to buy an undervalued asset. In addition, buybacks help EPS growth and raise dividend yield at the same time as the buyback lowers the EPS denominator; fewer shareholders own the same piece of pie. What's not to love?

Leveraging the company to buy back stock is not as attractive as if it was done from free (discretionary) cash flows for two reasons:

1. Higher return comes with higher risk, thus possibly putting downward pressure on a company's P/E and offsetting benefits from a share buyback.
2. Leveraging a company's balance sheet has limitations; the company can take on only so much debt, whereas share buybacks from free cash flows over time are limited only by shares outstanding (assuming the company keeps generating free cash flows)—a nice problem to have.

Technically, buying back stock is leveraging the balance sheet, because it lowers equity (cash balance declines, lowering equity and raising the ratio of debt to total assets). Also, with this logic, paying a dividend is leveraging the balance sheet as well, as it forces cash balances and retained earnings to decline, having a similar impact on debt ratios as buying back stock.

However, when a company increases debt for a stock buyback (high leverage scenario), in absolute terms the dollar amount of debt and interest expense rises. Stock buybacks that are sourced from free cash flows (lower leverage scenario) result in more sustainable earnings growth and are arguably less risky (everything held constant), as they don't raise the absolute levels of debt. As long as free cash flows keep rolling, a company can keep buying stock.

Here is a look from the credit analysis perspective (measuring a company's risk of bankruptcy):

- High leverage scenario does the following: raises debt-to-assets ratio and lowers interest coverage ratios.
- Lower leverage scenario does the following: raises debt-to-assets ratio (but by a lower degree than in the first case) and has no impact on interest coverage ratios (it may have a small negative impact as cash paid out earns interest).

Stock buybacks may create shareholder value, but if not done right may destroy it as well.[1]

CASE STUDY: Westwood One's Share Buybacks

Westwood One is a great example of a company that bought back stock at a high valuation and for the wrong reasons.

Westwood One is a creator of content like traffic updates and radio shows, selling the content to both terrestrial and satellite radio stations. It showed little revenue growth from 2001 to 2005. Actually, *little* doesn't do it justice—there has been zero revenue growth since 2002. In real terms (after inflation), revenues actually declined.

Instead of reinvesting money and growing the business, Westwood One bought back stock as if it was going out of style. Unfortunately, the stock itself has been declining for a while, from $35 (a P/E of 35) in 2002 to $7 in January 2007 (a P/E of 13), and earnings also declined over that time. Sadly, the company was buying the stock all the way from the top to the bottom, paying an incredibly high P/E multiple in the process.

I can understand when a company buys back undervalued stock and it subsequently gets cheaper; timing those things is difficult. However, buying back stock that is trading at a high valuation—and I would argue that 25 to 35 times earnings is high, especially for a company that isn't growing revenues—and leveraging its balance sheet (debt increased from $232 million to $406 million by September 2006) to support those purchases shows management misallocation of capital. All EPS growth from 2002 to the first half of 2006 came from share buybacks—none of it was organic (until the earnings took a dive in the second half of 2006).

I cannot fault management for this no-growth company's ridiculous prior valuation; investors had everything to do with that. But I can fault management for buying back stock at very high valuations, instead of reinvesting earnings to grow its core business or paying a nice fat dividend (the company started to pay a dividend only in 2005).[2]

You should analyze stock buybacks on a case-by-case basis asking these four questions:

1. Is the stock purchased when it is undervalued?
2. What is management's motivation for the stock buyback?
3. Is the company leveraging its balance sheet to buy back stock?
4. Is there a better use of the company's cash?

Increase in Asset Utilization

One of the first things that Bob Nardelli did when he came from GE Power Systems to run Home Depot in 2000 was to stretch the time Home Depot took to pay its suppliers. Accounts payable days went from 21 days to 31, and then a year later to 41 days. You may ask, so what? This small change created billions of dollars of cash flow for Home Depot overnight. Nardelli shifted the burden of paying for inventory from Home Depot to its suppliers, who basically extended interest-free loans (the best kind) to Home Depot, freeing up Home Depot's cash flows. This move was justified because Home Depot's smaller competitor, Lowe's, paid its suppliers in about 40 days at the time.

Dell has been shifting the burden of inventory to its suppliers for years. If suppliers want to do business with Dell, they have to deliver inventory to Dell in a matter of days, if not hours. As a result, Dell carries only several days of inventory—a crucial factor in an industry that faces constant price deflation. This historically provided Dell with a competitive advantage against less efficient competitors like Gateway and Hewlett-Packard, which carry 20 and 40 days of inventory, respectively. At the same time, Dell pays its suppliers 60 to 80 days after it purchases parts from them. Dell's management of working capital strategy forces its suppliers to pay for its growth.

Improvements in management of working capital efficiency may lead to value creation for shareholders in many different ways: a company may increase dividend payout, buy back stock, pay down debt, invest for future growth, and so forth.

PAST HAS PASSED

Just because a company was able to rely on a source of growth in the past doesn't mean it can count on it in the future. I strongly recommend you not project past growth into the future with blind linearity. To forecast the future, you need to really understand the past.

On April 17, 2004, *Barron's* published an article called "Colgate's Revenge"[3] (we'll talk about that article in the Valuation chapter as well).

The article made a point that Colgate had a temporary hiccup, and the company would come back to its historical earnings growth again (which in the preceding five years stood at an impressive 13 percent a year).

On April 27, in response to this article, I wrote a piece for TheStreet.com, excerpted here:

> *Let's watch and try to understand what the drivers were behind impressive earnings growth (over the past five years)—what I call sources of growth.*

> - *Sales grew only 2 percent a year.*
> - *Net margins expanded from 9.5 percent to 14.4 percent. That contributed another 8.8 percent to annual net income growth. Most of the margin expansion came from cost cutting since operating leverage only kicks in when there is meaningful sales growth.*
> - *Colgate was buying back stock consistently year after year, which contributed another 1.9 percent to annual EPS growth. Thus, the company presumably paid as much as 33 to 34 times earnings in 1999 and 2000 for its stock.*
> - *The growth rate in overall EPS was close to 13 percent. That's a very impressive pace for a very mature company, but one I consider unsustainable.*

Looking at a 13 percent earnings growth number and projecting it in a straight line into the future is dangerous. Growth engines that were around before (the preceding five years) may not be around in the future. Margin expansion is a finite growth engine (you can cut costs only so much) and, unfortunately for Colgate, it had been its biggest source of past earnings growth. Unless Colgate started growing its top line at a meaningful rate, its past earnings growth rate would be unsustainable. The past has passed—be aware of the past but focus on the future.

FUTURE ENGINES OF GROWTH

Identifying the sources (engines) of future earnings growth and examine each source on an individual basis provides a deeper understanding of the company's growth drivers and it forces you to be more objective and forward-looking in analysis.

Forecast the rate of growth for each engine separately at first, and only after that put them together. This will help you to maintain a rational mind when things don't go as expected. You'll be able to quantify the impact of each growth engine on the company's valuation.

For instance, in my analysis of Jackson Hewitt, a tax preparation company, I identified the following five growth engines:

1. *Young store base.* Over half of Jackson Hewitt stores are less than five years old; this is important because as newer stores mature they process more tax returns, providing 3 to 6 percent of volume growth.
2. *Inflation.* Price inflation in the tax preparation business was and is about 4 to 6 percent a year. It is a function of two factors: price increases and increased complexity of tax returns (Jackson Hewitt charges a fee per form filled out, and the number of forms per tax return has been on the rise forever).
3. *New stores.* New stores growth should bring 3 to 6 percent annual revenue growth. Jackson Hewitt has only a 4 percent market share in a fragmented and growing industry. Since most new stores growth is achieved through franchisees opening new stores, opening new stores doesn't consume much company capital. The company has almost infinite incremental return on capital, as incremental growth costs almost nothing, which leads to another engine of growth—margin expansion.
4. *Margin expansion.* Ninety percent of Jackson Hewitt's stores are oper-ated by franchisees. This business model lends plenty of room to margin expansion: this should contribute 2 to 3 percent to earnings growth on an annual basis.
5. *Share buybacks.* Jackson Hewitt has been using every penny of its free cash flows to buy back stock, which should help earnings per share growth by 5 to 7 percent a year, depending on the company's valuation. The company can achieve that while continuing to pay out 20 percent of net income in dividends, adding another 1 percent or so to total return.

Between all of its engines Jackson Hewitt can grow earnings per share somewhere between 17 and 28 percent a year.

Finding companies that have several growth engines at the core of their growth reduces investment risk; if one growth engine fails or temporarily stalls, the other engines may still be driving the company's growth forward, as is the case with Jackson Hewitt.

Finding the range of possible growth scenarios will help you to determine a range of possible values for the stock when you plug various growth rates into discounted cash flow, absolute P/E, and margin of safety models (discussed in depth in the next chapter).

DIVIDENDS

Dividends versus Stock Buybacks

Yogi Berra must have been talking about dividends and stock buybacks when he said: "In theory there is no difference between theory and practice. In practice there is." Though in theory there is no difference between dividends and stock buybacks, in practice there is. Management will sell their corporate jets and cancel their country club memberships before they cut the dividend, as dividend cuts send a negative signal to investors, in the extreme sending the stock into a tailspin and costing management their jobs. Even when earnings take a turn for the worse, companies often increase dividend payout to maintain the dividend.

Share buybacks, however, are optional. Though a company may have authorization to buy back a certain amount of stock, the execution is under management's control. Share buybacks are, in theory, as value-creative as dividends, but the absence of strict management accountability makes them unpredictable and thus less value-creative than dividends.

On a theoretical level, dividends are just a transfer from a company's corporate account (an account partly owned by shareholders but over which they have no control) to the shareholders' brokerage accounts (over which they have full control). Thus there is a transfer of hypothetical wealth to real wealth. Owning 0.00005 percent of the $10 billion residing in the company's account is hypothetical wealth, since it is not liquid. That 0.00005 percent paid out as a dividend becomes $5,000 in the shareholder's brokerage account: real wealth, as it is a liquid asset. Dividends are a superior choice to earnings growth, as once dividends are paid out they cannot be taken away from you, whereas earnings can be reversed if a company gets into trouble.

When a company pays a high dividend, you are getting paid to wait for the stock to come back to appropriate valuation. Often a significant dividend creates a floor under the stock, as any stock decline increases dividend yield (though dollar dividend per share doesn't change, a lower stock price raises its dividend yield), attracting more income-seeking investors and arguably reducing downside volatility.

Dividends and Range-Bound Markets

As we discussed in Chapter 3, the importance of dividends quadruples in range-bound markets, where they historically represent 90 percent of total return, as opposed to only 19 percent of total return in bull markets (see Exhibit 3.18).

In *The Future for Investors*, Jeremy Siegel says that dividends serve as bear market protectors: "The greater number of shares accumulated through reinvestment of dividends cushions the decline in the value of the investor's portfolio." He goes further: "But extra shares do even more than cushion the decline when the market recovers. Those extra shares will greatly enhance future returns. So in addition to being a market protector, dividends turn into a 'return accelerator' once stock prices turn up. This is why dividend-paying stocks provide the highest return over stock market cycles."[4]

In addition to quantifiable financial benefits, a decent dividend instills confidence about a company's business. Earnings represent a myriad of accounting assumptions. The dividend check is cut from cash flows, not earnings; thus an Enron-like accounting scandal is less likely to happen with a company that is paying a considerable dividend.

As we saw in Exhibit 3.19, in the twentieth century the average dividend yield was 4.3 percent. The current yield is less than half of that; it is at one of the lowest levels in 100 years. Thus dividends paid on an average stock or a broad market index (i.e., S&P 500) are unlikely to provide any salvation and will not help much to protect and accelerate returns in range-bound markets, whereas a portfolio of stocks with higher than average yields should achieve that objective.

Higher Dividend, Slower Growth?

There is a myth that is ingrained in our minds in academia: High dividend payout leads to slower earnings growth.

In theory, companies that have a relatively high dividend payout should grow earnings at a slower rate than those that don't pay dividends. Intellectually this makes sense: Paying out more earnings leaves less to be reinvested in growing the business. In reality this only makes sense at the extreme. For example, a start-up company generally produces little free cash flow, as a large portion of its capital is consumed by investment in future growth (R&D, infrastructure, sales force, factories). Any capital it diverts to paying dividends will hinder its growth. But the reality is that a great portion of publicly traded companies have passed that stage and generate plenty of free cash flows that are available to pay higher dividends.

A study conducted by Cliff Asness and Robert Arnott called "Surprise! Higher Dividends = Higher Earnings Growth," published in the *Financial Analysts Journal*, showed that companies that had a higher dividend payout actually grew earnings faster.

This is the summary of their findings:

The historical evidence strongly suggests that expected future earnings growth is fastest when current payout ratios are high and slowest when payout ratios are low. This relationship is not subsumed by other factors, such as simple mean reversion in earnings. Our evidence thus contradicts the views of many who believe that substantial reinvestment of retained earnings will fuel faster future earnings growth. Rather, it is consistent with anecdotal tales about managers signaling their earnings expectations through dividends or engaging, at times, in inefficient empire building. Our findings offer a challenge to market observers who see the low dividend payouts of recent times as a sign of strong future earnings to come.[5]

This study goes against theory, as theory doesn't factor in destruction of capital by corporate management. A company that has a high dividend payout operates in a different environment from the one that is swimming in shareholder cash, as rigid dividend payouts force management to maximize the value of every dollar retained. Higher dividend payout instills discipline but doesn't hurt the growth prospects.

Cash that has not been paid out is often squandered by management. Microsoft's large cash position throughout the 1980s and 1990s did not create much shareholder value, as it allowed Microsoft to waste billions of dollars on so-called strategic investments (a $5 billion investment in AT&T comes to mind). Or Mobil Oil, swimming in cash in the late 1970s, deciding to "diversify its cash flow" by buying Montgomery Ward, a now-bankrupt retailer, qualifying it as the dumbest waste of shareholder capital ever.

Dividends Are Very Important, But . . .

In his book *Contrarian Investment Strategies: The Next Generation*, David Dreman demonstrates that low P/E and high dividend strategies have performed considerably better in both range-bound and bull markets. A study he conducted from 1970 to 1996 covered 12 years of the 1966–1982 range-bound market, and captured 14 years of the 1982–2000 secular bull market. During that period, at the time when the average stock price dropped 7.5 percent, a portfolio of low-P/E stocks went down 5.7 percent and a portfolio of high-dividend-yielding stocks declined only 3.8 percent.[6]

Though dividends are an extremely important contributor to portfolio returns in the range-bound market, they should come secondary to other analysis. Dreman found that though a high dividend strategy beat the market from 1970 to 1996, it proved inferior to low P/E, low price-to-cash flows, and low price-to-book strategies. In other words, a stock should not be bought automatically just because it pays a high dividend. High dividends are a great help, but should not be looked at in isolation. They should be approached in the context of the aforementioned cornerstones (inherent P/E contraction and earnings growth).

GROWTH MATTERS — A LOT!

Though this book is titled *Active Value Investing*, this doesn't mean that the Growth element is unimportant. Quite to the contrary, there is value in growth! Growth is a very important value creator, as it helps to fight the P/E compression of the range-bound market. It should not be approached in isolation (i.e., buying companies with the fastest earnings growth and ignoring the Quality and Valuation dimensions), but it should be a very important component of your analysis.

CHAPTER 7

The "V"—Valuation

Even if a carpenter finds the hammer to be his favorite tool, he never comes on the job with just a hammer (at least not intentionally, not if he is sober). He brings his toolbox with a variety of tools in it. It's the same with investing: You have many valuation tools at your disposal, and they all have advantages and drawbacks. However, by using them in conjunction with one another and being aware of their strengths and weaknesses, you may make a more accurate (multiangle: relative and absolute) valuation of any given company.

TEVYE THE MILKMAN'S APPROACH TO VALUATION

Note: If you feel that you have a fairly good understanding of discounted cash flow analysis and use of relative valuation tools and you want to jump right into the meat of the valuation discussion, you may skip the Tevye the Milkman section and go straight to the next section, "Review of Relative Valuation Tools."

The application of relative and absolute value could hardly be demonstrated on less glamorous objects than cows. A farmer (let's call him Tevye the Milkman) has many ways of figuring the right price when making a cow purchase decision. Tevye lives in a small village similar to the one we saw in *Fiddler on the Roof*. Tevye is a simple fellow, not familiar with the financial maxim that the value of any asset (and a cow is an asset) is the present value of the asset's future cash flows.

Tevye was thinking about buying a young cow, which he'd name Golde, after his first wife. He expected Golde to produce about 2,500 gallons of milk a year, which he'd sell for about $1.20 a gallon, bringing him about $3,000 in revenues a year (see Exhibit 7.1). After paying for a heated barn,

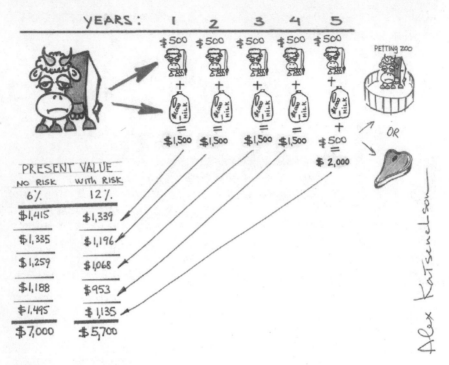

EXHIBIT 7.1 Golde's Cash Flows According to Tevye

high-quality feed, stud fees, top-notch veterinarian services, his nephew to take care of and milk Golde, and finally taxes, he expected to pocket about $1,000 a year just from the milk.

Golde would give birth to a calf every year (not unusual for cows), which Tevye would sell at a livestock auction for $500. After five years of hard work, Golde's milk production would likely fall off—she is not a robot, after all. Tevye could sell 700-pound Golde to his friend the butcher for $0.70 per pound, netting him about $500. For those who don't want to see Golde slaughtered, he might sell her to a local petting zoo—he is a kind man, after all. Tevye is not aware of it, but that final good-bye, Golde's liquidation value, is called her terminal value.

What's She Worth?

Tevye believed that at the most, Golde would be worth about $8,000 to him. He figured that between milk ($1,000) and a calf ($500) she would generate about $1,500 of cash a year for five years—that is, $7,500 plus another $500 from a butcher or petting zoo at the end of year 5. So at first, Tevye thought that in the worst possible case he would not pay more than $8,000 for Golde.

The $8,000 he'd receive over the five-year period would not be the same as $8,000 today—a lot of things could happen in five years. There is inflation and opportunity cost. The $8,000 value of the cow did not account for inflation and opportunity cost.

Tevey's son-in-law, a banker, found out that Tevye was contemplating buying Golde. Wanting to win the heart of his father-in-law he offered (on behalf of the bank he worked for) to finance Golde's future cash flows by giving Tevye a lump sum today of $7,000.* In exchange, Tevye would have to agree to pay the bank $1,500 a year for five years and an additional $500 at the end of year 5 from selling Golde. In other words, the son-in-law's bank would finance Golde's purchase at 6 percent a year.

Tevye did not require the financing, but his son-in-law gave him an important insight: If Tevye could predict and forecast Golde's cash flows with absolute certainty, taking all the risk out of the transaction, then he could accept his son-in-law's offer and buy Golde at the livestock auction for $7,000 at the most. (But why bother buying Golde for $7,000? He could just give the money to his son-in-law and let earning 6 percent a year be his son-in-law's problem.)

Tevye thought the purchase of Golde would be riskless if:

- Golde did not get sick with the crazy disease—the mad cow.
- Feed prices did not fluctuate.
- Milk prices and demand were not subject to competition from farmers across the pond.
- The "other" milk was not stealing shelf space from "real" milk in the local supermarket (Tevye never had much respect for soy milk, which he called soy juice. He told his daughters, "When you find an udder on a soybean, I'll call it milk").
- The taxes could not be increased on a whim to finance things that Tevye did not really understand or care about (he never had much interest in politics).

If Tevye bought Golde for $7,000, he would be compensated for inflation and opportunity cost (6 percent earned by his son-in-law) but would not be compensated for the extra risk.

---

*$6,6912.17 to be exact.

Fair Value and Risk Premium

Tevye's gut and experience were telling him that he should at least demand double the riskless rate that his son-in-law offered him, and require a 12 percent rate of return for Golde's risky cash flows. This would bring Golde's fair value (also called intrinsic value) to about $5,700.* In other words, instead of discounting Golde's cash flows (bringing future cash flows to today's value) at 6 percent—what the son-in-law did when he offered Tevye $7,000—Tevye should use 12 percent. Some may say it would be asking for a 6 percent premium to a risk-free rate of 6 percent (see Exhibit 7.2).

If Tevye bought Golde for $5,700, the value of Golde's cash flows discounted at 12 percent, he would be compensated for inflation, opportunity cost, and risks that arrive with owning a cow.

Yes, the risk—unpredictability of future cash flows could always turn in his favor. Milk prices might increase, feed prices and taxes could decline, beef prices could climb, Golde could turn out to be a super cow and produce a lot more milk than he expected, or the petting zoo could go wild and pay several times what he expected for Golde. However, his years of experience have taught him to hope for the best and prepare for the worst. If the future turns out brighter than he expects, that will be a nice bonus and he can install indoor plumbing in his house.

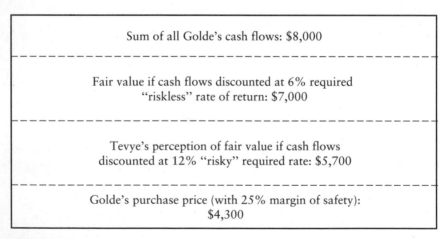

Sum of all Golde's cash flows: $8,000
Fair value if cash flows discounted at 6% required "riskless" rate of return: $7,000
Tevye's perception of fair value if cash flows discounted at 12% "risky" required rate: $5,700
Golde's purchase price (with 25% margin of safety): $4,300

EXHIBIT 7.2 Golde's Absolute Valuation Stats

---

*$5,690.88 to be exact.

Margin of Safety

*The margin of safety is dependent on the price paid. It will be large
at one price, small at some other price, and nonexistent at some
higher price.*
                                    —Benjamin Graham, *The Intelligent Investor*

Tevye never met Benjamin Graham, nor did he read his book *The Intelligent
Investor*; he never heard of the "margin of safety" (buying at discount to fair
value) that Benjamin Graham popularized in his writing. However, Tevye
had several daughters' weddings to pay for, and this transformed him into a
cautious farmer. Some would have called him a value investor; however, for
Tevye it was just common sense. He thought if he bought something at fair
value (Golde at $5,700 would be fairly valued after factoring in the risk),
then he had a little margin for being wrong. Even if his forecasts were right
on the money, there were still many variables that he could not control or
forecast.

Discounting Golde's cash flows using the 12 percent risky rate (6
percent above the riskless rate) provided Tevye some buffer for being wrong.
The 6 percent risk premium provided a $1,300 risk premium buffer (the
difference between $7,000 and $5,700). However, if Golde was purchased
at fair value ($5,700) and cash flows came in below Tevye's estimates, he
would not be fully compensated for the risk taken.

But he needed protection (a margin of safety) for two reasons:

1. *As a source of returns.* If things turned out as expected (or better),
   then he would have made extra return from buying Golde below her
   estimated fair value of $5,700. For instance, if he purchased Golde at
   $4,500 (about a 20 percent margin of safety) and all assumptions played
   out as he expected, then in addition to earning a 12 percent annual rate
   of return Tevye would make $1,200 from the margin of safety.
2. *As a risk absorber.* More important, if Tevye made a mistake in
   forecasting future cash flows, or some of the risks that he had no
   control over surfaced and impacted the cash flows, he'd have a margin
   of safety to fall back on. At a 20 percent margin of safety, (discounted)
   cash flows could have been off by $1,200 and he still would have made
   his 12 percent annual rate of return.

Diversification

Tevye was not a naive farmer. He knew that Golde could become sick and
possibly die, and then he would lose a large portion of his investment. And
though the margin of safety could still soften the blow, it would not offset

the total loss (and we are not even talking about the emotional scars of seeing the cow named after his first wife die). This was the reason Tevye never put all his cash in one cow (or eggs in one basket), and bought cows from different regions of the country to mitigate this remote but possible risk. With these thoughts, Tevye went to the livestock auction (not much different from the stock market) looking for his Golde.

The Livestock Auction

Tevye did not buy Golde on day one. The weather was sunny, his fellow farmers were excited about the prospects of the cattle market, and the bidding for cows went too high—many sold above their intrinsic value (in Tevye's opinion). Expecting that the sun would be shining all the time, many farmers got caught up in the moment of excitement, forgot that they were farmers, and bought cows ignoring the expected cash flows and hoping that other farmers (who are known in investments as "bigger fools") would buy these cows at higher prices tomorrow.

The second day was more productive than the first, but still Tevye did not buy his Golde. The prices were still too high, but instead of obsessing over prices Tevye did research on the cows that were available for sale. He identified the best of breed, the ones that would be less susceptible to getting sick and had the potential to surprise him with their milk production.

The third day was Tevye's day—the day when he bought his Golde. It was a rainy day, and cattle prices did not go up as everybody expected. Many disappointed farmers who had just bought cows at prices above their intrinsic values with a hope of selling them at a profit were selling them at any price just to recover some of their investment. In addition, all this coincided with the liquor store next door having a huge sale, and many disenchanted farmers went to take advantage of it.

Tevye found his Golde. She was not the star of the show, but was definitely the best of breed; she met all Tevye's stringent quality criteria, and the best part was Tevye bought her with a 25 percent margin of safety to her intrinsic value—he paid only $4,300!

Value Creators and Destroyers

Without giving it a second thought, Tevye was using a discounted cash flow model to analyze Golde's purchase. He estimated the drivers of value:

- The revenues—milk, calves, and beef (or proceeds from selling Golde to a petting zoo) she'll produce over the years.

- The costs associated with taking care of his favorite cow, which had all the personality traits of his first wife (calm, cooperative, low-maintenance).
- Her longevity—aside from personal attachment, the longer Golde can keep producing high-quality milk, the more valuable she becomes.
- The external risk factors—the whims of consumer demand, taxes, political risks, regulation of the dairy industry, and so on.

Estimating all these creators (and possible destroyers) of value was an immensely important mental exercise, as it kept Tevye in the boots of a farmer, not a speculator. He believed that if, at the livestock auction on day one, his fellow farmers had been making their decisions based on expected cash flows from the cows, they would not have been buying cows as if milk was about to become "the new vodka." The discounted cash flow analysis would have cooled down the euphoria that came with a sunny day and rising cattle prices, and kept the farmers from turning into speculators.

Relative Valuation Tools

There were other techniques at Tevye's disposal that assisted him in buying Golde. To him they were the shortcuts, his rule-of-thumb tools: the "price to anything" ratios (more accurately, price divided by anything), where anything could be earnings, cash flow, revenues, gallons of milk, or anything else! His son-in-law called them relative valuation tools, as they established a relative value link between a price and a value creator ("anything").

Relative valuation tools were not an intuitive pricing resource to Tevye at first, but after using them for a while he learned to appreciate their simplicity and ease of use.

After a while, price to cash flows started to appeal to Tevye's intuitive sense. At $5,700 (Golde's fair value in his estimate), he would have paid 3.8 times Golde's annual cash flows of $1,500 ($5,700 divided by $1,500). It would take him just a bit less than four years to break even (make his money back) on Golde's purchase, and if his estimates of Golde's cash flows were right, Golde would pay for herself in four years (see Exhibit 7.3).

Whereas estimating and discounting Golde's cash flows provided Tevye with an insight into Golde's value in absolute terms, relative valuation tools provided a relative assessment for pricing value creators when considering Golde's history or in relation to the valuation of other cows. Tevye found that often "price to anything" measures were an adequate shortcut to figure out the appropriate price of a cow.

Despite the provinciality of Tevye's livestock auction, farmers still had to disclose the cash flows and revenues that their cows generated in previous

	Price to Cash Flows
Golde's fair price according to Tevye: $5,700	3.8 times
Lowest price over previous five years: $4,050	2.7 times
Highest price over previous five years: $12,000	8 times
Young farmer purchased Golde-like cow for $10,500	7 times
Golde's purchase price (with 25% margin of safety): $4,300	2.8 times

EXHIBIT 7.3 Golde's and Similar Cows' Relative Valuation Stats

years in accordance with rules of the Cow Exchange Commission (CEC), a government agency not much different from the Securities and Exchange Commission (SEC) in the United States. The CEC checked the accuracy of farmers' claims, and those who had the audacity to deceive their fellow farmers were publicly whipped.

From his wealth of experience, Tevye knew that at 3.8 times cash flows a typical two-year-old cow (and Golde had just turned two) was fairly valued. A quick look at historical price-to-cash flows ratios confirmed that a cow of Golde's stature on average changed hands at about 4 times cash flows. Also, over the previous five years, similar cows changed hands at as low as 2.7 times cash flows (putting a price tag of $4,050 on Golde), and went as high as 8 times (putting a $12,000 price tag on her). In Tevye's estimation, at 8 times cash flows ($12,000 price tag), Golde would change hands at a higher value than the sum of all the cash flows she could possibly produce for her owner over her entire productive life ($8,000). Bingo! Tevye had an epiphany. He saw one of the greatest limitations of "price to anything" measures: In the heat of the moment these measures can lose their meaning for farmers, and turn them into irrational speculators.

On day two, while at the livestock auction, Tevye overheard two farmers having an interesting conversation. The younger one argued that at 7 times cash flows ($10,500) Golde was a great buy, as only yesterday (day one) she demanded as much as 8 times cash flows. Another farmer, substantially older than the first, who had experience and common sense written all over his wrinkled face (just like Tevye's), said:

"Son, just because one fool found a bigger fool to buy a cow for a ridiculous price doesn't mean that's what the cow is worth. Knowing what happened in the past doesn't tell us what will happen tomorrow. After the dust settles and everybody comes down from all the excitement, prices will swing back to their true value. How long will it take? Well, it may or may not take a while; the answer will be obvious to us only after the fact. That's why I stop bidding on sunny days when everybody's got a smile on their face. True value gets real hard to peg on days like that. And of this I'm certain: The cash flows that this cow will bring for its owner in the future don't support the 7 times cash flows multiple that she's trading for at the moment."

The younger farmer shrugged, and bought a Golde-like cow anyway, expecting to sell it the next day (day three) at a higher price. As the older farmer predicted, the dust did settle, and it didn't take long at all. In fact, it settled the very next day.

Tevye believed that the past price-to-cash flows ("price to anything") ratio had its advantages, as it showed the valuation road on which Golde had traveled in the past. However, don't forget that he was a cautious fellow. He believed that knowing the past is helpful, but understood that the valuation road that farmers will take cows down in the future may not be at all like the roads gone by.

And as it turned out, the price-to-cash flow ratio did have its advantages: It quickly helped him to identify undervalued cows on the livestock auction. In addition, when farmers started to panic and cattle prices began to decline, he could without difficulty gauge the level of cheapness of the overall cattle market. He objectively determined the required margin of safety for Golde—25 percent—and figured that he wanted to buy Golde at about 2.9 times cash flows (3.8, the fair value price to cash flows, reduced by a 25 percent margin of safety). Then he just waited for prices to drop and bought his Golde.

Tevye did not buy Golde at the lowest price, but he bought her at a significant discount to her intrinsic value. Maybe if he had waited a little longer he could have gotten her a bit cheaper, but Tevye did not mind, because he knew he'd bought a great cow (his Golde) at a great price. Besides, trying to outsmart the auction by scraping the bottom had emotional appeal but little practical use. He could brag to his neighbors about how smart he was, but that was not Tevye. The bragging rights were of little value to him, as they would not help him to pay for his daughters' weddings, and after all—that is what this purchase was about.

REVIEW OF RELATIVE VALUATION TOOLS

Relative valuation tools such as price to cash flows (P/CF), price to earnings (P/E), price to sales (P/S), price to dividends (P/D), price to book (P/B) and others are good, quick, and easy shortcuts to analyze and screen stocks. Their ease of use and simplicity of calculations have made them very popular among investors.

For simplicity of this discussion I'll use P/E (the most popular of the bunch) to demonstrate application of relative valuation tools and their use in the range-bound markets.

Relative valuation analysis allows investors to see how the current P/E stacks up against other competitors, industry averages, and the market or itself on a current or historical basis. The P/E ratio is an important tool, if for only one reason—almost everybody uses it. The market has a view on stocks, and it expresses that view in the price it pays for a unit of earnings.

An investor buying a stock wants to assess whether the stock is cheap or expensive. One way of doing it is to see at what P/E this company has changed hands in the past. If a company is trading at a P/E of 15, but in the past it never traded at a P/E higher than 12, it may not appear to be expensive on the surface, but may be expensive relative to its past history. The market participants constantly vote with their actions (buying and selling) and inactions on how much they'll pay for one company's earnings versus its competitors. Relative valuation analysis provides insight into how the market has voted on a company's valuation in the past.

CASE STUDY: Why Banks Trade at Low P/Es

In the past large banks have consistently traded at a discount to market P/E. In Exhibit 7.4, I assembled some historical and current statistics on the largest banks in the United States. With the exception of Fifth Third Bancorp, based on their relative P/Es banks traded between 0.66 and 0.90 (industry average of 0.84, a 16 percent discount) of market P/E over the past 10 years. Why? Does it have to do with financial leverage? Or complexity of the financial statements? Maybe the answer is a lot simpler—they are slow growers.

I looked at some larger banks to see whether they had been slow growers in the past, and I couldn't reach that conclusion. Many of these banks, in fact, had achieved respectable earnings growth and paid above-average dividends in the process (see Exhibit 7.4). I then looked at expectations for future earnings growth, and they appeared not to be below average, either, while dividend yield of most banks is double the average S&P 500 company. With the exception of Fifth Third, which Wall Street once loved to love and now loves to hate, the rest of the pack was trading at a substantial discount to the market (they still are).

EXHIBIT 7.4 Historical Bank Valuations: Do Banks Deserve to Trade at a Discount?

	10-Year Historical			Current		
	Median P/E	Average EPS Growth Rate	Relative P/E Ratio	P/E	Dividend Yield	First Call Projected EPS Growth
Citigroup Inc.	15.3	16.4%	0.82	12.0	3.6%	10.0%
U.S. Bancorp	14.3	17.3%	0.89	12.7	4.5%	10.0%
Fifth Third Bancorp	22.7	14.5%	1.25	13.9	4.1%	10.0%
Wells Fargo & Co.	15.6	14.4%	0.90	13.2	3.1%	10.9%
Bank of America Corp.	13.4	9.2%	0.66	10.4	4.4%	9.0%
Regions Financial Corp.	13.7	4.6%	0.76	12.7	4.0%	8.0%
Wachovia Corp.	13.6	2.8%	0.73	11.2	4.0%	10.0%
JPMorgan Chase & Co.	15.0	−2.7%	0.73	12.2	2.7%	10.0%
Group Average	**15.5**	**10%**	**0.84**	**12.3**	**3.8%**	**9.7%**

Data Source: Standard & Poor's Compustat.

The answer must be more complex than just the growth rates. I believe the answer to banks' lower P/Es lies in other factors, each of which I'll cover: cyclicality, financial leverage, interest rate volatility, complexity of financials, and quality of growth.

Cyclicality

The banking business is closely tied to the health of the economy. As the economy expands, demand for loans increases and bad debts decline—a combination that improves banks' profitability. In a contracting economy, of course, the reverse takes place.

Because investors pay up for predictability, they rarely pay a full market multiple for the volatility that comes with cyclical companies. Cyclical heavy-industrial companies like Caterpillar and Ingersoll Rand, for example, usually trade below the market P/E, just as many banks do.

Financial Leverage

We have not had a bank crisis in the United States for a while, so most investors have forgotten just how risky banks can be. But as Warren Buffett has said, by the time you find out a bank has a problem, it will be too late. The equity at most banks stands at a meager 6 to 10 percent of total assets, so when a bank does make a mistake, its high leverage amplifies the problem.

Interest Rate Volatility

Banks are subject to the risks that come with changing interest rates. They prosper when the difference between long-term and short-term rates—in other words, the interest rate spread—is high. However, when that spread narrows, it becomes increasingly difficult for banks to make any money. Many banks have addressed the problem by boosting their fee businesses. For example, fees account for a full 46 percent of U.S. Bancorp's income, thereby making the company less susceptible to swings in interest rates.

Complexity of Financials

I could teach my six-year-old son Jonah to analyze retailers' financials in about 20 minutes, if I could get him to sit and concentrate for that long. Okay, maybe I'll have to wait a couple of years. But the point is, retailers' financials are easy to understand. A quick look at the income statement and a glance at the balance sheet (especially the part that focuses on inventories) will quickly tell you what happened during a retailer's most recent quarter.

Banks and insurance companies are very different animals. Where analyzing a retailer is like playing checkers, analyzing a bank is akin to playing chess. (I'll save the 3-D chess analogy for insurance companies; their financials are even more complex than banks.) Investors need to look at financial statements and at dozens of other sources to assess a bank's true performance. And that's a problem, since investors tend to embrace simplicity and shy away from complexity.

To make things even worse, banks' financials are riddled with assumptions. Although all companies have to make some assumptions in their financials, the complexity and magnitude of those assumptions increase exponentially with banks. Consider, for example, that it's not uncommon for a high-growth bank to have its expected credit losses understated because of the immaturity of its portfolio (in other words, new loans predominate). However, as growth decelerates and a large portion of the loans matures, credit losses may skyrocket beyond the estimated provisions.

Quality of Growth

The very size of large banks often gets in the way of their ability to continue producing high-percentage growth. Instead, the bulk of growth for large banks comes from acquisitions. An acquirer is able to fold most of the acquired bank's operations into its existing infrastructure, which, in turn, results in huge cost savings and, of course, higher earnings.

That sounds great on paper. However, acquisitions come with risks, including integration challenges. Bank One (now part of JPMorgan Chase) learned about that problem firsthand when it acquired First USA. Soon after the acquisition, Bank One ran into huge problems with the incompatibility of the combined companies' computer systems, and the stock tumbled as a result. Regions Financial had similar integration problems after making successful acquisitions for a long time. To sustain its growth, it eventually had to start marking larger and larger acquisitions, and that's when the problems began.

In addition to the integration risks, bank executives' egos and their attendant desires to manage bigger and bigger (though not necessarily better) empires often get in the way of common sense. Ultimately, the acquirer overpays for the acquired.

Still, despite all of the potential pitfalls, acquisitions have been the main source of EPS growth for most large banks. In fact, I can't think of a large bank that became large by way of organic growth. Not one!

Bottom Line

Growth by acquisition is much riskier and usually more expensive than organic growth is. Investors recognize that risk, and thus they put a lot less value on large banks' growth. So, to a large degree slow organic growth is, in part, responsible for banks' below-market valuations. However, higher risk caused by cyclicality, high financial leverage, and the complexity of financials contributes to the lower P/E as well.[1]

A multitude of factors could have impacted past valuation, many of which may or may not repeat in the future, such as:

- Historical P/Es may be benchmarking events during a period of time that may or may not recur in the foreseeable future. For instance, the stock market bubble of the late 1990s drove stock valuations to unprecedented levels. Unless you expect the bubbly valuations to return again soon, stocks (and cows) are unlikely to revisit those exuberant valuations.
- Past sales and earnings growth rates may be different from the future ones. P/Es are impacted significantly by investors' expectations for future earnings and cash flows growth. If future growth for the company is expected to be higher than observed in the past, then future valuation levels may exceed the ones of the past, and vice versa.
- Significant changes have taken place that will change how investors look at the company. The changes may take the form of divesting highly cyclical, low-growth, or high-risk businesses. The divestitures may also simplify and make a company's business more understandable and transparent to investors.

Past valuation is not a guarantee of where the company will trade in the future; it is just a guide to future valuation.

ABSOLUTE VALUATION TOOLS—DISCOUNTED CASH FLOW ANALYSIS

Discounted cash flow (DCF) analysis—the "common sense" model that Tevye used to estimate the value of Golde—is the honorary member of the absolute valuation tools club. We'll discuss the absolute P/E model, its lesser-known member, in a bit, but for now let's focus on DCF model.

The DCF model makes a multitude of company projections: future sales, profit margins, capital expenditures, networking capital requirements (accounts receivable, inventory, and accounts payable), and many other variables to determine its future cash flows, including a terminal value of the company at the end of the forecasting period. Once future cash flows are estimated, they are discounted back to the present at an appropriate discount rate to find the estimated value of the stock. This result is then compared to an actual price. Many would stop at this point, but this is just a start.

The DCF model output—the estimated intrinsic value of a company—is sensitive to the assumptions that went into the model, and there are plenty of those. As a result, expecting precise answers from the model is impractical. At best, it shows the direction of a stock's value.

The DCF model is a "vaguely right" model, and should be used that way. Thus, the final step in applying the DCF model should be changing the assumptions that went into the model to find the range of likely values. Range of values doesn't have the sex appeal of a precisely crafted number, but again we are only trying to be vaguely right with our end result.

I often see sell-side analysts use the DCF model as a precise tool in research reports, saying something along the lines of: "XYZ stock at $10 appears to be undervalued by 7 percent as our DCF model shows that it's worth $10.70." Often all that analyst has to do is increase a discount rate by a fraction of a percentage point to see the estimated value of the stock drop and therefore become fully valued.

The DCF model is in most part a forward-looking model. Though the inputs that go into it often take into consideration what happened in the past, the gap between the past and the future is reached through the analysis. Tevye, for instance, looked at what milk production and the cost of raising a Golde-like cow were in the past and took that information into consideration, and then he projected (using his understanding of farming) what they would be going forward.

Golde's intrinsic value was estimated by using the "common sense" model, and was absolute as it was tied to the cash flows Golde was expected to produce in the future. It was not tied to relative market metrics (i.e., past valuation or comparative valuation that similar cows were selling for).

Great Barometer of Expectations

The DCF model is also a useful tool for measuring market expectations that are built into a stock's valuation. By plugging different assumptions into the model and trying to equate the end result to the price of the stock, you should be able to gauge the assumptions that are priced into the stock by the market, and then evaluate the stock's attractiveness based on achievability of the assumptions.

The DCF model is useful in extreme circumstances, in much the same way Tevye's analysis kept him out of the livestock auction on days one and two, when the Golde-like cows were selling for prices higher than the cash flows they'd be expected to generate over their useful lives. DCF models would have kept investors away from high-flying dot-coms and many other grossly overvalued stocks during the 1990s bubble.

Even if investors discounted their cash flows using the risk-free rate, as if these companies had a license from the U.S. government to print money (making them default riskless entities, which they were not), it would show investors that expectations built into these bubbly stocks were not from this planet.

The DCF model serves as a great barometer of expectations built into a stock on the other end of the emotional spectrum, as well—when the stock is beaten down. In 2004, Nokia traded as low as $11 after it reported disappointing earnings, loss in market share in the United States, and shrinking margins. However, the market overreacted (at it often does), and DCF analysis revealed that even at 3 percent lower margins and pricing in little sales growth, the stock was 40 to 50 percent undervalued—and that was not counting $3 of net cash per share (cash less debt) Nokia had on the balance sheet.

The Value of the Process

There is another hidden benefit of the DCF model—the practical process of constructing the model. Putting the model together should help you better understand the value creators and destroyers for a company. DCF also works as a great prioritizing tool in company analysis, focusing your energy on the inputs that have the largest impact on value creation (i.e., DCF variables like profit margins, sales growth, capital expenditures, accounts receivable, inventories, forecasted period length, etc.).

When in the early 2000s I analyzed Dollar General, a retailer focusing on the low-income consumer, the company had 4,300 stores and was planning to open 15 percent more stores a year for the foreseeable future. After I constructed a DCF model for Dollar General, I realized that inventory turnover (or inventory days outstanding) is a lot more important than almost any other input into the model. For example, changing the sales growth rate assumption from 17 percent to 12 percent (over the next 5 to 10 years) had a lot less impact on estimated intrinsic value of the company than increasing inventory days from 100 to 120.

This made sense—Dollar General was opening 700-plus stores a year, and each new store needed inventory. A 20 percent increase in inventory impacted the cost of opening new stores and inventory costs at the existing 4,300 stores, and significantly impacted free cash flows. Therefore, in the Dollar General analysis, I spent more time focusing on inventory management than on sales growth.

RELATIVE VERSUS ABSOLUTE TOOLS

Though relative valuation tools are simple and intuitive, they have to be used with caution in range-bound markets, as the valuation the future holds is likely to be different from the past. Relative valuation tools benchmarked to valuations achieved in a past bull market are unlikely to be observed for a long time ahead. They may produce false positives (give false buy signals) in a range-bound market and lead investors into the relative valuation trap.

Here is an example of the relative valuation trap. In the April 17, 2004, article I mentioned in the preceding chapter, "Colgate's Revenge," *Barron's* wrote:

> At a recent $56, the stock [Colgate] trades at 21 times expected '04 earnings of $2.62 a share and 19 times next year's estimates of $2.92. That's far below the 29 P/E the stock sported three years ago and among the lowest multiples in the consumer-products realm.[2]

My response to the *Barron's* article was published by TheStreet.com in an article entitled "Barron's Is Wrong on Colgate":

> The Barron's *article argues that [Colgate] stock is cheap since the current P/E is 21 times '04 earnings and is low relative to where it*

was in 1999–2000. This argument holds as much water as arguing that Yahoo! is cheap at 60 times earnings since during the bubble it traded at 600 times earnings. Even a high-quality company that actually is growing earnings at 11–13 percent a year doesn't deserve to trade at 29 times earnings.... Our discounted cash flow model shows that if reasonable (achievable) expectations are factored in, the company should trade at a P/E around 15–16 times earnings at the most. That is after we factored in the quality and sustainability of Colgate's cash flows.

This *Barron's* reporter fell into the typical relative valuation trap. Yes, the stock did appear inexpensive relative to the high valuation it commanded in the late 1990s. However, the valuations observed in the late stages of the bull market are not a good proxy to determine the appropriate valuation for a stock, as they are unlikely to be observed in the future. In fact, before Colgate's P/E was pushed into oblivious to logic territory in the late 1990s, the stock traded at around 16 to 17 times earnings (see Exhibit 7.5). (I don't have a bone to pick with *Barron's*; it is a fine business newspaper that often defies conventional thinking with its excellent articles. It has gotten a lot more things right than wrong. The relative valuation trap is seductive and lures even the finest in the business to fall into it on occasion.)

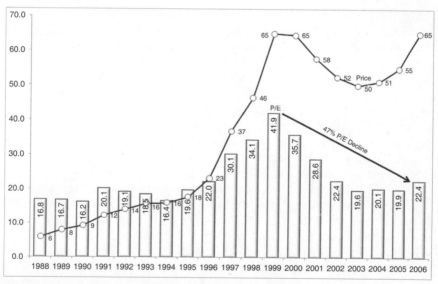

EXHIBIT 7.5   Colgate-Palmolive's P/E and Price History
Data Source: Standard & Poor's Compustat.

Absolute valuation models (i.e., discounted cash flow analysis, dividend discount model, and similar multiple-variable input-driven models) serve as better tools for stock valuation since they don't suffer from benchmarking errors.

ABSOLUTE MODELS OVERVIEW

Through absolute P/E, discount rate, and margin of safety models, we will explore how you can use the Quality, Valuation, and Growth framework as an equalizing tool, putting stocks with different risk and return characteristics on the same comparative scale (footing) in the portfolio.

I was often asked by students taking my investment class at the University of Colorado what constitutes appropriate (fair value) P/E for a given company. Despite being more complex than a P/E ratio, students found the discounted cash flow model intuitive, as after a magnitude of assumptions it spits out a precise intrinsic value for the company.

I had an intuitive feel for an appropriate P/E ratio for a company, gained mostly from the experience of looking at a lot of them over the years, but I found it hard to express my intuitive understanding in general terms. At the same time, I believed that the traditional P/E to growth rate (PEG) ratio is too simplistic (flawed) and does not do justice to capturing the risk differentials between industries and stocks. It assumes a linear relationship between P/E and earnings growth. The PEG aficionado is looking to buy stocks with low PEG ratios. A 30 percent earnings grower trading at a P/E of 20 and a PEG of 0.66 (20 divided by 30) is more attractive than a stock trading at a P/E of 2 but growing earnings at 1 percent a year, resulting in a PEG of 2 (2 divided by 1). That did not seem logical to me.

Higher growth of earnings usually comes at higher risk; thus the relationship between P/E and a company's growth rate is far from being linear, and the PEG ratio doesn't address this issue. In addition, the traditional PEG ratio is focused solely on earnings and ignores dividends. On top of all that, it assumes that a company that is not growing earnings is worthless (P/E divided by 0 percent growth = 0 value).

At first, keeping my students in mind, I created a multifactor models (a fancy word for a model with multiple inputs) to help them gain insight into what goes into the P/E ratio, margin of safety, and discount rate. These models quantified how my firm and I looked at these variables. Similar to the discounted cash flow model, the process of going through the models brought clarity, as it put different value creators and destroyers together. Later I found that these models removed a lot of subjectivity from the analytical process, and I started using them in my day-to-day research.

THE FALSE PRECISION OF MATH

We are about to talk about several quantitative models: absolute P/E, discount rate, and margin of safety models. I'll be throwing around precise numbers like "low business risk factor of 0.9" and "financial risk factor of 1.25." I implore you to understand that there is nothing unique or "future telling" about these numbers. My goal in this discussion is to provide the qualitative framework and illustrate its possible use with quantitative examples. Using the so-called precision of math, I am trying to illustrate the process of analysis, not a secret formula that will answer investors' prayers (sorry). The quality of any model is as good as the inputs that go into the model, and this one is no different.

We love elegant equations that are supposed to explain complex systems. As an undergraduate finance student I fell in love with modern portfolio theory (until I faced the real world), where the one number—beta—put into a simple and elegant capital asset pricing model (CAPM) equation holds the key to the investment kingdom. Okay, at least in theory.

$$\text{Required Rate of Return} = \text{Risk Rate} + \text{Beta} \\ \times (\text{Market Return} - \text{Risk-Free Rate})$$

However, the reality of real-world investing is much different from theory. Let's take beta for instance. Beta on the individual security level has a lot of noise that makes it often an irrelevant (random) as a measure of risk and a predictor of returns. Often it represents just a coincidence in time. Beta speaks of the past but is mute about the future. It is unstable and can move up or down by a large amount in months, where the risk of underlying company has not changed at all.

Looking at Exhibit 7.6, historical beta for Wal-Mart, we see that it was as high as 0.99 in March 2002 and declined to as low as 0.40 in March 2005. The company risk profile has not changed much, whereas beta's decline of almost 60 percent would tell us that the stock became 60 percent less risky during that time frame.

Everyone calculates beta differently, which often leads to different results. For instance, in January 2007 the following services reported the beta for Wal-Mart:

- Value Line Investment Survey: 0.9
- Yahoo! Finance: 0.17
- Standard & Poor's Compustat: 0.57

These are diverse betas for a stock that has not moved much in six years. The difference may come from the time period used to calculate beta and

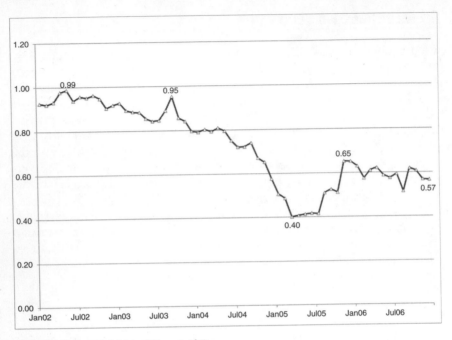

EXHIBIT 7.6 Wal-Mart Historical Beta
Data Source: Standard & Poor's Compustat.

different index benchmarks used to compare the movements of the stock against. Which beta should investors use? From what time period?

I am not trying to build a rebuttal here against modern portfolio theory—not at all. But I emphasize that investing is often an ambiguous exercise and should be approached this way. The comfort that the precision of math brings to investing should be received with a healthy dose of skepticism.

I've found that it's easier to explain an interaction between different variables by quantifying them. In the following discussion I assume that the financial risk factor of an average company is 1.00. In the model, a lower-risk company would have a lower risk factor number (i.e., less than 1.00), and vice versa.

Let's say Company B has higher than average financial risk. Its financial risk factor would increase to a level above 1.00. It could be 1.10 or 1.20. If Company C has even higher financial risk than Company B, its financial risk factor would increase to any number at your discretion, as long as it is above Company B's financial risk factor.

In the following discussion you'll have to make a fairly subjective decision on picking a company's risk and earnings predictability factors. However, though you rarely quantify these factors, you may already be doing this in your head when you analyze companies on a subconscious, fuzzier, less quantified level.

I often hear investors (and myself) say: "This company is loaded with debt; I'd only own it at a significant discount to its peers or the market." Or "I am willing to pay extra for this company's quality." Or "I am not paying much for this company's growth, as I don't trust its growth numbers (lack of earnings visibility)." Investors do it all the time. *Significant*, *much*, *extra* (and many others) are all subjective terms. Does *significant* mean 20 percent? Does *much* mean 10 percent? Or does *extra* mean 30 percent? Somehow, without giving it much thought, our natural inclination is to mentally assign fairly precise numerical values (quantify) to vague terms.

As with discounted cash flow analysis, going through the process of quantifying risk factors and earnings predictability is as important as the final outcome of the process. The process forces you to look at the company from a three-dimensional view, and not get stuck in one dimension (i.e., this is a great company; it made a lot of investors happy in the past; I want to own it at any price).

Though the inputs that go into the absolute P/E, discount rate, and margin of safety models are subjective (I hope you are detecting a pattern here), as long as we are consistent in our use of the precise math, these models provide a good starting point for absolute valuation analysis. If you find them useful you'll make your own modifications, adapting the models to your investment style and your view of the investment landscape.

ABSOLUTE P/E MODEL

There are three basic factors that influence P/E of any company:

1. Fundamental return, comprising earnings growth rate and dividend yield.
2. Perceived (business and financial) risks to future earnings.
3. Long-term visibility of earnings growth rate.

The Growth Rate

The higher the rate of fundamental return (i.e., the higher the earnings growth rate and the dividend yield), assuming everything else is held constant, the more valuable is the company to investors, leading to a higher P/E. Growing earnings and dividend payments are tangible and often the most observable value creators. In the longer run (not minutes, days, or months but years) stock prices go up in part because a company earns higher profits and/or raises its dividend. I have to qualify this statement: I am making an assumption that P/E doesn't change up or down during this time frame.

Business and Financial Risks

Risks are present in every company; otherwise investors would receive a risk-free (Treasury bill–like) rate of return when they invest in common stocks. Understanding the risks that impact a company's cash flows is essential in investment analysis, and this is where the previously discussed quality analysis comes in handy. The two most common risk categories present in public U.S. listed companies are business and financial risks.

Business risk analysis is centered on a company's position within its industry and all the factors that we discussed in the Quality chapter. The financial risks analysis has a more narrow focus on how a company is financed and its ability to make interest and principal payments.

Though business risks and financial risks could be combined and called simply "risk," I believe it helps the analytical process to break down risk into the two distinct categories. Business risk is more of a by-product of a company's operating environment, whereas financial risk is a function of how the company is financed and the strength of its cash flows in relation to debt and interest payments. These risks are interrelated, as the operational environment has a significant impact on a company's ability to make good on its debt, and vice versa.

Company financial structure is often driven by its position within the industry. For instance, chicken producers Pilgrim's Pride and Sanderson Farms have structured their balance sheets to reflect different risks of their business models. Pilgrim's Pride has focused on supplying chicken to fast-food restaurants. It has entered into cost-plus arrangements with many fast-food restaurants, where the company's revenues are stable and to a large degree insensitive to volatile chicken prices. This is a lower-risk type of business, but produces a lower return on capital as well. This relatively low-risk business model affords the company a more leveraged balance sheet than others in the industry, with debt standing at about 20 percent of its assets.

Sanderson Farms has taken a different route: It mainly sells chicken to retailers at the market price—a more volatile (riskier) but higher return on capital business model. This strategy exposes Sanderson Farms to volatile chicken prices; therefore, to mitigate that risk it lowers the balance sheet (financial) risk by refraining from using much debt to finance its operations.

For every identifiable risk* you want to see a company with a very strong balance sheet to overcompensate for the possibility of the risk playing out, which is often just a matter of time.

The higher a company's total risk, the lower P/E investors are willing to pay for its stock. This ties in well with the DCF model as well, as the riskier the company, the higher (discount) required rate of return investors would ask for when discounting company cash flows. Higher required rate of return would lead to lower present value of future cash flows, making the company less valuable and in turn leading to a lower P/E.

Please note there is an inverse relationship between discount rate and P/E ratio; this will become important closer to the end of the chapter when computation of absolute P/E and required rate of return will be discussed.

Earnings Visibility

Taking a page out of the DCF model, the further ahead you can confidently look to project a company's cash flows (or earnings) growing at supernormal (faster than the economy/industry) rates, the greater is the present value of

---

*There are other business risks that are briefly worth mentioning:

- *Foreign political risk*—risk associated with a foreign government taking over the company (e.g., American investments in Cuba in 1959).
- *Concentrated product risk*—for instance, often seen in large pharmaceutical companies' exposure to a few blockbuster drugs that account for a large portion of their profitability.
- *Concentrated customer risk*—one customer accounting for a large portion of revenues.
- *Litigation risk*—risk that a legal judgment against the company will result in substantial losses. Tobacco companies come to mind here.
- *Environmental risk*—a lot of things can fall into this category: an oil spill, dumping chemicals into the water supply, increased environmental standards.

I can see some other risks that don't fall into business and financial risks but could be added to these analyses: liquidity, for private or very small capitalization companies; and currency risk, which usually comes with ownership of foreign securities.

future cash flows and the more valuable the company becomes to the investor. Visibility of growth is dependent on two broad factors: presence of growth opportunities and ability to capitalize on those opportunities.

Ability to capitalize on the growth opportunities ties back to quality factors, which is primarily the company's sustainable competitive advantage and high-quality management. The company will need it to defend against competition; a strong balance sheet will help it get through tough times; and high return on capital exceeding the cost of funds will allow the company to grow without relying on usually more costly and fickle outside financing. All these factors are prerequisites for visibility of growth, but without growth opportunities they usually don't lead to that visibility of growth.

Earnings visibility of an average company would be 1.00; superior earnings visibility results in a lower number (e.g., 0.90, or 10 percent premium); and absence of earnings visibility brings a higher number (e.g., 1.2, or 20 percent discount).

I suggest looking at the business risk, financial risk, and earnings predictability factors in terms of percentages, as most people find it easier to relate to percentages than to decimals.

The Math

The rest of this chapter will require you to slow down your reading pace a little, as the material covered becomes temporarily dense and requires increased concentration. However, it is extremely important to your valuation analysis in the range-bound market. Don't operate heavy machinery while you are reading it.

The objective of the model is to derive a fair value P/E for a stock based on five variables: earnings growth rate, dividend yield, business risk, financial risk, and earnings visibility. The qualitative factors that go into a model are not carved in stone; they are as subjective as anything in investments. However, the following points illustrate the core principles of the absolute valuation model:

- As we discussed, though the PEG ratio would suggest otherwise, a company that is not growing earnings is not worthless. A new management team may come in and unlock the value, or it could be acquired by a competitor—bringing cost savings and synergies to the acquirer. I assumed an average company that doesn't grow earnings and pays no

Expected EPS Growth Rate	P/E		Dividend Yield	Add'l P/E Points
0%	8.00		0.0%	0.0
1%	8.65		0.1%	0.5
2%	9.30		0.5%	0.5
3%	9.95		1.0%	1.0
4%	10.60		1.5%	1.5
5% →	11.25		2.0%	2.0
6%	11.90		2.5%	2.5
7%	12.55	Δ0.65	3.0%	3.0
8%	13.20		3.5%	3.5
9%	13.85		4.0% →	4.0
10%	14.50		4.5%	4.5
11%	15.15		5.0%	5.0
12%	15.80		5.5%	5.5
13%	16.45		6.0%	6.0
14%	17.10		6.5%	6.5
15%	17.75		10.0%	10.0
16%	18.40			
17%	18.90		etc.	
18%	19.40	Δ0.50		
19%	19.90			
20%	20.40			
25%	22.90			
etc.				

EXHIBIT 7.7 Factors Determining Basic P/E

dividend would trade at a P/E of 8 (you may choose another number). Benjamin Graham in his book *The Intelligent Investor* suggested a P/E of 8.5 for a zero growth company.[3]

- A company that is growing earnings at a higher rate will trade at a higher P/E, and the reverse is also true. However, the relationship between earnings growth and P/E in this model is not linear. This model assumes that for every unit of earnings growth from 0 to 16 percent P/E increases 0.65 points. The relationship would have been linear if for every percent of growth P/E went up 1 point (see Exhibit 7.7).

- As growth accelerates above a certain level, investors are willing to pay less for the incremental unit of growth in P/E units, as risk increases with higher growth. Therefore, starting at 16 times earnings (to infinity), for every incremental percent of earnings growth, P/E increases only 0.5. This is a 0.15 (0.65 − 0.50) reduction from 0 to 16 percent earnings growth.
- Earnings growth projections are made for five years or longer.
- Higher earnings visibility leads to a higher P/E, and the reverse is also true. Again, this is taken out of the DCF model: The value of the company that generates return on capital that exceeds the cost of capital increases as the horizon of supernormal earnings growth is extended. Highly cyclical companies, almost by definition, will have lower earnings visibility.
- Investors place a higher value on dividend yield than on earnings growth. Dividends are more tangible, as a company needs to have real earnings (cash flows) to pay dividends. Also, dividends paid out cannot be taken away from the investor (well, at least not by the company), whereas today's earnings growth could be taken away by tomorrow's losses at any time. Therefore, the model assumes a linear relationship between dividend yield and P/E. For every percent increase in dividend, P/E increases 1 point. A company with a 3 percent dividend would receive a 3-point boost to its P/E, for example.
- A company's business and financial risk are inversely related to its P/E ratio (e.g., higher risk, lower P/E; lower risk, higher P/E).
- Though I don't put any constraints on how much a company's P/E could be reduced by the level of riskiness or lack of earnings visibility, to put a safeguard against my own emotions (i.e., falling in love with the stock), I limit the premium (a combination of business risk, financial risk, and earnings visibility) to basic P/E to be no more than 30 percent. For instance, if you find the company's basic P/E to be 10, the highest adjustment it can receive due to being a higher-quality company is three P/E points (30 percent of 10), so it could have an adjusted P/E of no more than 13.
- Two important caveats of this model are inflation and interest rates. It assumes that inflation and interest rates are in their average state and not expected to rise or fall to a new level dramatically different from the average level. If you expect inflation or interest rates to rise and stay elevated for a prolonged period of time, the starting, zero growth P/E of the model and thus subsequent growth P/E should be adjusted down. If you expect inflation and interest rates to fall for a prolonged period of time you should do the opposite. I want to caution

against using current interest rates without regard of their long-term direction.

To make sure that I was not off base with this model, I looked at the P/E of the market—an average stock. The stock market, defined as the S&P 500 or Dow Jones Industrial Average, is an average. It is a basket of above-average, below-average, and just average companies. As we discussed in previous chapters, over the last hundred or so years the market's earnings have grown at about 5 percent a year, average dividend yield has been about 4 percent, and the market has traded on average at about 15 times earnings. Thus an average company growing earnings at 5 percent would receive a P/E of 11.3; adding 4 points for a 4 percent dividend yield would bring a target basic P/E to 15.3 times earnings (see Exhibit 7.7).

Once we determine a basic P/E for an average company solely based on expected earnings growth and dividend yield, we move on to qualitative adjustments for business risk, financial risk, and earnings visibility. Since the market is an average, we would not adjust its basic P/E for any of those factors (all business risk, financial risk, and earnings visibility are equal to 1.00). However, these factors become important in determining absolute P/Es of individual stocks. Quality and growth analysis should lend you a hand in at least vaguely quantifying these factors.

$$\text{Fair Value P/E} = \text{Basic P/E} \times [1 + (1 - \text{Business Risk})] \\ \times [1 + (1 - \text{Financial Risk})] \times [1 + (1 - \text{Earnings Visibility})]$$

Let's say you are analyzing three companies: Well-Mart, Average-Mart, and OK-Mart. They have the same expectations for earnings growth (10 percent a year) and dividend yield of 1.5 percent, and have the same average earnings visibility, but are of different quality.

- *Well-Mart*—the industry leader, with a strong balance sheet and great competitive advantage. Scores high marks on the Quality dimension:
  - Business risk: 0.90
  - Financial risk: 0.95
  - Earnings visibility factor: 1.00
- *Average-Mart*—not the crème de la crème but has an okay competitive advantage; its balance sheet is not spectacular but decent. Scores average on the Quality dimension:
  - Business risk: 1.00
  - Financial risk: 1.00
  - Earnings visibility factor: 1.00

- *OK-Mart*—used to be an industry leader, but new management lost its focus; the company got overextended, balance sheet got leveraged up, and competitive advantage has being marginalized by Well-Mart. Scratching the lows on the Quality analysis:
  - Business risk: 1.25
  - Financial risk: 1.25
  - Earnings visibility factor: 1.00

To figure out their fair value P/Es, you perform the calculations shown in Exhibit 7.8.

The very large difference in fair value P/Es makes sense. Though these companies have the same expected fundamental rate of return (earnings growth and dividend yield), they are of very diverse quality. Therefore, you are willing to pay a premium of 2.5 P/E points for Well-Mart's quality versus Average-Mart. You are not willing to pay Average-Mart's P/E for a substantially riskier company—OK-Mart—and therefore its fair value P/E is 7 points above that of OK-Mart.

Nobody Is Perfect

This multifactor absolute P/E model suffers from the same problem as almost any model: It produces results only as good as the numbers that are input. However, it does have a lot of advantages:

- It will prevent you from stepping into a relative valuation trap. Similar to DCF, this is a forward-looking model, so it doesn't suffer from the benchmarking error that handicaps relative valuation tools, making it an important tool in the range-bound market.
- It systematizes the investment process. Though inputs are still subjective, the model forces you to look at quality (business and financial risks) and growth (expectations for earnings growth, dividend yield, and earnings visibility), the criteria that determine a company's P/E.
- It keeps your emotions in check. Similar to the discounted cash flow model, you may look at the stock P/E and estimate what growth rate and risk assumptions are priced into the stock. This model can prevent you from significantly overpaying for a stock. Conversely, it can provide needed confidence when buying a beaten-down stock.
- It's easier to use than DCF. Though it lacks the depth of the DCF model, a multifactor P/E model is easier to use. I recommend using it in conjunction with the DCF model, as it shares similar inputs.

EXHIBIT 7.8 Fair Value P/E Application

	Well-Mart Given	P/E Adjustments
Earnings Growth	10%	14.5
		+
Dividend Yield	1.50%	1.5
		=
Basic P/E		**16.0**
		×
Business Risk Factor	0.90	[1 + (1 − 0.90)]
		×
Financial Risk Factor	0.95	[1 + (1 − 0.95)]
		×
Earnings Predictability Factor	1.00	[1 + (1 − 1.00]
		=
Fair Value P/E		**18.5**

	Average-Mart Given	P/E Adjustments
Earnings Growth	10%	14.5
		+
Dividend Yield	1.50%	1.5
		=
Basic P/E		**16.0**
		×
Business Risk Factor	1.00	[1 + (1 − 1.00)]
		×
Financial Risk Factor	1.00	[1 + (1 − 1.00)]
		×
Earnings Predictability Factor	1.00	[1 + (1 − 1.00)]
		=
Fair Value P/E		**16**

(Continued)

EXHIBIT 7.8   (*Continued*)

	OK-Mart Given	P/E Adjustments
Earnings Growth	10%	14.5
		+
Dividend Yield	1.50%	1.5
		=
Basic P/E		**16.0**
		×
Business Risk Factor	1.25	$[1 + (1 - 1.25)]$
		×
Financial Risk Factor	1.25	$[1 + (1 - 1.25)]$
		×
Earnings Predictability Factor	1.00	$[1 + (1 - 1.00)]$
		=
Fair Value P/E		**9.0**

- It will provide justified and logical buy, hold, and sell P/E targets for a stock. This application of P/E targets becomes handy in the range-bound market (discussed further in Chapter 12 on the sell process) as it allows you to set P/E (price) targets on stocks in your portfolio and personal wish lists.
- After making adjustments for growth rates, risk factors, and earnings visibility, it puts stocks that you hold in your portfolio or have on your watch list on the same scale.
- It is easy to integrate and cross-reference with a relative P/E model. Since relative and absolute P/E models are both focused on estimating the P/E ratio, you can compare estimated absolute P/E versus competitors and the company's historical valuation. However, I'd let the DCF and absolute P/E models have the final vote.

DISCOUNT RATE MODEL

The "E" in the P/E

What "E" should you use in the absolute P/E model? Personally I like to project earnings several years into the future, doing it in parallel with constructing a DCF model. I do this intentionally as it forces me to think long-term (as the wise investor should), and keeps me from living and dying by the volatility of company's short-term (quarterly) performance.

The future EPS estimate, be it three or five years into the future, I then discount back to today. If you like to look forward one or two years, I still suggest discounting future earnings (the ones that are more than a year from now). This puts all stocks in your portfolio on the same scale, irrespective of the time period you use to forecast future earnings.

The Math

What discount rate should be used to discount earnings and cash flow in the DCF model? There is nothing scientific or precise about the discount rate, despite what modern portfolio theory would tell you. Just for fun (you cannot really use it for anything else), if you computed a discount rate for Well-Mart using the capital asset pricing model (assuming a risk-free rate of 5 percent and market return of 11 percent) and aforementioned betas from the Value Line Investment Survey (0.9), Yahoo! Finance (0.17), and Standard & Poor's Compustat (0.57), you'd receive discount rates of 6.9 percent, 8.8 percent, and 10.5 percent, respectively—a 3.6 percent variance from high to low. Which one should you use? I have no idea.

Tevye used 12 percent to discount Golde's cash flows. His logic was simple—to take a cow-raising risk he needed double the risk-free rate of 6 percent that his son-in-law offered him. It was not a precise, scientific logic, but it made sense. In the creation of a discount rate model, my goal is to put together a framework that is logical, takes into consideration specific company risk, and makes analysis consistent across all companies I am analyzing.

We'll start with a basic rate—a concept similar to the basic P/E. This is the annual rate I'd like to receive for the portfolio—my (risk-unadjusted) opportunity cost. I like a nice round but not a magic number of 15 percent. (You may pick any other round or less round number of your choosing if you like. My logic behind picking 15 percent is that this is the opportunity cost for an average quality stock to remain in my portfolio.) Then using the same business and financial risk factors used in the absolute P/E model, I adjust the basic rate up or down for company business and financial risks.

The computation of the discount rate looks like this:

$$\text{Discount Rate} = \text{Basic Discount Rate} \times \text{Business Risk Factor} \times \text{Financial Risk Factor}$$

EXHIBIT 7.9 Adjusting Discount Rate for Risk Factors

	Well-Mart	Average-Mart	OK-Mart
Risk-Unadjusted Discount Rate	15.0%	15.0%	15.0%
	×	×	×
Business Risk Factor	0.90	1.00	1.25
	×	×	×
Financial Risk Factor	0.95	1.00	1.25
	=	=	=
Risk-Adjusted Discount Rate	**12.8%**	**15.0%**	**23.4%**

Sticking with Well-Mart, Average-Mart, and OK-Mart, given a basic discount rate of 15 percent and the business and financial risk factors from the example, a discount rate for each company is shown in Exhibit 7.9.

As you would expect, OK-Mart required a higher discount rate than Well-Mart and Average-Mart, as it is a lower-quality, higher-risk company.

Looking at Well-Mart's discount rate of 12.8 percent (see Exhibit 7.9), should it be 12.1 percent or 13.6 percent? There is nothing magical or precisely accurate about this number. However, it is not computed based on random variables (movements of company's stock price or a market index), and it will not change from 8.8 percent to 6.9 percent or 10.5 percent for a random reason. This number will be adjusted up or down when your qualitative research shows that the company's risk profile is changing.

In my analysis, discount rate doesn't have a ceiling, but it does have a floor. Again it is done so I don't fall in love with the stock and lose my head. No matter how much I love a company's business, its stock must be riskier than the highest-quality (AAA) corporate bonds. Facing a choice between receiving the same return (let's say 7 percent) from a company's stock or its bond, the rational investor will always choose bonds—less risk, same return.

I use the same discount rate formula when I estimate a discount rate for the discounted cash flow model.

In my current analyses I establish a floor of 8 percent for a discount rate (AAA bond rate plus a couple of points of stock risk premium). This applies to any company, no matter how minimal its business and financial risks. You may choose a different floor number, of course.

Also, when my analysis cranks out high business and financial risks, somewhere above 30 percent (1.30), I ask myself if I want to own any company that is that risky.

Note that earnings visibility is absent from the discount rate model, as it will be absent from the margin of safety model. Earnings visibility is not a risk factor; its objective is to capture the sustainability of a company's above-average earnings growth rate, whereas in the discount rate and margin of safety models the objective is to capture risk that is unique to this company.

MARGIN OF SAFETY MODEL

How Much Margin of Safety Is Enough?

In any market, margin of safety provides a nice cushion in case a company disappoints investors' expectations, which is just a matter of time. However, when a company that is trading at a discount to its appropriate valuation (margin of safety) disappoints (missing earnings estimates, generating lower return on capital, achieving lower margins) the stock is likely to respond less violently to the disappointment (the punishment rendered to the stock is not as severe) than if the stock was fully valued (no margin of safety).

A large margin of safety transforms a company into what amounts to a defamation-proof entity. In short, it can be compared to a person with such a terrible reputation that it is very difficult to say anything to defame or damage that person's reputation further. For example, it is hard to say anything, really anything, to damage the reputation of Hitler. Calling him a fascist and murderer could not possibly harm his social standing, as it is already damaged beyond repair, to say the least. (Have you ever thought of Hitler having a large margin of safety?)

A company with a large margin of safety has already been defamed—it already has volumes of bad news priced into it, and another round of bad news will probably get lost in the shuffle. However, just a sliver of unexpected sunshine may lift the stock up. Imagine *USA Today* writing a short article about the kind side of Hitler. Okay, it is hard to imagine anything nice to say about Hitler, but you get the point.

Margin of safety is a function of the following factors:

- Company's quality—business and financial risks.
- Investor's required rate of return for a stock.
- Company's expected earnings growth rate.
- Company's expected dividend yield.

Company Quality

Should you require the same margin of safety for stocks of differing quality? The answer is of course not. It is just a matter of time before a company stumbles. The strong ones (Well-Mart, for instance) will get up, regroup, and move forward. The weak ones (OK-Mart, for instance) may never get up; they may be liquidated or go bankrupt, leading to a permanent loss of invested capital.

Source of Returns

When you own a stock you are compensated in two ways: from the stock going up in price and from dividend payments. In the long run, stock appreciation can be explained by earnings growth and/or P/E expansion. If a stock is undervalued and likely to revert to the fairly valued level, P/E expansion is really just a margin of safety working in its "source of returns" role.

Companies that have higher returns from dividends and earnings growth will require a lower margin of safety, as earnings growth and dividends are important sources of returns. This doesn't mean that you should not attempt to buy companies at a large margin of safety even though they pay high dividends and grow their earnings at fast rates. Finding a portfolio full of these companies may prove to be difficult. Also, a company that lacks growth or a dividend should overcompensate with a larger margin of safety, as it will serve an important role as a source of returns.

The Math

Let's say you demand a 15 percent annual return from your portfolio (aforementioned risk-unadjusted opportunity cost). You realize that though you are a smart individual (I won't argue on this point, especially since you have already read half of this book!), not every stock idea you come up with will work out. Some will do well, while others will not perform and will either deliver below-expected returns, break even, or worse—lose money. Based on this premise you set a high 30 percent first-year performance hurdle for each (average) new stock introduced to the portfolio. Your thinking goes—if I aim to achieve a 30 percent return from every stock, the worse half, the nonperformers, will offset the returns of the better half, the performers, and thus bring the return of the overall portfolio to the desired 15 percent a year.

However, once a stock's margin of safety is exhausted (the stock appreciates to fair value), for the average stock to remain in the portfolio it should continue to deliver at least 15 percent of annual return from earnings and dividend payments (assuming that you don't have more attractive—higher risk-adjusted return—opportunities on the horizon).

If you were looking for a 30 percent (initial required) annual return from an *average* individual stock introduced to the portfolio, dividends and stock appreciation driven by earnings growth and margin of safety (P/E expansion) are the generators of that return.

Returning to the math, the expected return from an average-quality stock can be expressed as:*

$$\text{Dividend Yield} + \text{Earnings Growth} + \text{Margin of Safety}$$
$$= \text{Initial Required Rate of Return}$$

Subsequently, required (risk-unadjusted) margin of safety for an average-quality stock would look like this:†

$$\text{Risk Unadjusted Margin of Safety} = \text{Initial Required Rate of Return}$$
$$- \text{Dividend Yield} - \text{Earnings Growth}$$

The greater the dividend yield and/or expected earnings growth, the lower the margin of safety required for an average stock, as the earnings growth and dividend yield will be providing a greater portion of the return.

We also know that not all companies are of average quality: higher-quality companies require a lower margin of safety and lower-quality companies require a higher margin of safety.

Borrowing the business and financial risk factors from the absolute P/E framework, our required margin of safety needs to be adjusted for the company's risk factors. Therefore:

$$\text{Required Margin of Safety} = \text{Risk Unadjusted Margin of Safety}$$
$$\times \text{Business Risk Factor}$$
$$\times \text{Financial Risk Factor}$$

---

*Mathematically precise formula

$$(1 + \text{Dividend Yield}) \times (1 + \text{Earnings Growth}) \times (1 + \text{Margin of Safety}) - 1$$
$$= \text{Initial Required Rate of Return}$$

†Mathematically precise formula

Risk Unadjusted Margin of Safety =

$$\frac{1 + \text{Initial Required Rate of Return}}{(1 + \text{Dividend Yield}) \times (1 + \text{Earnings Growth})} - 1$$

Or:

Required Margin of Safety = (Initial Required Rate of Return
$\qquad$ − Dividend Yield − Earnings Growth)
$\qquad$ × Business Risk Factor
$\qquad$ × Financial Risk Factor

For instance, Well-Mart, Average-Mart, and OK-Mart have the same expected dividend yield and earnings growth rate of 1.5 percent and 10 percent, respectively. Therefore, using the required initial return of 30 percent established earlier and their unique business and financial risk factors, the risk-unadjusted required margin of safety calculation would look as follows

Risk Unadjusted Margin of Safety = 30% − 10% − 1.5% = 18.5%

Risk-adjusted calculations for these companies are shown in Exhibit 7.10.

Since Well-Mart's financial and business risks are lower than Average-Mart's and OK-Mart's, it requires a lower margin of safety. OK-Mart has the same growth prospects but much higher risk factors, so it requires a 10.4 percent higher margin of safety than Average-Mart (28.9 percent − 18.5 percent) and 13.1 percent higher than Well-Mart (28.9 percent − 15.8 percent).

Is this 28.9 percent margin of safety enough to buy shares of OK-Mart? It would not have protected investors in a company with a similar name (Kmart) in the late 1990s. This is another example of the subjective side of investing: For some lower-quality stocks, sometimes no margin of safety will be big enough. Common sense is important; don't ever go shopping (for stocks) without it.

EXHIBIT 7.10 Adjusting Margin of Safety for Risk Factors

	Well-Mart	Average-Mart	OK-Mart
Risk-Unadjusted Margin of Safety	18.5%	18.5%	18.5%
	×	×	×
Business Risk Factor	0.90	1.00	1.25
	×	×	×
Financial Risk Factor	0.95	1.00	1.25
	=	=	=
Risk-Adjusted Margin of Safety	**15.8%**	**18.5%**	**28.9%**

THE MARRIAGE OF ABSOLUTE P/E AND MARGIN OF SAFETY

The gambling expression "know when to hold 'em and when to fold 'em" applies to stocks as well. You need to know at what valuation (P/E) to buy and at what valuation to sell a stock.

The marriage of margin of safety and absolute P/E produced a child (buy P/E) and a stepchild (sell P/E—we love buying, selling not so much).

Buy P/E is a fair value P/E adjusted for margin of safety.

$$\text{Buy P/E} = \frac{\text{Fair Value P/E}}{(1 + \text{Margin of Safety})}$$

In theory you should buy a stock at the buy P/E and sell it at the fair value P/E. However, the problem with this is that it ignores the value of growth. Let me illustrate. Say you bought a stock at a buy P/E with the intention to owning it for a long time (years) and selling it when it got to fair value P/E. However, the day you bought it the stock market went crazy, and by the end of the day it had reached your fair value P/E. Should you sell it?

Remember that the total return from the stock comes from fundamental return (earnings growth and dividends) and P/E expansion (margin of safety). If you sell at the end of the day you'd capture the return from the P/E expansion, but leave fundamental return on the table.

Investors are looking-forward creatures. In January they value companies based on the next December's earnings, but sometime around August or September they start giving glances toward the following December. In the second half of November they usually (mentally) close the year and start looking more directly at the following year's earnings.

Since our buy model incorporates both margin of safety and fundamental return, our sell model should do the same. I suggest incorporating (one year) look-ahead bias into sell P/E. Here is how:

Sell P/E = Fair Value P/E
$$\times (1 + \text{Expected Dividend Yield} + \text{Earnings Growth Rate})$$

Let's apply these concepts of buy P/E and sell P/E to our Well-Mart, Average-Mart, and OK-Mart (see Exhibit 7.11).

BRING OUT THE TOOLBOX

Now that we are equipped with various valuation tools, let's try to get some synergy out of using them together.

EXHIBIT 7.11   Determining Buy and Sell P/E

	Well-Mart	Average-Mart	OK-Mart
Expected Earnings Growth Rate	10%	10%	10%
Expected Dividend Yield	1.50%	1.50%	1.50%
Fundamental Return	11.50%	11.50%	11.50%
Required Risk-Adjusted Margin of Safety	15.80%	18.50%	28.90%
Fair Value P/E	18.50	16.00	9.00
	÷	÷	÷
Required Risk-Adjusted Margin of Safety	(1+15.8%)	(1+18.5%)	(1+28.9%)
	=	=	=
Buy P/E	16	13.5	7
Fair Value P/E	18.50	16.00	9.00
	×	×	×
Fundamental Return	(1+11.5%)	(1+11.5%)	(1+11.5%)
	=	=	=
Sell P/E	20.6	17.8	10

I recommend doing a relative valuation analysis first, as it can tell you if a company has always traded at a premium or discount to its peers. Similar to the large bank analysis I completed, relative valuation tools are important hints that are unlikely to bring you complete answers, at least not at first, but will put you on the path of asking the right question—why? Why did a company (or industry) trade at a premium or discount to the industry or its peers (or market)? It could be because of difference in growth rates, perception of management quality, capital structure, return on capital, and many other variables.

Then I'd do a DCF analysis, as it is great at determining ranges of value and measuring sentiment at the extremes. So, after playing with different good, bad, and ugly scenarios, for instance, you estimate a stock's fair value at $50 to $70. Then if the company is trading in the lower part of that range, the relative and absolute P/Es should help to narrow down that range.

If you were to take what we learned from large banks' relative valuation analysis and apply it to absolute models, you'd increase business risk, financial risk, and earnings predictability factors to reflect that they are riskier (high-debt, more complex) enterprises with less predictable (cyclical, heavily reliant on ability to make large acquisitions) earnings than an average company. I'd increase each factor (financial risk and earnings predictability especially) to be above 1.00. How much? 1.05 (5 percent premium) or 1.15 (15 percent premium) or any other number—it is your call.

I find it is a lot easier to identify risk and earnings predictability factors in relation to other companies I closely follow or already own, especially if they are in the same industry. For instance, if I were to assign risk and earnings predictability factors to Bank of America, I may take a look at U.S. Bancorp's factors—stock I already own. Without going into deep analysis here, I'd say that the fact that Bank of America has a large proprietary trading operation that can potentially blow up, wiping out years' worth of profits in a day, makes Bank of America a riskier company than U.S. Bancorp, which doesn't have that risky exposure. Therefore, if U.S. Bancorp's business and financial risk factors were at 1.05 (5 percent discount to average company), I'd set Bank of America's risk factors at above 1.05.

Merging all valuation techniques covers all the valuation angles and provides clear insight into what the company's true worth is. Buying companies at the right price, at the right margin of safety, is not enough to succeed in the range-bound market, but it is at the core and an important part of the formula for success.

I am sure anyone (especially academics) could find a lot of holes in these models, but these are Tevye-like common sense models, not scientific Nobel Prize-winning equations—and are intended as such. Most of us make similar adjustments in our heads; I've just quantified them and put them into a framework.

THE P/E COMPRESSION AND HOW TO DEAL WITH IT

A Glimpse at the 1966–1982 Range-Bound Market

How do we deal with the P/E compression that is inherent in the range-bound market? This is the hardest question yet to answer. I've spent a lot of time experimenting with Standard & Poor's Backtester™, a one-of-a-kind, state-of-the-art product developed by Standard & Poor's Compustat. As a time machine, Backtester flawlessly took me back in time to the 1966–1982 range-bound market and gave a clear understanding of the impact the overall market P/E corrosion had on companies with different P/Es. The results astonished me. I had a good hunch that a value-based, low-P/E approach was superior to a higher-P/E growth approach in the range-bound market. David Dreman's study, *Contrarian Investment Strategies: The Next Generation*, which covers the 1970–1996 time period, made that clear. But I did not realize the true superiority of a low-P/E (value) approach to a high(er)-P/E (growth) strategy until I started using Backtester.

To start, I broke up the market into quintiles (five groups) based on companies' P/Es from high to low, high P/E being quintile 1 and low P/E being quintile 5, with three quintiles in between. Then in each quintile I instructed Backtester to identify 80 companies whose P/Es lay around the mean of the respective quintile (40 below and 40 above). All together, among five quintiles I had 400 companies. This doesn't sound like much, but in 1966 there were only 726 publicly traded companies tracked by Standard and Poor's Compustat database. That was a good sample of the market considering that in 2007 the S&P 500 index, which includes 500 companies, is considered to be a sample of the market and there are close to 10,000 companies trading in the United States today.

Next, I wanted to see what would happen to the average P/E of each quintile if I bought each quintile in the beginning of the range-bound market (January 1966) and sold it at the end in December 1982 (see Exhibit 7.12). The highest-P/E quintile exhibited a P/E compression of 50.3 percent. The P/E of the average stock dropped from 29.3 in 1966 to 14.6 in 1982. That portfolio generated a total annual return of 8.6 percent. The lowest-P/E quintile, to my surprise, had a P/E *expansion* of 34.8 percent. Yes, you read it right. The P/E of the average stock in my lowest-P/E quintile actually went up from 11.8 to 15.8 throughout the range-bound market. That portfolio produced a nice bull market–like total annual return of 14.16 percent, although this is counterintuitive—you'd expect the P/E to decline or at

EXHIBIT 7.12 Low P/E versus High P/E, 1966–1982—Low P/E Wins!

P/E Quintile	High 1	2	Median 3	4	Low 5	Growth ÷ Value Quintile 1 ÷ Quintile 5
1966	29.3	19.3	16.0	13.6	11.8	2.5
1982	14.6	14.4	15.1	14.4	15.8	0.9
Change 1966–1982	−50%	−25%	−6%	6%	34%	
Annual Total Return	8.6%	9.4%	9.4%	9.4%	14.2%	

Data Source: Standard & Poor's Compustat.

best remain the same. The 1966–1982 range-bound market started after a great 1950–1966 bull market. As usually happens during bull markets, growth stocks got all the glory (this explains the very high P/Es of the high-P/E quintile), but value stocks were as popular as last month's news, with valuations about one-third of those of growth stocks. It was simply value stocks' time to shine.

I thought maybe these results were a post–bull market fluke, so I repeated the same exercise for seven more time periods starting in January of 1968, 1970, 1972, 1974, 1976, 1978, and 1980 (see Exhibit 7.13) and ending in December of 1982. I used the same methodology, dividing the market into five quintiles, buying five baskets of stocks, and holding them

EXHIBIT 7.13 Low P/E versus High P/E—Low P/E Wins! Again, Again, Again, and Again

P/E Quintile	High 1	2	Median 3	4	Low 5	Growth ÷ Value Quintile 1 ÷ Quintile 5
1968	28.2	18.0	13.4	11.5	9.3	3.0
1982	18.3	12.3	12.8	10.7	13.0	1.4
Change 1968–1982	−35%	−31%	−4%	−8%	40%	
Annual Total Return	7.9%	9.4%	10.5%	9.4%	10.8%	

P/E Quintile	High 1	2	Median 3	4	Low 5	Growth ÷ Value Quintile 1 ÷ Quintile 5
1970	39.7	22.0	16.9	12.4	9.8	4.1
1982	19.4	16.6	12.7	10.1	9.0	2.2
Change 1970–1982	−51%	−25%	−25%	−18%	−8%	
Annual Total Return	8.2%	10.3%	10.1%	10.6%	12.0%	

P/E Quintile	High 1	2	Median 3	4	Low 5	Growth ÷ Value Quintile 1 ÷ Quintile 5
1972	41.1	21.9	16.8	12.4	12.4	3.3
1982	19.4	16.1	12.7	10.0	10.0	1.9
Change 1972–1982	−53%	−27%	−25%	−19%	−19%	
Annual Total Return	9.5%	10.3%	10.6%	10.9%	12.2%	

(Continued)

EXHIBIT 7.13 (*Continued*)

P/E Quintile	High 1	2	Median 3	4	Low 5	Growth ÷ Value Quintile 1 ÷ Quintile 5
1974	19.5	11.4	8.7	6.5	5.4	3.6
1982	14.6	13.2	10.7	13.0	12.4	1.2
Change 1974–1982	−25%	16%	23%	100%	131%	
Annual Total Return	8.0%	16.9%	15.0%	18.7%	24.6%	

P/E Quintile	High 1	2	Median 3	4	Low 5	Growth ÷ Value Quintile 1 ÷ Quintile 5
1976	18.3	11.4	8.1	7.4	5.3	3.4
1982	15.7	15.2	12.2	12.8	14.0	1.1
Change 1976–1982	−14%	33%	51%	72%	163%	
Annual Total Return	15.5%	19.8%	19.8%	20.9%	30.2%	

P/E Quintile	High 1	2	Median 3	4	Low 5	Growth ÷ Value Quintile 1 ÷ Quintile 5
1978	12.4	9.4	7.6	6.4	5.3	2.3
1982	16.6	12.5	11.2	12.6	12.2	1.4
Change 1978–1982	33%	33%	47%	95%	131%	
Annual Total Return	17.7%	18.3%	17.4%	20.3%	24.2%	

P/E Quintile	High 1	2	Median 3	4	Low 5	Growth ÷ Value Quintile 1 ÷ Quintile 5
1980	13.2	8.2	6.2	5.4	5.3	2.5
1982	18.5	14.4	11.5	9.7	13.6	1.4
Change 1980–1982	41%	75%	87%	81%	155%	
Annual Total Return	15.5%	17.7%	21.3%	23.8%	29.3%	

Data Source: Standard & Poor's Compustat.

until the range-bound market ended in 1982, and studied the results. I had a holding period as long as 16 years (1966–1982) and as short as two years (1980–1982).

The results were consistent across all eight time periods:

- The high-valuation stocks performed worst in terms of change of the P/E from the market's P/E contraction.
- Lowest-P/E stocks consistently outperformed highest-P/E stocks, in many cases by a margin of 2:1.
- Lower-valuation stocks consistently dominated higher-valuation stocks, producing much better returns than their high-valuation comrades. They suffered lower P/E decline at the time of P/E compression. They also achieved higher P/E expansion at the time of P/E expansion (remember that several massive cyclical bear, bull, and range-bound markets took place during the 1966–1982 secular range-bound market).
- For high-P/E stocks, despite being higher-growth companies (at least that is what high P/E implied), growth (earnings growth and dividends) did not offset the massive P/E erosion brought by the range-bound market.

Historically, range-bound markets have not been friendly toward P/Es in general. If what we learned about the 1966–1982 range-bound market is representative of other range-bound markets, the range-bound market is brutally toxic to high-P/E or so-called growth stocks. The ratio of the average P/E of expensive stocks (fifth quintile) to cheap stocks (first quintile) declined from about 3:1 at the beginning of the range-bound market in 1966 to about 1.4:1 at the end in 1982.

If we can agree that the difference between low- and high-P/E stocks is the expectation of growth, this means that in the beginning of a range-bound market investors are willing to pay 200 percent premium for growth, whereas at the end of a range-bound market investors are willing to pay only a 40 percent premium.

A warning: Whenever you deal with data that goes back 40 years, as data in this study did, you face an issue of survivorship bias. Remember, in 1966 the stock market was not a pastime hobby for the average American and a computer's cost did not rival the price of a sewing machine. Fundamental data (e.g., earnings, price, sales, etc.) on many companies was collected more or less by hand. At the time, for a company to make it into a data set it had be a successful (read: large) company. Also, there is another bias: the absence of negative P/Es. In creating the quintiles, I excluded companies that did not have positive earnings, as interpreting negative P/Es is a fruitless exercise.

These biases skewed the results of all quintiles to the upside, as they excluded the weaker links from the simulation, and, therefore, companies that made it into the study (Backtester database) were above average. As you may notice from the results in Exhibit 7.12, for instance, every quintile delivered a respectable return that exceeded the 6.3 percent (1966–1982) return of the S&P 500. Despite these limitations, the results of this study are still significant, as these biases impacted all P/E quintiles from low to high the same way.

Adjustments

You need to adjust the absolute P/E (an average scenario) model shown in Exhibit 7.7 for the range-bound market's P/E deflation. These are the following approaches you can use:

You can gradually deflate the no-growth P/E in the absolute P/E model. In Exhibit 7.7, P/E of no-growth stood at 8—an average scenario. With every passing year you can deflate the no-growth P/E by the rate of P/E deflation.

$$\text{P/E in Year X} = \text{No-Growth P/E} \times (1 - \text{P/E Deflation Rate})^{\text{Year X}}$$

As you can see from Exhibit 3.2, historically P/E deflation has been as low as −7.4 and as high as −2.2 percent. So if you pick a number close to the middle, let's say a P/E deflation rate of 4 percent, you'd calculate a no-growth P/E for year 5 of the range-bound market in the following way:

$$\text{P/E in Year 5} = 8 \times (1 - 4\%)^5 = 6.5$$

As no-growth P/E declines, the rest—the growth P/E—will follow. Let's say you are looking at a company with average business and financial risk that doesn't pay dividends and you expect it to grow earnings 10 percent annually. You'd add 6.5 growth points (0.65×10) to a no-growth P/E of 6.5 in year 5 and you'd get a fair value P/E of 13 (1.5 point decline in P/E from base case of 14.5).

This is not my favorite approach, as it impacts all stocks the same and thus doesn't address the main issue—P/Es of high-growth stocks decline at a faster pace than P/Es of slower-growth stocks.

The following approach (possibly combined with the previous one) makes a bit more sense, as it impacts higher-P/E stocks by a greater degree than lower-P/E stocks. Gradually reduce P/E points that you are willing to pay for growth. In Exhibit 7.7, for 1 percent of earnings growth between

1 percent and 16 percent I granted 0.65 P/E points. Thus a company that is expected to grow earnings 10 percent a year would trade 6.5 points (10 × 0.65) higher than a no-growth company (at a P/E of 14.5, assuming the no-growth P/E is 8, average quality, no dividend).

I suggest gradually deflating growth points by a P/E deflation rate of your choosing:

$$1\% \text{ Growth Point in Year X} = 1\% \text{ Normal Growth Point} \\ \times (1 - \text{P/E Deflation Rate})^{\text{Year X}}$$

If you choose a 4 percent P/E deflation rate, five years into the range-bound market you'd deflate (average scenario) incremental 1 percent growth point in the following way:

$$1\% \text{ Growth Point in Year } 5 = 0.65 \times (1 - 4\%)^5 = 0.53$$

Therefore, a company that is expected to grow earnings at 10 percent a year would expect to have a P/E of 13.3 (no-growth P/E of 8 plus 5.3 points for 10 percent growth). This approach has little impact on a company that is not growing earnings, but a much a greater impact on companies that grow earnings at a faster pace. Consistent with our findings of what transpired in the 1966–1982 range-bound market, the P/E of a company that is expected to grow earnings at a faster rate will suffer more using this approach than a slower-growth company.

Finally, the easiest way to combat the P/E corrosion is to increase the initial required rate of return for stocks. In the previous example I used a rate of 30 percent. Considering that more stocks will fall into the nonperformers category in a range-bound market than in a bull market, an increase in initial required rate of return is justified.

Every one of the adjustments just described will make finding new stocks to buy in the range-bound market harder, but that's as it should be! You are trying to assemble a portfolio of much-above-average stocks. Remember, the road taken by average stocks in past range-bound markets led to meager (zero plus dividends) returns.

In summary, I cannot stress enough that you should be very cautious of how much you pay for growth. As a range-bound market persists, investors become more indifferent to growth and are willing to pay less and less for it. If you own some of those high-P/E stocks, you want to be absolutely sure that their growth (earnings growth and dividends) will overcompensate for the P/E contraction that they are about to face.

CHAPTER **8**

Let's Put It All Together

THE ADDED CLARITY

In the previous chapters we reviewed each dimension of the Quality, Valuation, and Growth framework on an individual basis. In this chapter we'll take the framework to the next crucial step: We'll put these three dimensions together and explore their interactions with each other. Also we'll answer a question: Should you compromise on any dimensions of the QVG framework for a stock to make it into your portfolio? And if yes, what dimensions? (Okay, two questions.)

ONE OUT OF THREE IS NOT ENOUGH

You found this "great" company/stock that receives high scores on only one QVG dimension. Should you buy it?

Quality — Yea; Valuation and Growth — Nay

A company that has a high quality score (all or at least most of the factors that we discussed in the Quality chapter) but lacks meaningful earnings growth and/or dividend yield and is overvalued is not a good investment, no matter how high-quality that company is.

H. J. Heinz, for instance, was a great high-quality company in the late 1990s: Although it had some debt, it had stable, noncyclical cash flows that provided respectable interest coverage; its return on capital exceeded 20 percent; it had the ketchup market mostly to itself worldwide, as its brand was synonymous with ketchup—an indisputably high-quality company. However, it was lacking on the growth and valuation fronts. In 1998 it was trading at over 23 times trailing earnings—not a shocking number, at least in relation to other highfliers. But considering that its growth prospects were in the low single digits (which the company still failed to achieve, possibly due to poor execution by management), as it already owned the ketchup market, the stock was not cheap by any stretch of the imagination.

Most of those who invested in Heinz in the late 1990s either lost money or barely broke even on the stock. Even if, starting in 1998, Heinz had grown earnings at 3 percent a year (which was not the case; earnings were flat over that time period) and continued to pay a 3 percent dividend yield, assuming Heinz traded at 20 times earnings, the stock would be at about the same level in 2006 as it was in 1998. Eight years later, in 2006, the estimated value of Heinz would not be much higher than in 1998. Therefore, the dividend payment was the only return shareholders received for owning H. J. Heinz for almost eight years.

High quality may prevent a company from disappearing as a business, but its overvaluation is likely to turn the stock into a dreadful investment. In addition, subpar growth will not bring to this quality company much-needed salvation from overvaluation. The religion stocks that we discuss in this chapter often fall into this category.

Valuation — Yea; Quality and Growth — Nay

A company that scores high valuation marks but lacks growth or quality faces a different fate. Time is like a ticking bomb stacked against this company. Those hoping for the value gap to close—for the stock to go up—may find themselves lucky or not. The possibility of a low-quality business suffering a stroke and dying increases proportionately to the time passed. Since this stock scores low marks on the growth front, earnings growth and dividends will not come to the rescue. Thus, akin to catching a falling knife (or ax if you like), one may catch it by the handle—or by the blade.

General Motors (GM), for example, has been consistently trading at a P/E of 6 to 10 for over 20 years, excepting the few times when its earnings dropped and its P/E either went up or turned negative. On the surface GM is a cheap stock. Unfortunately, GM, once an exemplar of U.S. ingenuity and success, is now crippled by its unions and faces a continuous loss of market share to more efficient, better-run Japanese competitors. In 2006 the S&P bond-rating agency cut GM's bond rating to junk. GM has not been either a quality or a growth company for decades. Its stock price is at 1960s levels, and its earnings are no higher than they were in 1970s (see Exhibit 8.1). Unless GM's management pulls a miraculous turnaround, something it has struggled to do for decades, GM may not exist in its current legal form in the next decade.

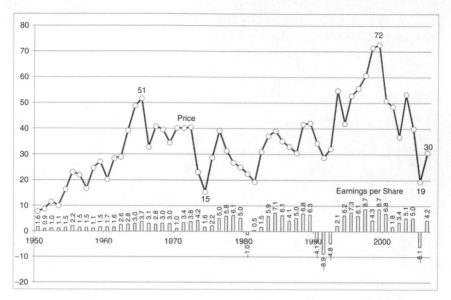

EXHIBIT 8.1   General Motors—Forever Cheap
Data Source: Standard & Poor's Compustat.

Growth—Yea; Quality and Valuation—Nay

Let's look at a low-quality, overvalued company with fast-growing earnings (and/or above-average dividends). It may appear that time is on the company's side, as growing earnings and dividends may lessen the valuation gap. Similar to a previous case, low quality may get the company before it has a chance of growing out of its overvaluation. Or perhaps the company will grow out of its quality and valuation problems, but that road is full of surprises and, similar to a previous scenario, comes with a lot of risk.

A lot of dot-com companies of the late 1990s fell into this category; they were growing their revenues at fast rates, their valuations were high, and their competitive advantage was difficult to uncover. We know the fate of those companies; many of them went bankrupt and few survived.

TWO OUT OF THREE IS BETTER, BUT IS IT ENOUGH?

A company that receives high marks on at least two dimensions should have a disproportionately better risk/return profile than the company that scores high on only one dimension. There are three possible combinations where two dimensions are at their highs and one is lagging:

1. Quality and growth are at their highs, while valuation is not.
2. Quality and valuation are at their highs, while growth is not.
3. Valuation and growth are at their highs, while quality is not.

Quality and Growth—Yea; Valuation—Nay

Many investors don't make the distinction between a great company and a great stock—an important cognitive error, perhaps one of the most common fallacies in investing. It is often easy to identify a great company. It easily meets the Quality and Growth test: It has great brands, a bulletproof balance sheet, often great margins (though this may not be true for retail stocks), and high return on capital; it consistently has grown revenues and earnings and is expected to continue to do so. But a great company may or may not be a great stock.

We just established an important link and relationship among valuation (the required margin of safety); quality (company-specific risk factors); and growth (earnings visibility, expected earnings growth, and dividends). A company scoring high quality and growth marks but lacking on the valuation front (lack of margin of safety) has to overcompensate by having very high quality and growth marks. A combination of earnings growth and dividend payment has to be high enough to offset the impact of possible P/E compression (inherent in stagnant markets) and lack of margin of safety—a company's overvaluation.

It is important to realize that high quality and growth marks may not be enough to offset a company's overvaluation. High quality and growth marks may be an indication of a great company, but overvaluation (low score on the Valuation dimension) may make this great company not a good stock! There are plenty of companies that score high marks on quality and growth tests in any market environment. However, the number of companies passing the value test often is dependent on the market valuation at the time of the analysis.

There is a certain type of company that fall into the religion stock category. A basic property of religion is that the believer takes a leap of faith: to believe without expecting proof. Where emotion is concerned, it takes a while for a company to develop this type of religious following: Only a few high-quality, well-respected companies with long track records ever become worshipped by millions of unquestioning investors. When it happens, however, everybody recognizes these great companies, turning them into so-called religion stocks, the you-cannot-go-wrong-owning-this-company type of stocks, pushing their valuations to ridiculous levels.

To achieve the religion stock designation, a stock has to make a lot of shareholders happy for a long period of time, sufficient for them to form that psychological leap of faith. Having high-quality brands readily identified with products or services that are widely used in everyday life is helpful, but not necessary. The stories (which are often true) of relatives or friends buying a few hundred shares of the company and becoming millionaires have to percolate a while for a stock to become a religion. Little by little, the past success of the company turns into an absolute—and eternal—truth. Investors' belief becomes entrenched: Past success paints a clear picture of the future, pointing the way to investor salvation.

Gradually, investors turn from cautious shareholders into loud cheer-leaders. Management is praised as visionary. The stock becomes a one-decision stock: buy! This happened to the Nifty Fifty stocks of the mid-twentieth century and select technology stocks in the late 1990s. This euphoria is not created overnight. It takes a long time to build, and a lot of healthy pessimists have to be converted into believers before a stock becomes a religion—and a hefty P/E reflects that.

Though I don't want to single out and pick on Coca-Cola, in the late 1990s it was a classic example of a religion stock. There are very few companies that had delivered such consistent performance for so long and had such a strong international brand name as Coca-Cola. It was hard not to admire the company. But admiration of Coca-Cola achieved an irrational level in the late 1990s.

Throughout the 1990s Coca-Cola grew earnings in the mid-teens, impressive for a 100-year-old company. It had little debt, great cash flow, and top-tier management. This admiration came at a steep price: Coca-Cola commanded a P/E of 47.5. That P/E was 2.7 times the market P/E. Even after discounted future cash flows using Treasury bills (a risk-free rate, not something a rational investor should ever do, as Coca-Cola's cash flows are not risk free and, unlike the U.S. government, Coca-Cola doesn't have a license to print money or unconditionally raise taxes or have a nuclear weapons arsenal) could no longer justify Coke's valuation, analysts started to price hidden assets, such as Coke's worldwide brand. No money manager ever got fired for owning Coca-Cola. The company may not have had a lot of business risk, but by 1999 the high valuation was pricing in expectations that were impossible for this mature company to meet.

"The future ain't what it used to be"—Yogi Berra never lets us down. Success over a prolonged period of time brings a problem to any company—the law of large numbers. Old age and arthritis eventually catch up with religion stocks. No company can grow at a fast pace forever. Growth in earnings and sales eventually decelerates. Enormous domestic and international market share, combined with maturity of the soft drink market, made it difficult for Coca-Cola to grow earnings. Its famed consistent double-digit earnings growth also failed its faithful believers: From 1995 to 2005 its sales and earnings per share grew at a meager 2.5 percent and 5.6 percent, respectively.

For Coke, the descent from its status as a religion stock resulted in a drop from a price of $89 at the high of 1998 to $42 in 2006. And after no capital appreciation, the stock was still not cheap by any means. It traded at 18 times earnings in 2006, despite expectations for sales growth in the mid-single digits and EPS growth in the high single digits.

It takes a while for the religion premium to be totally deflated, because faith is a strong emotion. A lot of frustration with subpar performance has to come to the surface. Disappointment chips away at faith one day at a time.

Religion stocks are not safe stocks. Irrational faith and false perception of safety come at a large cost: the hidden risk of reduction in the religion premium. The risk is hidden because it never showed itself in the past. Religion stocks by definition have had an incredibly consistent track record. Risk was rarely observed. However, this hidden risk is unique because it is not a question of if it will show up but a question of when. It is hard to predict how far the premium will inflate before it deflates—but it will deflate eventually. When it does, the damage to the portfolio can be tremendous. Religion stocks generally have a disproportionate weight in portfolios because they are never sold—exposing the trying-to-be-cautious investor to even greater risks.

Religion stocks often pass the quality test with flying colors, as past success was driven by a strong sustainable competitive advantage. The greatest danger with religion stocks? Faith that was built on past performance, which leads investors to believe that growth is still ahead of the company, whereas this is often not the case. The next greatest danger of religion stocks is that, without earnings and cash flow growth, there is nothing to cushion the fall from contracting P/Es. The stock behavior when P/E premium deflates depends on many factors, but stock market performance and company's earnings growth are at the top of the list.

Let's take a look at Wal-Mart, for instance. Its stock was a member of the religion stock temple, as it was trading at 54 times earnings in late 1999. However, it did not fail the faithful, at least on the earnings growth side, as its earnings more than doubled from 1999 to 2005. As its P/E declined from its 1999 highs, most of the decline was cushioned by consistently growing earnings that lowered its P/E to 16 in 2006. In fact, I argued in one article that Wal-Mart stock was actually undervalued at that time.

Wal-Mart and Coca-Cola were the epitome of religion stocks: Although they were not technology companies, they traded to unjustifiably high valuations in the late 1990s. However, Wal-Mart and Coca-Cola were not alone in this exclusive club. General Electric, Gillette, and many others were at least at some point in their lives proud members of the Temple of Religion Stocks.

Past members also include: Polaroid—bankrupt; Xerox—earnings have not grown in 20 years; Eastman Kodak—in a major restructuring; AT&T—swallowed by its own offspring. The most dangerous types of religion stocks are the ones that have their moats eroded by time and competition. Kodak, Polaroid, and Xerox were in the religion stocks hall of fame for quite a while, but technological change eroded their moats. Their quality was eroded (though by different degrees), and growth disappeared as earnings and cash flow collapsed. Unfortunately, it happened at a time when they were trading at high valuations.

Range-bound markets are agnostic deflators of the religion premium, turning religion stocks into a subpar (to say the least) class of investments.

You need to maintain an agnostic view of religion stocks, since the comfort and false sense of certainty that these stocks bring to the portfolio come at a huge cost—prolonged underperformance. As I hope is clear by now, in addition to facing a general market P/E compression, they'll face deflation of their religion premium by the relentless range-bound market.

Quality and Valuation—Yea; Growth—Nay

It happens quite often: You find a great company that has a great brand, strong competitive advantages, a solid balance sheet, nice return on capital, and more. It has attractive valuation, at least on the surface. It dominates the market where it competes, but its market is not growing fast and it has taken the entire market share that was there for the taking—it is a slow-growth company.

What should you do? Avoid slower-growth companies altogether? Maybe not, but you can do these two things:

1. Require increased margin of safety.
2. Look for a catalyst—an event that would close the margin of safety gap within a specific time frame.

How Much More Margin of Safety?   Let's say you believe that this company can grow earnings 3 percent a year and can sustain a 3 percent dividend yield. After doing relative and absolute valuation analysis, you determined that this company trades at a 20 percent discount to its intrinsic value (margin of safety). Extensive analysis leads you to believe that the company has an average business risk and financial risk.

You calculate the required margin of safety:

$$\text{Required Rate of Return} = 30\% - 3 - 3\% = 24\%$$

Though the company has scored low on growth, it has scored average on quality—meeting (though not exceeding) quality requirements. You find the stock has a 24 percent margin of safety—in line with the required margin of safety, at least on the surface. However, the risk with this quality but slow-growth company is that though the company has a significant margin of safety, this investment may turn into a subpar performer because time is not on your side.

If it takes four years for the market to realize the true value of the company and drive up the stock to its fair value (margin of safety disappearing), it would go up roughly 36 percent (24 percent due to P/E expansion and 12 percent due to earnings growing 3 percent over the four-year period). In addition, you collect a 3 percent annual dividend over the four-year period, bringing cumulative dividends collected to about 12 percent. Between the 36 percent price appreciation and 12 percent dividend payments, you receive a rough total cumulative return of 48 percent (ignoring compounding), or 12 percent annual return. Though 12 percent is a decent return (many would kill for it), it fell below your 15 percent required annual rate of return for a stock to be kept in your portfolio (as we discussed in the Valuation chapter).

Growing earnings and dividends collectively brought only 6 percent a year, and a 24 percent return from the margin of safety was spread out over four years, amounting to 6 percent a year—time was not your best friend, as it was fracturing a 24 percent margin of safety into smaller 6 percent annual pieces. If it took longer than four years for the market to realize that true value of the company, the annual rate of return would only decline further and further as return from the margin of safety would be granulated over a longer period of time.

Let's start with an increased margin of safety. Since you believe that a company's earnings growth and dividend will not increase any more than 6 percent a year, required margin of safety has to offset the subpar growth from earnings and dividends.

$$
\begin{aligned}
\text{Required Margin of Safety} &= (\text{Required Annual Rate of Return} \\
&\quad - \text{Expected EPS Growth} - \text{Dividend Yield}) \\
&\quad \times \text{Years to Fair Value} \\
&= (15\% - 3\% - 3\%) \times 4 = 36\%
\end{aligned}
$$

A 36 percent margin of safety (as opposed to 24 percent) would have offset the subpar growth from earnings and dividends, and this stock would have delivered a 15 percent target annual growth. A company that could deliver subpar growth for a long period of time should be considered only if the stock is cheap enough to compensate the investor for a long wait.

Look for a Catalyst   The catalyst is an event that would bring investor interest back to the undervalued stock, driving the stock to its fair value. It could take many different forms, such as:

- Corporate restructuring, whereby selling of underperforming or noncore assets enables a company to unlock shareholder value—arguably what happened to General Electric (among other things) when Jack Welch took it over in the 1980s.
- Management change, as new management may turn the company's operations around. It could be bought by another company or taken private through a leveraged buyout by current management.

Here are two catalyst questions to be asked:

1. How certain are you that the catalyst will take place?
2. Will the catalyst attract enough investor interest to drive the price of the stock to fair value?

Valuation and Growth—Yea; Quality—Nay

This is the most dangerous combination of all: A company is growing earnings at a fairly fast rate and/or paying a dividend; it is attractively priced (at least relative to the growth rate), but has a quality flaw. Its competitive advantage may be thin, it is overleveraged, its return on capital may be below the cost of capital, or revenues may not be recurring.

It is difficult to generalize about this scenario, as quality issues are diverse in nature. Looking for salvation in a higher growth rate or an increased margin of safety may or may not be enough. For instance, if the incremental return on capital is below the company's incremental cost of capital, high growth is only going to hurt the company, as investment will be destroying shareholder value.

The exception here is when a company's return on capital suffers from lack of scale. Growth could save the company by bringing the needed scale (spreading higher revenues over the same asset base) and improving return on capital.

A heavily leveraged company cannot afford to make even a small mistake, as the consequences could be dire, and even a huge margin of safety may not provide a safe haven if disaster strikes. The investor's focus should be on severity (depth) and diversity of the quality issues. One quality flaw should be overcompensated by the strength of another quality factor. For instance, a company's volatile or unpredictable revenues should be compensated for by having as low operating fixed costs and/or as little interest-bearing debt as possible.

Let's take Claire's Stores—a retailer selling low-priced jewelry and fashion accessories to teenage girls. A fad risk could strike this company at any time. Pink earrings or purple bracelets could become cool or uncool in a New York second, and Claire's could find itself with sales taking a dive at any moment. Teenage girls are not known for their stable taste.

However, Claire's management is aware of that risk, and that is why the company stayed away from using interest-bearing debt (except when making acquisitions, and then its number one priority was to pay off debt, which it did fairly rapidly) and maintained a large cash pile on the balance sheet. Claire's doesn't own its stores, as most of them are located in shopping malls and have long-term leases—another form of long-term obligation (i.e., another risk). However, unlike traditional interest-bearing debt, a large portion of this cost could be mitigated by terminating a lease and paying a penalty or subletting the space to another tenant.

In Claire's case, the fad quality flaw is more than offset by a strong interest-bearing-debt-free and cash-rich balance sheet. Some may argue that a $400 million cash pile (close to 40 percent of total assets) is a waste of shareholder capital, as cash is earning a meager return for shareholders. However, I'd argue that a large level of cash (it may not have to be $400 million) is needed to mitigate the unpredictable nature of Claire's business.

As we discussed in the previous chapter, chicken producers use their balance to mitigate the risk of uncertain chicken prices. The ones that have taken the safer (lower return on assets) route of providing chicken at a cost-plus arrangement to the restaurant industry have a more leveraged balance sheet, as opposed to the ones that risk selling chicken to retailers at the more volatile current market prices.

Little could help a company that has no competitive advantage. A strong balance sheet may prolong its life expectancy, but it will not save the company from its less than happy fate. Even if a company has high return on capital, it is likely to be a temporary phenomenon, as a competitive moat is not there to protect the return on capital from competitors encroaching on the company's turf.

CONCLUSION

As a general rule, you should not compromise on more than one Quality, Valuation, or Growth dimension, as it introduces too much risk and/or subpar returns (to say the least) into the mix.

Each of the Quality, Valuation, and Growth dimensions is an important source of value creation. Valuation and growth (as Warren Buffett put it) are joined at the hip, being the source of returns, whereas quality makes sure that the company is still around to collect the fruit of its work. We'll discuss how to apply the framework to buy and sell processes in the following chapters.

Strategy

Introduction to Strategy: The Value of Process and Discipline

Rule No. 1: Never lose money.
Rule No. 2: Never forget Rule No. 1.
                —Warren Buffett

Warren Buffett's admonishment not to lose money sounds as useful as Will Rogers's advice, "Don't gamble; take all your savings and buy some good stock and hold it till it goes up, then sell it. If it don't go up, don't buy it." However, we do know that in bull markets, the strong tailwind of rising P/Es provides a boost to the performance of many stocks in one's portfolio, helping to offset large losses of a few. The opposite takes place in range-bound markets, where the headwind caused by general market P/E compression forces the whole portfolio to work a lot harder, leaving a lot less room for error. To continue the wind analogy, in a range-bound market you are sailing into a very stiff gale.

Stock valuations in bull markets usually overshoot their fair value by a very large margin, as their volatility has a pronounced upside bias. An ocean of optimism that is characteristic of the bull market easily overwhelms the puddle of pessimism, and thus stocks (on average) explore valuations far above average.

Valuation of the range-bound markets is not as rewarding, as occasional bursts of optimism are cooled down by the pessimism that predominates in the range-bound market. Over the very long term, optimism and pessimism more or less cancel each other out, resulting in even handed volatility to the upside and downside (see Exhibits 2.5, 2.6, and 2.7).

In the range-bound market, losers and underperforming stocks have a significant impact on performance of a portfolio, as overall flatness of the market is driven by widespread long-term P/E contraction, compounded by the declining birthrate of superstar stocks. Indifference and lack of mass excitement serve as the contraceptives mainly responsible for this decline in the creation of new superstars. Stock selection and disciplined investment process—the strict buy-and-sell processes—are a lot more important in the range-bound market than in a bull market, as all stocks in the portfolio have to work harder to produce the desired returns.

Once you buy into the range-bound market mentality, you should shift your focus from the broader market to individual stocks. In broad strokes, the goal is to get three things right:

1. Assemble a portfolio of the right companies.
2. Buy them at the right prices.
3. Sell them at the right prices.

... and repeat steps 1 through 3 over and over again. This will be the focus of the following chapters: to carry out these three objectives correctly.

CHAPTER 9

Buy Process—Fine-Tuning

Any time you make a bet with the best of it, where the odds are in your favor, you have earned something on that bet, whether you actually win or lose the bet. By the same token, when you make a bet with the worst of it, where the odds are not in your favor, you have lost something, whether you actually win or lose the bet.
— David Sklansky, *The Theory of Poker*

THE VALUE OF THE PROCESS AND DISCIPLINE

Over a lifetime, active investors will make hundreds, often thousands of investment decisions. Not all of those will work out for the better. Some will lose and some will make us money. As humans we tend to focus on the outcome of the decision rather than on the process.

On a behavioral level, this makes sense. The outcome is binary to us—good or bad, which we can observe with ease. But the process is more complex and is often hidden from us.

One of two things (sometimes a bit of both) can unite great investors: process and randomness (luck). Unfortunately, there is not much we can learn from randomness, as it has no predictive power. But the process is something we should study and learn from. To be a successful investor, what you need is a successful process and the ability (or mental strength) to stick to it.

Several years ago, I was on a business trip. I had some time to kill, so I went to a casino to play blackjack. Aware that the odds were stacked against me, I set a $40 limit on how much I was willing to lose in the game.

I figured that a couple hours of entertainment, plus the free drinks provided by the casino, were worth it. I have never been a big gambler (as I never win much). However, several days before the trip I had picked up a book on blackjack on the deep discount rack in a local bookstore. All the dos and don'ts from the book were still fresh in my mind. I figured if I played my cards right, I would reduce the house advantage from 2 or 3 percent to 0.5 percent.

Wanting to get as much mileage out of my $40 as possible, I found a table with the smallest minimum bet requirement. My thinking was that the cheaper the hands I played, the more time it would take for the casino's advantage to catch up with me and take my money.

I joined a table that was dominated by a rowdy, half-drunken fellow who told me several times that it was his payday (literally: he was holding a stack of $100 bills in his hand) and that he was winning. I played by the book. But it did not matter. Luck was not on my side, so my $40 was thinning with every hand.

Meanwhile, the rowdy guy was making every wrong move. He would ask for an extra card when he had a hard 18 while the dealer showed 6. The next card he drew would be a 3, giving him 21. Then the dealer would get a 10 and then a 2 (on top of the 6 that already showed), leaving him with 18. The rowdy guy barely paid attention to the cards. He was more interested in saying "Hit me."

Every "right" decision I made turned into a losing bet, while every "wrong" decision he made turned into a winner. His stack of chips was growing while mine was dwindling. His loud behavior and consistent winnings attracted several observers. Some were making comments such as: "This guy is good." Nobody paid attention to me—I was not loud and I was losing.

The rowdy guy had no process in place. He was just making half-drunken bets that had statistical improbabilities of success. And he was winning, at least for a while. I was armed with statistics, making every bet to maximize my chances of winning (or rather to minimize my losses—the odds were still against me), but I was on the losing side of the game.

After a couple of hours, and after consuming more of the free alcohol, my rowdy companion was increasing the size of his bets with every successful hand. The law of large numbers caught up with him. He gave up his winnings and his paycheck as well; two weeks of hard work sadly but predictably went into the casino's coffers.

I was down to a couple of dollars at one point. But then my luck changed and I won the bulk of my money back. In the end I lost only $10. This was a successful deal. I'd had a couple beers, spent a couple of hours gambling, and learned a valuable gambling/investing lesson.

What is the lesson? Spend more time focusing on the process than on the end results. If it were not for randomness, every decision we made would be right or wrong based solely on the outcome. If that were the case, the process could be judged solely on the end result.

But randomness is constantly present in investing (as it is in gambling). Although we are drawn to judge our decisions and those of others on their outcomes, it is dangerous to do so. Randomness may teach us the wrong lessons.

It is important to realize the duality of definition (at least as it applies to investing) of the word *discipline*:

- First, a system of rules, a systematic method.
- Second, control obtained by enforcing compliance.

The first definition can be interchangeably used with *process*—a system of rules. The second is really about being in control and sticking to the process. To avoid confusing the issue with phrases like "disciplined discipline," for the first meaning of discipline I'll use the word *process*, and for the second, *discipline*.

In previous chapters we discussed the process of stock analysis. The following chapters will focus on strategy execution—the buy and sell processes. I believe that the less ambiguous your investment process, the more likely you'll have the discipline to stick to it. My rowdy gambling companion did not have a process, unless you call yelling "Hit me" one. He had no process to be disciplined to, unless ordering free beer twice an hour counts as a discipline. Even if he won that day, in the long run, unless the gods of randomness decided to play a cruel joke, after playing for tens of hours he'd have no chance of succeeding (defined here as minimizing your losses)—because he had neither a process nor a discipline.

THINK LONG-TERM, ACT SHORT-TERM

Investing for the long term is not about a time horizon. Anybody who invests in stocks should expect to commit capital for five years or longer. Long-term investing is an attitude, an approach to analysis. By that, I mean focusing the thought processes on deciding whether to make an investment in the company (the business) at the right price, not on trying to make a speculative trade in the stock. This investment philosophy, the way you approach company analyses, doesn't need to change in the range-bound market. But the buy and sell processes, the execution of one's investment philosophy, do require some tweaking.

Buy-and-hold is really just a code name for a "buy and forget to sell" strategy. A stock likely went through a fairly rigorous buy process, but "hold" is really just camouflage for the absence of tangible sell process, unless you call "I'll own it until death do us part" a sell process. "Buy and forget to sell" works great in a prolonged bull market. P/Es keep expanding from much below to much above average as they did most of the time during the twentieth century. Stocks of so-so companies rise. Stocks of great companies shoot up, not touching the stars but coming close. Passive investing, buying and never selling, is rewarded.

However, as we've seen in the first part of the book, the complete opposite to bull market behavior takes place during the range-bound market.

There is a good reason this book is called *Active Value Investing*, not simply *Value Investing* (aside from the fact that the shorter name was already taken). In the range-bound market you should employ an active buy-and-sell strategy: buying stocks when they are undervalued and selling them when they are about to be fully valued (as opposed to waiting until they become overvalued).

MEET YOUR NEW BEST FRIEND—VOLATILITY

Presented in retrospect with two choices in Exhibit 9.1, which one would you choose?

> Option 1—an opportunity to sell into rallies (cyclical bull markets and their concurrent gains) and buy into sell-offs (cyclical bear markets).
> Option 2—an absolutely straight line providing no possibility of making money (other than collecting dividends, which in the current post-2000 market environment will not amount to much).

Despite range-bound markets being directionless, as we discussed in Chapter 2, they are as volatile as bull markets. The major difference is that the volatility of bull markets has a pronounced upward bias—you get compensated with a healthy return for the ride—whereas volatility in range-bound markets is mainly evenly distributed to the upside and the downside; the ride is still exciting (which can pose a psychological risk!), although the returns are not.

You need to befriend volatility; it should be respected and used to your advantage. I am not suggesting that you try to time the market by going to cash at the top and becoming fully invested (e.g., mortgaging the house, pawning your favorite cat) at the bottom. Although tops and bottoms are

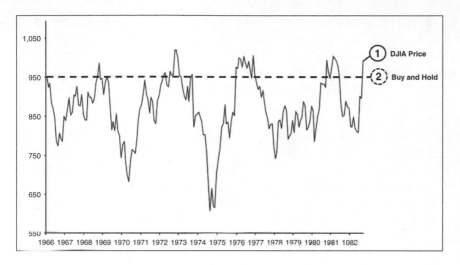

EXHIBIT 9.1 Dow Jones Industrial Average, 1966–1982 Range-Bound Market

obvious by looking at historical charts, they are not as precisely evident in real-time.

A market timer's buy and sell decisions are made based on predicting the short-term direction of stock prices, interest rates, or the condition of the economy. It is hard if not impossible to create a successful market-timing process. Aside from the fact that it demands that you be correct twice—when you buy and when you sell—emotions are in the driver's seat of the market, especially at the tops and bottoms. These emotions are driven and reinforced by events that are often unpredictable (random) in nature and cannot be accurately forecast. The timing of the inflection points that create tops and bottoms in the market is simply random.

In fact, the worst thing that can happen to you is being right once about a change in market direction. You'll think that you figured it out, although you really have not. Randomness was just playing a trick on you, and you will lose (or not make) money if you fall for it.

TIME STOCKS, NOT THE MARKET

There is a better way. Instead of trying to time the market, my answer to volatility is to time individual stock valuations through a strict buy-and-sell process. If you don't like the word *timing*, call it *pricing*—you need to price individual stocks. You buy them when they are undervalued and sell them when they become about fully valued.

To time stocks, first break stock analysis into the three dimensions of Quality, Valuation, and Growth, and then combine the analyses. To avoid falling into the alluring "good company/bad stock" trap, or even worse, the "religion stock" emotional trap, make company analysis (quality and growth) and stock analysis (valuation) two separate steps and then ask two separate questions:

1. Is XYZ a good company?
2. Is XYZ a good stock (investment)?

To take this a step further, if both (good company and good stock) conclusions lead to "yea," the stock is bought. If the good-company test is failed, move on to the next stock—there are lots more stocks where that one came from! However, for the companies that pass the good-company test but fail the good-stock test, the wish list or "Companies I Would Love to Own at the Right Price" list is a great place to keep track of them without making emotional decisions by overcommitting or abandoning them altogether.

For every company you find worthy of owning (high quality and growth marks), set the optimal price or valuation levels at which it transforms into a good stock. First, determine the fair value of the company using the combination of relative- and absolute-valuation tools discussed in the Valuation chapter. Then, settle on the required margin of safety (the discount to the fair value) that will lead to the buy P/E. And finally (the hardest part), sit and patiently wait for the stock to come down to the predetermined target valuation level and/or price.

Depending on the time that has passed since the stock was placed on your wish list, the company's fundamentals (Quality and Growth dimensions) may well need to be reviewed to make sure that they have not changed (deteriorated) since the original analysis.

Using a valuation target such as P/E (or price to cash flows, price to book, etc.) has an advantage versus a price target. As time passes and earnings grow, the specific price target becomes less meaningful, as it was created at a time when earnings power was lower (or higher). Thus, even as the price goes up, if earnings power increases at a faster pace the stock could still be an attractive purchase.

A benefit of the aforementioned exercise is that the valuable time spent on analysis doesn't go to waste, even if no stock is purchased immediately. The opportunity will often present itself at a later time to buy a good company on attractive terms at a good price. Assembling your list will liberate you from emotional attachment to good companies, aligning emotion with the truth that investing is not about feeling good owning good companies at any price, but rather is specifically about making money while taking a reasonable amount of risk.

CASH IS KING

The number-one objective should be not to lose money, and thus you should try to avoid making marginal decisions (i.e., buying stocks that have not scored appropriate marks on all three dimensions of the Quality, Valuation, and Growth framework). Blaise Pascal said, "All man's miseries derive from not being able to sit quietly in a room alone." You need to be able to sit on your hands and do nothing unless or until a great investment opportunity presents itself. Sitting and doing nothing is a difficult thing to do, especially when stocks are constantly moving up and down, news is released, earnings get reported, and so on.

In 1998, at Berkshire Hathaway's annual meeting, Warren Buffett said: "We don't get paid for activity, just for being right. As to how long we'll wait, we'll wait indefinitely." Buffett plays bridge in his "do nothing" time, whereas his righthand man Charlie Munger works on his mental models by reading books on different intellectually stimulating subjects.[1]

In a raging bull market, cash is your biggest enemy, because that boat doesn't rise with the tide of a rising market. As we saw in Chapter 4, the lost opportunity cost of being in bonds or cash (short-term bonds or money market funds) is high during bull markets, but that is not the case in range-bound markets, when fixed income instruments are a fair contender for your capital in the absence of attractive stocks.

As a *market* timer your cash balance is a function of what you think the market is about to do. However, the *stock* timer's cash balance is a by-product of investment opportunities you see in the market. If you can't find good companies (quality and growth requirements being met) to own at the right price (valuation commensurate with quality and growth), cash or short-term bonds are good alternatives until a new opportunity presents itself. Again, this is not about market timing, but you should not be buying stocks for the sake of being fully invested.

I have no desire to attempt to forecast short-term and long-term interest rates or the yields of money market funds (the modern-day equivalent of cash—almost without risk, very liquid, and interest paying). No matter what money market yields are, as long as they are not negative (an improbable scenario), they should still be preferred to a marginal investment. Unless you find stocks that offer superb returns that are commensurate with the level of risk taken, your money should be parked in cash.

BE READY TO STRIKE WHEN THE TIME COMES

Professional investment managers don't have the luxury of playing bridge or reading books on subjects unrelated to investing (e.g., the history of civilization, perhaps, or the ice age), at least on the company's dime. Employers will not understand that just by doing nothing we are following in the footsteps of great investors! "Do nothing" time should be used to increase one's areas of expertise. You should prepare for the battle by researching companies that score high quality and growth marks and by finding companies that should be put on your wish list; and when the time comes and the company hits the target buy valuation, you should strike without hesitation (as I mentioned, although depending how much things changed since the last analysis, a review might be required).

CHAPTER 10

Buy Process— Contrarian Investing

The third-rate mind is only happy when it is thinking with the majority. The second-rate mind is only happy when it is thinking with the minority. The first-rate mind is only happy when it is thinking.

—A. A. Milne

You are neither right nor wrong because the crowd disagrees with you. You are right because your data and reasoning are right.

—Benjamin Graham

CONTRARIAN IS THE NAME OF THE GAME

What does it really mean, being contrarian? Doing the opposite of what everybody else is doing, all the time? What if you agree with what everybody else is doing? Should you disagree for the sake of being contrarian?

Being contrarian means being able to think and act independently of the crowd and not being swayed by crowd thinking. It means staying on your own autonomous track, independent of the direction the crowd is taking, even if that requires going against the crowd. It means not accepting (although respecting) the market's wisdom unconditionally, but rather attempting to develop an opinion of your own.

This is another case where the saying attributed to Yogi Berra could not be truer: "In theory there is no difference between theory and practice. In practice there is. " In theory it is easy to be able to think and act independently; however, in practice it becomes a lonely and trying experience. Emotions that we don't experience in the theoretical state overcome us in the practical circumstance.

Being a contrarian or an independent thinker is vital for success in the secular range-bound market. This is a time when you must exercise disciplined buy and sell processes for an extended period. A contrarian state of mind is needed when selling into the rallies as stocks become fully valued, since this is usually a time of great excitement about stocks in general and the crowd is buying. Conversely, buying into sell-offs, when conventional wisdom says the market is not where you want to be—but the stocks on the watch list start hitting the buy valuations—requires an unemotional and often courageous contrarian mind-set.

The majority of investment decisions are made when the future is uncertain, whether we want to admit it to ourselves or not. We feel more comfortable and more certain about the future when the investment crowd (especially in our immediate surroundings) is on our side of the market fence. We want to feel good about decisions, so doing what the crowd does provides the comfort that we constantly seek. Not following the crowd or, even worse, making decisions that are contrary to the crowd's, may try your convictions and bring self-doubt and a lack of certainty.

It was easy to follow the crowd in the late 1990s. For instance, that crowd loved Sun Microsystems to death. Remember: It was one of Kenny's "must own" fantastic five stocks. Sun Microsystems reached a high above $63 in 2000 (see Exhibit 10.1), but then settled into the single digits by early 2002 and stayed there well into 2007. Following is an excerpt from a 2003 *BusinessWeek* interview with Scott McNealy, the CEO and founder of Sun Microsystems, in which he questions the crowd's thinking when it bid up Sun's stock to above $63.

> **BusinessWeek:** Sun's stock hit a high of $64. Did you think what tech stocks were doing two years ago was too good to be true?
>
> **McNealy:** ... Two years ago we were selling at 10 times revenues when we were at $64. At 10 times revenues, to give you a 10-year payback, I have to pay you 100 percent of revenues for 10 straight years in dividends. That assumes I can get that by my shareholders. That assumes I have zero cost of goods sold, which is very hard for a computer company. That assumes zero expenses, which is really hard with 39,000 employees. That assumes I pay no taxes, which is very hard. And that assumes you pay no taxes on your dividends, which is kind of illegal. And that assumes with zero R&D for the next 10 years, I can maintain the current revenue run rate. Now, having done that, would any of you like to buy my stock at $64? Do you realize how ridiculous those basic assumptions are? You don't need any transparency. You don't need any footnotes. What were you thinking?

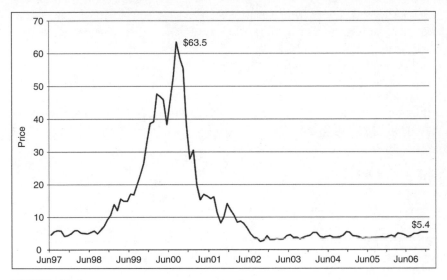

EXHIBIT 10.1 Sun Microsystems Price Performance

This exchange makes it clear that there are times when the investing crowd behaves in irrational ways; this is a time when being an independent thinker is crucial, because following the crowd, although it provides emotional comfort, often has a cost associated with it—financial losses.

YOU DON'T HAVE TO OWN IT

It is the stock that is on everybody's lips. It is hot. It is a "must own," or so you've been told. The usual comparisons are being thrown around—this one is the next Starbucks or Microsoft. All this craziness about a stock, and it is not even a full-blown bull market. And finally, if you are a professional investment manager, clients start to call asking why you don't own it. Microsoft, Starbucks, Amazon, eBay, Google, Tazer, Whole Foods—at some point they were all the talk of the town (the country, to be more accurate). However, there is a very high survivorship bias when talking about hot stocks. We remember only the companies that succeeded, as they are still around to remind us of that; we don't remember the ones that have failed. For every Microsoft and Starbucks there are hundreds of companies (if not more) that sank into oblivion.

When everybody is talking about the hot stock, it looks expensive to a value investor. It has no margin of safety to speak of; only hoped-for return is priced into the stock, but very little risk. The future industry structure and achievable growth rates are unclear, but the price assumes they are favorable!

The good news is—you don't have to own it! It is okay to say, "I don't know." It may be the next Microsoft, or it may be the next Atari (and statistically, chances are it is the latter). You want to own stocks on your terms, not when everybody wants you to own them, and only when they meet your QVG criteria.

BE A MYTH BUSTER

My son Jonah's favorite TV show is *Myth Busters*. On this show, special-effects experts use their skills to test the validity of urban legends—myths. Using modern-day science they separate truth from fiction. Instead of just explaining how something is scientifically possible, they test it.

The show might test, for example, if running in the rain instead of walking would keep you drier. That myth was confirmed to be true, but another well-worn myth—"a shotgun barrel plugged by a human finger will backfire and explode, injuring or killing the shooter instead of the intended victim"—that myth was busted.

Just as the perfect retirement home in sunny Florida cannot exist without a bingo night, Wall Street cannot survive without myths. The dictionary defines *myth* as a widely held but mistaken belief. The key words are *widely* (impacting the stock price) and *mistaken* (creating an opportunity). If just mentioning a stock name elicits a widely accepted/off-the-cuff reason for why the stock should not be owned, you may have a myth on your hands. For instance, if I say "Wal-Mart," I hear: "Grew too big; slower growth looms"; Home Depot: housing slowdown will cripple its profitability; Boston Scientific: overpaid for Guidant; Intel: AMD is stealing its market share in servers; Washington Mutual: too much mortgage exposure; Kodak: digital pictures will undermine its core film revenues.

A myth may start its life from a company's press release, a news story, or an analyst comment. Just because an opinion is widely accepted doesn't mean that it is de facto a myth, but you already have half of the required ingredients for it to be one. The second half, of course, is that it be wrong. To bust a myth you need to prove that a widely accepted opinion is wrong. Also, to make sure you bust the right myth, it has to be properly defined. The following line is an example of a properly defined myth statement:

XYZ stock is not a good buy, because ABC will enter the industry and will drive it out of business.

Properly phrasing the myth is crucial to being able to test it. Otherwise, you may miss an attractive buying opportunity. Make sure you are testing the myth in relation to a company's stock, not the company itself, as a much worse scenario might already be priced into the stock. For instance, perhaps your myth-busting phrase is "Wal-Mart grew too big; slower growth looms." Well, this may not be a myth, as Wal-Mart's sales growth will probably slow down from historically achieved levels. However, if you phrase a myth correctly (about a stock), the phrase becomes "Wal-Mart stock is not a good buy because its sales growth will slow down"; you may find, for instance, that although Wal-Mart's great size will slow down its sales growth from 15 percent to 9 percent, the market is already pricing in only 5 percent growth, making Wal-Mart stock a great buy.

QUANTIFY EVERYTHING AND BE A CONTRARIAN HEADLINE INVESTOR

The *Myth Busters* program busts myths by testing everything, not taking anything for granted, and you should do the same. They often do it by conducting experiments that may result in bodily injury if not done right, but don't worry, you won't be asked to do the same. Whenever you detect a myth surrounding a particular stock, phrase the myth correctly and then quantify! Build vaguely right models, test different what-if scenarios, and be prepared to buy or sell based on the inconsistencies between consensus and revealed truths—the myth and what the numbers say. Once armed with facts and research, you are less likely to be swayed by the pressure of crowd thinking. Quantifying will help you to manage your own emotional impulses and will give you an edge against the crowd.

As we discussed in Chapter 7, the discounted cash flow model is a great quantifying contrarian tool, as it provides good intelligence on the expectations built into the stock. But often analysis doesn't have to be that complicated. Sometimes the real story is just beneath the surface.

In September 2006 Wal-Mart announced that it would start selling 300 generic drugs for $4 each in its stores in the United States. This news sent stocks of stand-alone pharmacies Walgreens and CVS crashing down as much as 10 percent on the day of announcement, further declining in the next two months by another 10 to 15 percent. The myth headlines sounded like Wal-Mart, a company responsible for driving many retailers out of business, was about to have stand-alone pharmacies for lunch.

The properly phrased myth to be tested was: "Walgreens and CVS are not good stocks because Wal-Mart's $4 generics will substantially impact their profitability."

However, once you quantified the myth, you'd realize that the Wal-Mart program had the biggest impact on consumers who were paying for prescriptions out of their own pockets, which accounted for a small portion of CVS's and Walgreens' sales. In fact, only 5.9 percent and 7.1 percent (per 2005 annual reports) of CVS's and Walgreens' pharmacy sales were paid by consumers directly; the bulk was paid by third parties (insurance companies, government, and states). Out of this 5.9 percent and 7.1 percent, only a portion went to branded drugs and the rest went to vitamins and generics. Therefore, the impact of Wal-Mart's $4 generics program on Walgreens' and CVS's future sales was likely to be negligible. That myth was busted!

TIME ARBITRAGE

Wall Street is inherently short-term oriented. This is not because it is dumb. Quite the contrary, some of the brightest minds in this great country labor in the investment industry. But somewhere along the way of explosive growth in the mutual fund industry, our innate desire for short-term gratification has altered the nucleus of the investment business, turning it into a marketing one. There is nothing wrong with marketing; some of my good friends are marketers. But a good marketer's job is to find what customers want and try to fill that need. Unfortunately, to their detriment, the investing public wants instant gratification. They want to keep up with the (Dow) Joneses, and they want their fund to beat the other funds and comparable indexes on an instant basis—quarterly and annually. That is not what investing is about; it is about reaching your long-term financial goals while taking the least amount of risk.

Mutual funds' individual inflows and outflows are driven by how they rank against their peers on a short-term basis. Many mutual fund managers' and analysts' compensation packages are structured to meet goals (maximize inflows, minimize outflows) with great emphasis on short-term performance, creating faulty incentives. Hedge fund managers face an even trickier dilemma, as they need to show absolute positive return month after month.

A fund manager is often forced into making a short-run-oriented decision despite knowing that it is a wrong strategy for the long run—as his tenure may not survive the short run. Oakmark Fund manager Robert Sanborn, for instance, was replaced in 2000 because his value-oriented fund had underperformed the market and had lost $7 billion in asset outflows.[1] His difficult, but right, decision not to jump on the dot-com wagon and instead to stick to what he was hired to do—value investing (not speculating)—was vindicated several months later when the NASDAQ collapsed and value stocks came back into vogue, for what has so far been a run of more than six years! Unfortunately, his tenure did not survive the short run.

Investors chase last year's performers, and that in large part is the reason equity fund investors (according to a Dalbar study) have historically underperformed the mutual funds they have invested in by a huge margin. Media hype doesn't help the issue, either: Every January last year's mutual fund winners are paraded through glossy year-end publications. But don't blame the media; they publish what people want to read!

The shortsightedness of investors creates an embedded incentive for market participants (Wall Street) that control an enormous amount of capital to favor stocks that are expected to do well in the shorter run. They will sell (or avoid) those whose immediate future is ambiguous, but that may have a great risk/reward profile in the long run (which of course always lies past the short run). Therefore, if you can stomach the short run and have a longer time horizon than several quarters, as any sensible investor should, an opportunity is created: time arbitrage.

Time arbitrage is often created when a stock is sold off on missing its analyst guidance (which often doesn't have to be by much), fails to meet the Street's earnings estimates, or simply has a short-term stumble (which will happen to any company; it is just a matter of time). We don't live in a sterile world of linearity and should *not* expect linear performance from the companies we invest in. Despite the Street's perception, these short-term events have little or no impact on the long-term stream of company cash flows, and thus have little if any impact on a company's actual *value*. However, Wall Street with its huge mass will dump a stock as a bad curse (often driving it far below its intrinsic value) if the stock stands between fund managers and their annual bonuses (or their keeping their jobs)—a dangerous place to be.

Though time arbitrage is not a riskless opportunity, odds are that if you have the contrarian mind-set and are not afraid of being on the lonely side of the fence (owning a stock that is not loved by Wall Street at the time or that may be dead money for a while), you have a great opportunity to take advantage of Wall Street's habitual and recurring irrationality.

FINDING NEW IDEAS

How do you find stocks to buy? Sorry, but looking at the front pages of the *Wall Street Journal* and the *Financial Times* for myths to be busted may be a lot of fun, but it's not enough. What you really need is a continuous new-idea discovery process. As we'll discuss in Chapter 12, a strict sell discipline will increase portfolio turnover, and replacing stocks that are on the way out with new ones will become a priority. Here are some ideas on how to find new stocks.

Map the Market

Contrarian investors are usually drawn to the sectors that are not hitting all-time highs but are instead staring into the abyss of the multiweek, -month, and -year lows. These are the stocks that usually have a lot of myths surrounding them that need to be busted. An easy way to identify an entire group of stocks the market has decided to divorce is by looking at exchange-traded funds.

Though ETFs have been in existence for more than a decade, their popularity has exploded in the early 2000s. I don't know if they were mentioned on *American Idol* or were featured in the latest Britney Spears video, or ETFs are simply a financial product whose time has come. Nevertheless, they provide an elegant and easy way to map the market by slicing and dicing global markets in every conceivable way (and some previously inconceivable ways)—by sector; stock characteristic (e.g., market capitalization, P/E, dividend yield); investment style (value, growth); asset class (stocks, bonds, gold, oil, currency); markets—covering the globe in every plausible way, including which stock exchanges they trade on.

Periodic review of ETF performance provides a rapid but useful global intelligence report on what different pockets of the market are doing, helping you to be selective about where you spend your energy looking for ideas and enabling you to spend your time in places where opportunities are more likely to exist.

Screens

I have yet to meet a value investor who did not run stock screens. Value investing to stock screening is what America is to apple pie. Here I'll just mention some of my favorites. All of these can be supplemented with your own qualifiers, by throwing in your own magic by adding debt ratios, dividend yield, return on capital thresholds, or anything else that would help you find companies that fit your approach.

- *The Little Book That Beats the Market.* This stock screen was introduced in a book of the same name by Joel Greenblatt (John Wiley & Sons, 2006). In this stock screen, companies are ranked by P/E (lower P/E gets a lower score) and by return on equity (ROE) (higher ROE gets a lower score), and then scores are added together. The top candidates on the list (the ones that have the lowest scores) are your latest and greatest ideas. This simple but brilliant formula has beaten the market since the 1980s.

- *Low price to anything screens.* These are the most popular screens, where you simply look for cheap stocks; the lower the number, the better. Here are just some variations that come to mind: P/E, price to cash flow (P/CF), price to book, price to EBITDA, price to dividend, and price to sales;* "anything" could really be anything. You can make adjustments to price by calculating a company's enterprise value (market value less cash plus debt).

- *Hitting the bottom screen.* This search screens for stocks that are hitting multiweek, -month, or -year lows.

- *Low price to normalized anything screen.* The low price to anything screen may miss stocks that have suffered a short-term setback, or are on the wrong side of the economic cycle, or simply took an accounting charge. Therefore, company earnings or cash flows will be depressed (below their normal level) and the stock will fall through the price to anything screen as its P/E or P/CF, for instance, will be overstated. To run a P/E screen, for example, you should compute P/E not based on the current earnings, but by taking an average net profit margin over three or five years and applying it to current sales (or average sales over the same time period, if you like).

- *Net-net stocks.* This is a classic Benjamin Graham screen where you look to buy stocks as close to or preferably below their net current assets (current assets less all liabilities including debt and preferred stock). Or you could look for companies that trade close to their net cash (cash including short-term investments less all interest-bearing debt). These companies usually have a lot of myths surrounding them. (In most markets since the 1950s, relatively few stocks pass these screens at any one time.)

- *Analyst sentiment screen.* Stock prices are impacted by Wall Street analysts' recommendations. It is common for a stock to be up or down several percentage points on change of analyst recommendations (e.g., from buy to sell, hold to buy, etc.). A stock that has every piece of bad

---

*The price to sales screen deals with some of the problems of profit margins, but it often provides a lot of false positives and negatives as profit margins vary significantly across different industries. For instance, software or pharmaceutical companies that inherently have high profit margins will rarely show up on that search, but general retailers that usually have low profit margins will always look cheap.

news plus some priced into it usually has a lot of analysts' disapproving sell ratings stamped all over it.

With few exceptions, analysts' recommendations are reactionary to the news. Analysts serve short-term-oriented masters—institutional investors. Therefore, despite often doing original research, the quarterly performance rat race skews analysts' recommendations. Michael Conn—my partner at Investment Management Associates—told me if you want to understand what most analyst recommendations mean, add "was" in front of them. For example, when an analyst says a stock is a buy, most of the time it means it *was* a buy. If it is a sell, it *was* a sell.

Unique buying opportunities are usually created when an army of analysts comes out with a sell recommendation, or when a stock has little coverage by analysts. The latter becomes important for smaller companies that are still yet to be discovered by Wall Street.

There is more than one way to screen for analyst sentiment. You can calculate a percentage of sell and hold recommendations as percentage of total recommendations and screen or sort for highest percentages. For example, if a stock has seven sells, two holds, and one buy recommendation by sell-side analysts, you may interpret that as a 70 percent sell recommendation (7 out of 10) or a 90 percent nonbuy recommendation (7 sells plus 2 holds out of 10). Hold recommendations usually are weak sell recommendations: They provide a way for an analyst to tell investors not to buy the stock but at the same time not end up on the company's we-hate-that-ungrateful-analyst list. You can screen for recommendation changes from buy to hold or from buy and hold to sell. This analyst sentiment screen may complement any aforementioned screen.

Steal Ideas from Other Value Investors Whose Approach You Respect

My parents always taught me that stealing was bad; thus when I say "steal ideas from others," I really mean borrow them and just don't give them back. (Okay, it is still stealing, but it is public information, after all.) Most of us have value investors in mind whose investment approaches we admire and can relate to. Make a list of these investors and start following their holdings. The only rub here is that they have to manage over $100 million. The $100 million requirement is not because I think that anybody who invests less than that should not be followed, but because Securities and Exchange Commission (SEC) rules require institutional (non–mutual fund) investors that manage over $100 million to disclose their stock holdings on a quarterly basis; thus their holdings can be followed (although this rule doesn't apply to mutual funds).

The SEC web site, though improved over the years, is still a maze when it comes to uncovering needed financial documents. I have been using Stockpickr.com and GuruFocus.com to find the latest holdings by institutional investors. I have found both of the latter web sites very useful and easy to use.

Looking at the holdings of other value managers is really just another screen for attractive opportunities that are not caught by traditional screens. It is a start but not the end of your research process. You still want to do your own research, the same process you would have conducted if you had come to the idea on your own. If you mindlessly borrow ideas without doing your own research, you would not know what to do when things don't go as you planned—the stock declines or fundamentals deteriorate or both.

Notice I suggested following the holdings of investors "whose investment approaches we admire and can relate to." I did not say investors that have great track records. There are several reasons for that: First, their track records could simply be random phenomena—they've taken a lot of risk, and luck was on their side. Looking at the track records alone is not enough. Second, even if success was due to an excellent process, it may not fit *your* process. We should always be willing to learn from others, but in the end we still have to remain who we are.

Circle of Trust

Surround yourself with investors whose process is similar to yours and whose opinions you respect—your circle of trust. There will be a time when your flavor of value investing just doesn't work (temporarily, although at the time it will seem like forever)—you buy a stock that meets all criteria of our QVG framework with flying colors, yet it keeps going down, and that happens over and over again. Or the market will ignore your portfolio altogether, as it is paying attention to other asset classes or stocks with different characteristics. Something similar happened to value investors in the late 1990s when growth stocks were in vogue and value stocks were looked upon as second-class citizens. Julian Robertson, a legendary value investor, was a casualty of this crazy time period. He closed his firm, which had managed billions of dollars, in early 2000, just a few months before the NASDAQ collapsed and value investors were rewarded for their patience.

At the time when your emotions will make you doubt yourself and push you to do the popular thing, following the crowd is the worst thing you can do, because you are more likely to sell low (your stocks) and buy high (stocks that have been working so far). This is where the circle of trust will come in handy, as these investors will likely be going through similar pain (it is painful). Consider it group therapy, if you will.

The circle of trust is a good a source of ideas. Similar to looking at holdings of investors whom you respect, a circle of trust might be a source of new stock ideas—another set of eyes. But I'll issue my warning again: It should not substitute for taking the initiative to look for new stocks on your own, and is not a replacement for your own research.

A circle of trust will help to stretch your circle of competence. Assuming its members have diverse backgrounds, they'll know some industries better than you do and vice versa. Whenever I dive into analyzing energy stocks or pipelines, for instance, industries that lie on the fringe of my circle of competence, I always run my ideas past a couple of my friends who know these industries inside and out. They guide me to look at certain industry-specific factors that I might have missed.

Media, the Amplifier of Myths—Be a Skeptical Reader

Advertisements contain the only truths to be relied on in a newspaper.

—Thomas Jefferson

The media are great amplifiers of myths. If I learned anything from my economics classes it was the importance of incentives. Incentives are built-in biases, motivations that influence our decisions. Media have the incentive to amplify news. Reporting on a safe populace living quiet and totally legal lives doesn't sell newspapers, nor does it make you want to watch more TV. But media companies need to maintain sales. Company directors report to their shareholders, reporters need to keep their jobs, and media companies need to make money. Since newspapers are published every day, and web and TV reporting exist in a 24/7 continuum, the incentives and pressure to amplify news are tremendous. News needs to scare or excite you to stimulate sales, and a slow news day is not good for business.

Few business reporters have primary research knowledge of the companies they write about; don't fault them—they are reporters, not investors or even truly analysts. They have to write several articles a week, sometimes several articles a day. Many business reporters come from a liberal arts background and don't have the time or the expertise to do in-depth research on the companies they write about. And while a few reporters make the distinction between a good company and a good stock, in many cases it is not their job to do so; their job is to report the day's or week's news. The established pros have Rolodexes of articulate investment experts to whom they defer for knowledge and quotes, and who can be relied on to speak in dynamic sound bites that excite or scare you. (This paragraph guarantees that I'll never again get interviewed by a newspaper reporter who might read it.)

These experts spend a good portion of their time researching stocks, but cannot be experts on all stocks. Sometimes they know little about the company in question but, wanting to get their names in the paper, recite yesterday's headlines with a minor inflammatory twist—the amplification process at its worst.

I get approached from time to time for an opinion on a particular stock by reporters. If I don't have knowledge attained through primary (my own) research, I tell them so and decline to comment. Once I received an e-mail from a reporter asking me what I thought of firm XYZ (not its real name). My reply was, "I would love to help, but I don't follow XYZ so I don't really have an opinion on the company." So far so good, but then I added, "The company must be doing something right, as its results were very impressive in the last quarter."

The next day, to my surprise, I found myself quoted in that newspaper saying, "The [XYZ] company must be doing something right, as its results were very impressive in the last quarter." I was shocked, as I thought my first comment completely disqualified my second comment. I, now seemingly the expert, was quoted in the newspaper commenting about a company whose financial statements I had never even seen. My total knowledge about XYZ's "last quarter" performance came from a headline I vaguely remembered seeing in the *Wall Street Journal* that mentioned that sales and earnings were up in high double digits. This was a great lesson with two end results. First, now when I want to say "no comment" I say "no comment" and not a word more. Second, I know what the so-called expert's opinion is often worth in a newspaper.

The daily tsunami of headline amplifications creates strong myth awareness and influences investors' behavior, driving stocks above and below their intrinsic values. Media can be the value investor's best friend if you are willing to step into the shoes of a contrarian myth buster, since this effect can create great buying and selling opportunities.

Also, be aware of front-page articles of business magazines, as they are a good contrarian clue. Historically, a front-page "halleluiah" or "way to go" story in a business magazine is the kiss of death for a stock—a nearly flawless contrarian's sell signal. A negative front-page article on a company that suddenly and artificially depresses its stock price can potentially create a once-in-a-lifetime buying opportunity for the contrarian investor. These companies must be on the minds of many investors to qualify as magazine or newspaper sellers. The emotions must be at an extreme and so is the price—indications of an emotional climax. The first half of a possible myth is present!

DO IN-DEPTH PRIMARY (YOUR OWN) RESEARCH
AND DOCUMENT IT

To keep a sane head, independent of the direction in which the crowd is marching, write down your basis for every investment, identifying value creators and destroyers and your expectations for them. Similar to recording a valuation target for a stock at the time of purchase, an investment thesis committed to paper at the time of investment represents the unemotional you, made at a time when you were thinking clearly and rationally. It will provide you peace of mind. No matter how volatile markets become, how persuasive the emotive crowd's behavior, or how high the media turns up the volume when amplifying myths, you will have a lucid strategy for rational decision making.

CHAPTER 11

Buy Process—
International Investing

THE WORLD HAS FLATTENED: *HOLA, BONJOUR, GUTEN TAG, BUON GIORNO* TO THE REST OF THE WORLD

Behavioral finance studies show that investors are more likely to buy the stock of the local telephone company than stock of one in a different state (these studies were done before the day when Baby Bells committed incest and married their brothers and sisters, and there were still local phone companies to be bought). Investors feel more comfortable owning familiar stocks. They'll often buy shares of familiar telephone companies, even if it means not owning, on a risk/reward basis, the best telephone company stock.

The U.S. stock market has been a great place to be over the past hundred years. The U.S. economy has transitioned from agrarian to manufacturing and then to a service economy. The United States became the wealthiest and the most powerful nation in the world. What is not to love? In the past, investing in quality domestic stocks was a no-brainer decision. Owning U.S. stocks felt comfortable, like owning the local phone or electric company, and patriotic—Americans buying American.

Globalization has made the world a flatter place. It is close to impossible to find products in a store that were not manufactured at least in part in another region of the world. The world is more interconnected now than ever before. Looking at only U.S. companies limits one's investment choices tremendously. The United States has the largest stock market in the world, but the U.S. population accounts for only 5 percent of the world population, and the domestic stock market represents a little under half the global total.

Unscientific, unbacktested common sense tells me that over the years the overall benefits of international diversification have diminished as world economies have become more and more interrelated. The old adage "when New York sneezes Paris catches a cold" is truer today than ever before.

That said, the world is swarming with often-smaller publicly traded companies (e.g., a restaurant chain in France, a lawn service company in Spain, hospitals in Poland, a cable TV provider in Singapore, etc.) whose business is not impacted significantly by what takes place in the United States.

Even if international diversification is not all it was cracked up to be, by looking solely at U.S. stocks you are keeping yourself from exploring faster-growing economies, some high-quality companies that may be paying much higher dividends, growing earnings at more attractive rates than their U.S. counterparts, and at the same time trading at more attractive valuations. Since foreign markets may or may not have gone through a stock market cycle similiar to that in the United States, opportunities may be knocking on the investor's door and they may or may not be speaking "American English."

SAME DIFFERENCE

Analyzing international companies is not much different from analyzing U.S. companies. Of course there are generally accepted accounting principles (GAAP), cultural, political, currency, and language differences, and there is currency risk. But economics that drive company profitability in the United States are similar to those around the world.

On the accounting front it appears that we are entering a time of gradual convergence in global accounting standards, first with Europe and then with the rest of the world.

PricewaterhouseCoopers wrote the following in its introduction to "A Comparison of IFRS [International Financial Reporting Standards, accounting standards adopted by European Union member countries] and US GAAP" in February 2006:

> The International Accounting Standards Board (IASB) and the US Financial Accounting Standards Board (FASB) have been committed to converging IFRS and US GAAP since the Norwalk Accord of 2002. Preparers and others, including regulators, have called for convergence to simplify financial reporting and reduce the compliance burden for listed companies, especially those with a capital stock market listing in more than one jurisdiction.
>
> The SEC, in its more recent 'roadmap' towards removing the U.S. GAAP reconciliation requirement for foreign private issuers using IFRS, has cited the continuing convergence of IFRS and US GAAP as a key building block, and in the last few months the European Commission has thrown its weight behind convergence

as part of its strategy to better protect domestic investors who invest in non-European companies.[1]

In coming years, countries looking for access to European and U.S. capital markets will be adopting IFRS, making analysis, at least from the accounting numbers perspective, easier. In the meantime, while dealing with the accounting differences one should focus on the cash, not accrual, method of accounting, an approach appropriate and useful in the analysis of U.S. companies as well.

We as American investors want to believe the U.S. GAAP is the best in the world and that our companies are the most honest. But the overnight collapse of two Fortune 500 companies (Enron and MCI WorldCom), bankruptcy of one of the oldest and largest accounting firms (Arthur Andersen), the mutual fund timing scandal that touched many of the large mutual fund companies, accounting irregularities found in a few dozen Fortune 500 companies, and lately apparently more-than-isolated backdating of options for executives—all these took place in the United States, not in some third world nation. Some countries and governments are more corrupt than others, but not all countries outside of the United States should be painted with the same "higher risk" brush.

LOCATION OF CORPORATE HEADQUARTERS ABROAD MAY NOT CONSTITUTE A FOREIGN COMPANY

We often pay too much attention to a company's locality, usually defined simplistically as its headquarters location. By that definition Nokia is a Finnish company, but nearly all of its sales are made outside of Finland. By the same token, 3M (formerly Minnesota Mining & Manufacturing Company) is as American as apple pie, but now less than 40 percent of its sales comes from the United States. A U.S. investor may already own stock in foreign enterprises, as a large portion of sales for many companies is already coming from overseas.

In the late 1990s it was common to find a growth and an international mutual fund in the same family of funds with major overlaps in holdings. Since international companies were defined by where the company was headquartered, companies like Nokia, Nortel (Canada), Sony (Japan), and Ericsson (Sweden) showed up on both domestic growth and international managers' lists. If an investor owned an international fund in hopes of risk diversification, he/she was set up for a surprise when the market turned down in the late 1990s, as the international fund did not provide the international diversification it was purchased to provide.

In other words, investors holding a mutual fund that invests in large international companies may not receive the desired benefits of diversification, as these companies may derive a large portion of revenues from the United States.

YOU ARE EXPOSED TO MORE FOREIGN POLITICAL RISK THAN YOU REALIZE

Political risks often take a different and more drastic form overseas, but U.S.-based companies are not immune from that risk, either. A lot of them sell their products and services or source their production from overseas. It is difficult if not impossible to find a medium-size U.S. company that is not impacted by what takes place in the rest of the world.

In January 2007 Royal Dutch/Shell announced that it would be selling 50 percent plus one share of the Sakhalin-2 project to Gazprom for $7.5 billion. Several months before, the Russian government wanted to take Royal Dutch/Shell to court because it was allegedly ruining the environment. I suppose when the Russian government referred to the environment, it meant the *economic* environment, not Mother Nature. The environmental issue was simple: Product- sharing agreements (PSAs) with Shell signed some years earlier by the Russian government were not considered advantageous to Russia—at least not anymore.

The $7.5 billion question comes to mind: Did Gazprom buy a controlling stake in the Sakhalin-2 project at a fair price? It's hard to say. The $7.5 billion sale price is not chump change, but Shell didn't sell a controlling stake in the project of its own free will—which, by the way, ensured a replenishment of its dwindling oil reserves for years to come. You don't have to be a genius to figure out that after that sale (I use that term loosely because it assumes willing participants on both sides), the environmental issues will not be issues anymore.

The Russian government manipulated its environmental/legal levers to muscle an ownership stake in the project out of Shell, possibly at a significant discount. Mafia boss Al Capone was sent to jail not for his murderous crimes, but for tax evasion. Similarly, Mr. Putin & Co. went after Shell for environmental violations. However, in this case, Shell's crime is its profitability in the face of the Russian government's lust for oil money and control of natural resources. I don't know whether the environmental problems were really problems. Every time you drill for oil or gas in the middle of a wilderness, environmental issues could be found. But few things in Russia are done for the sake of the environment, and in my view this was no exception.[2]

Maybe I am just too cynical about Russian motives and Royal Dutch/Shell really is likely to pollute poor Mother Russia. However, if Gazprom was doing this, the government would be laying a red carpet under its pipelines to make sure that its executives don't get their feet wet.

This isn't the first time the Russian government has done something that has abridged the law. Using similar tactics, Russia stole (for lack of a better word) Yukos from its shareholders in 2004, sending its largest shareholder to jail, and has been gradually consolidating (deprivatizing) oil resources under the government (Gazprom) wing. Unfortunately, great amounts of natural resources are found in countries with often unstable political regimes like Russia, Venezuela, Nigeria, Iran, Iraq, and the list goes on.

Even if you always invested purely in the United States, though, you probably already had some foreign political risk in your portfolio but just did not realize it. Have you ever owned stock in an integrated oil company? If you have, then you've been exposed to plenty of foreign political risk.

WHAT ABOUT THE UNITED STATES?

Political risk is not limited to foreign countries. Although we may have one of the most stable political systems in the world, political risk, though arguably to less extreme degree, is present in the United States.

In 1993, after President Bill Clinton was elected, his wife Hillary Clinton tried to nationalize the health care system in the United States. Strictly putting political beliefs and biases aside, if her attempt had been successful it would have ultimately reduced profitability of pharmaceutical companies, and in the wake of this possibility pharmaceutical companies' shares plunged to multiyear lows. The nationalization attempt ultimately failed and stocks rebounded, but many investors who sold stocks into the declines lost money in the sector.

It seems that political risk shows up every four years during the presidential elections. In 2004, the issue of drug reimportation from Canada was hovering over the pharmaceutical industry, helping send pharmaceutical stock prices down. That time it did not lead to a law change to allow reimportation of drugs from Canada or European countries, but there is always a next time. Political risk is present in any country; it is just a matter of type and of degree. It is lower in the developed countries and higher in the developing countries.

PICK YOUR COMFORT ZONE AND GO FROM THERE

You don't need to become the Indiana Jones of international investing by diving into developing countries like Russia, where the rule of law is still in its infancy. Nor do I recommend investing in countries ruled by narcissistic egomaniacs. In *Adventure Capitalist* (Random House, 2003), Jim Rogers mentions his visit to an ex-Soviet Union republic, Turkmenistan. President Saparmurat Niyazov changed his name to Akbar Turkmenbashy, meaning "Great Father of all Turkmenistan." Not unlike Saddam Hussein in Iraq, Joseph Stalin in the Soviet Union, and Adolf Hitler in Nazi Germany, his pictures can be found everywhere: on money, on massive billboards, in the top righthand corner of the TV screen, and on various household products, including tea. He even tried to put his face on the national flag of Turkmenistan, but instead, after facing pressure from the international community opposing that idea, he renamed the months of the year after himself and his family members.

The country's economical infrastructure has been in a consistent decline since Turkmenbashy took over. In order to rid the country of Western influence, libraries and Western-style universities have been closed. The bulk of the country's revenues has been squandered by Turkmenbashy for self-glorification. Turkmenistan has one-fifth of the world's natural gas reserves, and for that reason, not for its humanitarian or economic achievements, the European Union has granted the country "most favored nation" trading status. This is a country that has been set by its president on the rocky road of the Stone Age.

(P.S. On December 21, 2006, shortly after I wrote this, Turkmenbashy died of cardiac arrest. One hopes, for the sake of the people of Turkmenistan, his replacement will not be a sequel—Turkmenbashy II.)

I wouldn't start my international investing voyage with Turkmenistan. I'd start with more stable political systems, the countries that we can relate to the most, maybe even with the United States' unofficial fifty-first state, our northern neighbor, Canada. Japan, Western Europe, New Zealand, Israel, and Australia are the next logical stops, followed by Eastern Europe and Mexico. I am sure that I missed a few dozen "must own" countries, but that is my comfort zone—countries in which *I* feel justified investing. We all will have a different comfort zone based on our experiences, but I hope you get the point: Start with your comfort zone and then tiptoe out from there.

Simply by starting within comfort zone countries will open your portfolio to several dozen places with relatively stable political and legal regimes. Once you become comfortable with international investing, I'd venture on a small scale into more exotic, faster-growth, emerging countries and maybe even into Turkmenistan . . . well, maybe not. Russia? I'd invest only as much money as I could afford to lose.

Usually, investors trade higher economic growth for stability of an economic and political system. I suggest creating a spreadsheet or table listing all countries of interest and ranking them by stability of economic and political systems, economic and population growth rates, demographic trends, inflation levels, indebtedness, access to capital, size and liquidity of capital markets, transparency of accounting system, overall stock market valuation, and the secular trend in the making (bull, cowardly lion, or bear). (And don't struggle to arrange countries in a perfect 1-to-25 ranking; instead, about four grades will do: low, below average, above average, and high.) Your goal is not to own a stock from every country, but to open your portfolio for some possibly better investment opportunities.

DON'T CONFUSE A FAST-GROWING ECONOMY AND A GOOD INVESTMENT

Of course I cannot write a chapter on international investing and not mention China, the most populous nation and one that has been on the growth wagon for a while now. However, similar to what often happens to fast-growing domestic growth stocks, investors may recognize the potential for high growth rates of a non-U.S. country, fall in love with its market, and bid up stock prices accordingly—making that country an unappealing investment. High growth should not be bought at just any price!

Although the Chinese economy has been growing at a rate exceeding 10 percent a year, double or triple growth rates in developed economies, its stock market has declined by more than half since it peaked in 2000—when its average stock changed hands at a P/E of 56 times earnings (see Exhibit 11.1). This decline took place despite the fact that earnings went up almost 50 percent from 2000 to 2005. Investors did what they do best: They got overly optimistic about the prospects of the Chinese economy and drove stocks to extreme valuation levels. This is another classic case where investors caught up in the moment of excitement failed to make a distinction between great companies and great stocks.

CURRENCY RISK

Currency risk should be diversified away. Predicting what currency is going to do in the future is usually a fruitless exercise (with few exceptions). Most of the economists, professionals who focus on that full time, still get

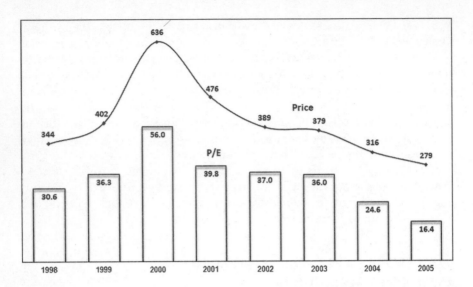

EXHIBIT 11.1 Chinese Stock Market: Shenzhen Stock Exchange

it wrong half the time. Diversifying the portfolio on a country and region level, in addition to the usual diversification techniques, should cancel out most of the currency risk.

If you have a strong opinion on the direction of a currency and want to amplify your portfolio exposure to a specific currency or want to hedge, you have a new investment option—currency exchange-traded funds. They are similar to index ETFs that investors have grown accustomed to but track performance of different currencies against the U.S. dollar. At the end of 2006, Rydex currency ETFs were tracking seven currencies against the U.S. dollar: euro, Mexican peso, Swedish krona, Australian dollar, British pound sterling, Canadian dollar, and Swiss franc. You can invest in these without the scary act of opening a commodities account.

HOW MUCH IS TOO MUCH?

Natural questions come to mind: how much should a U.S. investor have invested domestically? The answer will depend on the following: How many opportunities do you see in the United States? How much cash are you willing to hold? What is your comfort zone? How attractive are opportunities that are outside of the United States? Also, not all foreign countries have the same profile.

I'd argue that most Western European nations have a risk profile similar to that of the United States. For instance, if you cannot find an attractive bank stock in the United States and you buy a high-quality English bank stock—a stock that scored high marks on all dimensions of the QVG framework—did you increase the risk of the portfolio? I'd argue you *reduced* the risk. England is really no more risky than the United States, so you have not added any country risk. By refusing to skimp on any of the QVG dimensions and settle for just the best available U.S. bank stock, you reduced the risk of the portfolio by stepping across the waters.

CONCLUSION

As I mentioned in previous chapters, finding good companies is never the problem in any market. We are fortunate to have hundreds (if not thousands) of great "Made in the USA" companies to choose from. However, as I demonstrated earlier in Chapter 3, finding great companies at attractive valuations (appropriately high margins of safety) is a challenge that U.S. investors will be facing for quite some time, as overall market valuations are not cheap. As markets go through cyclical rallies and stocks that have exhausted their margins of safety are sold, new ones will need to be found. The search should not be a myopic one just out of old habits!

Finding good investments is exponentially more difficult at higher valuation levels. If you are unwilling to sit out the market in cash (some money managers are mandated to have low cash balances) will be pressed to buy marginal stocks—sacrificing quality, valuation, or growth—not a path that is worth taking in any market, but especially not in the range-bound market. Opening one's portfolio to international stocks may help those unwilling to resort to a higher cash position.

Simply stated, stocks should compete against each other for a place in your portfolio. The larger the pool of stocks you can choose from, the higher the bar—the opportunity cost—that a new stock has to overcome to make it into the portfolio. International stocks need not be seen merely as a necessary evil for diversification—they should contribute in a real way to raising that bar, as they increase the quality of the investment pool.

CHAPTER 12

Sell Process—Make Darwin Proud

If it is a great company at 50 times earnings, it will still be a great company at 15 times earnings!

Having a disciplined selling process cannot be emphasized enough in the range-bound market. An investor without a sell discipline is similar to a highway with on-ramps but no exits. The impact of losers or subpar performers in one's portfolio is usually muted in the bull market by the rise of the overall market's P/E levels. In addition, the portfolio is further helped by performance of a few superstars—stocks whose price appreciation exceeds the wildest dreams of most investors. The list of stocks that exceeded even the wildest expectations of many in the 1982–2000 bull market was long: Kenny's fantastic five are the obvious candidates that come to mind, but they only scratch the surface.

Stock selection, valuation, and diversification are the building blocks of risk management in the long-only portfolio, but a sell process is the cement (the glue) that holds them all together. Things change (not always for the better), and the defensive moat silts up, bringing quality of some companies down; fundamentals worsen, making a stock a riskier and less appealing investment; a stock appreciates, and though it's a good problem to have, it leads to a parallel deterioration of that precious margin of safety.

A disciplined sell process injects a healthy dose of Darwinism (survival of the fittest) into the portfolio, weeding out the weakest stocks—the ones that have deteriorated fundamentals or diminished margins of safety—in favor of stronger ones, thus improving the portfolio and making it less risky.

A great majority of stock sell decisions in the long-term investor's portfolio fall into one of two categories:

1. The stock price has gone up, depleting the margin of safety and hindering the Valuation dimension.
2. Fundamentals have deteriorated, so Quality, Growth, or both dimensions have deteriorated (or you expect them to deteriorate).

SELLING WHEN STOCK PRICE HAS GONE UP

Stocks should be purchased when the risk/reward equation is tilted in your favor and sold when that stops being the case. Stocks that became fairly valued, the ones that exhausted their margins of safety and in which expected total rate of return (earning growth plus dividends) now fall below your expectations should be sold—period!

You buy stocks to make yourself money. And when a stock, like a loyal pet, does what it was purchased to do—goes up—you are hesitant to part with it. The stock created your wealth, after all. Contemplating selling an overvalued stock feels similar to teaching your dog how to fetch and then as a reward sending it to a kennel. But a stock, unlike a pet, has no feelings to hurt and it should not be fallen in love with; it is just a tool to increase your wealth. Even when you decide to part with the stock, you want to squeeze every last penny out of it (sell at the top) before saying those final good-byes.

Selling is an emotional process, often more emotional than buying. After analyzing and holding a stock for some time, you've developed an emotional connection with it. Over time, you talked to management, listened to their presentations and conference calls, studied the company's financials, scanned press releases, built models projecting the company's future profitability, and more. Selling brings closure to the journey, and if the journey was successful (the price has appreciated) you don't want it to end.

However, stocks are not pets. The overvalued stock, once sold, can be bought back in the future when it starts meeting your criteria for ownership again. The stock doesn't know that you own it (an old Wall Street adage), and it will not hold a grudge against you for selling it.

Here are several strategies that should help you deal with your sell emotions.

Decide How the Game Will End Before It Starts

A phrase I heard from Minyanville.com contributor Rod David comes to mind: "I never owned a stock I was not willing to sell." For every stock there is a price at which you should be willing to part with it.

The easiest way to deal with emotional attachment to a stock is to decide and thereby know how the game will end before it starts. Arguably you are less emotional about a company at the time of purchase than at the time of sale. The emotions of the ownership attachment that come during the time you are holding the stock have not yet had time to develop. Setting a selling price (e.g., sell at $75) or, even better, a selling valuation (e.g., I'll sell this stock when it gets to a P/E of 17 or price-to-book ratio of 3.3) at the time of purchase and strictly following it when the stock reaches the sell target should help free you from your emotions (assuming risk/reward characteristics of the stock have not changed significantly).

When a stock reaches its predetermined sell target, the sell decision should become automatic and thus unemotional, a Nike-like "Just do it!" The stock should be presumed guilty of being fairly valued, and the burden of proof should be shifted to *keeping* the stock in the portfolio, not the other way around. It should be assumed that the price or valuation target chosen at the time of purchase was rationally based and had a lower emotional component attached to it, thus carrying higher weighting in the "to sell or not to sell" decision.

Personally, I'd like to set a sell P/E based on the absolute P/E model that we discussed in Chapter 7. In fact, for every company in my portfolio and on my watch list I determine and write down buy, fair value, and sell P/Es.

The difficulty of selling in the range-bound market is likely to be exacerbated by the fact that often you'll be selling when everybody else is buying. I suggest keeping Exhibit 2.4 in mind (frame it if you'd like) when a stock reaches its preset P/E target and you are having a hard timing saying good-bye.

Delegate Selling Responsibility

Depending on your investment environment (professional or personal), one way to get rid of the emotional baggage that usually accompanies the selling of a stock is to give sell authority to a person or entity less involved with the stock, a presumably less emotional and more capable party.

In the institutional environment, an analyst or a portfolio manager who was not responsible for selecting the stock in the first place should have the final authority to make the sell decision, of course only after hearing the defense (if there is one) for keeping the stock in the portfolio.

If the investment setting is your personal account, then a friend, spouse, or trusted adviser may step into the shoes of the sell authority. Of course, a major assumption is that the person to whom the sell authority was delegated is capable of making the appropriate decision. For instance, even though my six-year-old son Jonah and year-old daughter Hannah don't have an emotional attachment to my stocks, they're not the right people to be in charge of my sell decisions. I'll give them a couple of more years.

We Are Not as Smart as We Think

The secular range-bound market is full of cyclical bull, range-bound, and bear markets. You'll be doing a lot of selling during cyclical bull markets as temporary market ascents will be lifting more of your stocks. The investing public and the media will be excited about investing. You'll be getting a powerful feeling that everything you touch turns to gold, as every time you buy a stock, it goes up. You'll be thinking, "Did I finally figure out the stock market game? Did I find a secret to Will Rogers' advice to buy stocks that go up, and if they don't go up, don't buy them?"

Although you might have gotten smarter, you didn't get that much smarter (sorry). And your stock-picking skills haven't improved that much (sorry again). You were simply a willing participant in the cyclical bull market. A cyclical bull market makes us feel smarter than we are (overconfident) the same way a cyclical bear market makes us feel dumber than we are. Feeling smart makes us do the opposite of what we should be doing. The euphoria of the golden touch is a dangerous thing because it can make us careless. We forget about risk since we haven't seen it in a while and focus only on our rewards. You have to actively make yourself aware of the four-letter word *R-I-S-K*!

My favorite way is to remind myself how dumb I am. I pull out an annual report of a company on which I lost a boatload of money and masochistically try to read it from cover to cover, reliving my dumbness.

We all have these stocks, the ones we lost a lot of money on because we were overconfident. We tend to forget about them during the bull market phase. But I suggest you remember them during cyclical bull markets, so you'll have fewer of those names to remember in the future. Risk is still there; it is just hiding under the joyful sentiment of the cyclical bull market. Believe me, it will show its ugly face. It is just a matter of time.

In the (cyclical) bull market, it is easy to forget about our selling discipline and then turn into "buy and forget to sell" investors. Every time we sell a stock we feel dumb because it usually goes up afterward. We don't feel smart about our sell decisions (though we do feel smart about our buy decisions). You cannot worry about getting out at the very top in every sell. No, the proper objective is to buy a great company when it is cheap and to sell it when it is fairly valued![1]

"Growth Investors Gone Wild" Strategy

At the time a stock approaches its fair valuation, selling discipline should be kicked into high gear. However, it is common for the value investor (I can be guilty of this as well) to sell too soon, leaving additional price appreciation on the table. As a stock rises and reaches the fair valuation point in the eyes of the value investor, its starts showing up on the radar screen of momentum and growth investors, who usually take the stock out of the value investor's hands (i.e., buy it) and drive the stock price higher.

Using a traditional stop-loss strategy (selling if the stock declines below a predetermined point) in most cases is counterintuitive to a value investor (as it is to me). As the price of a stock declines, assuming fundamentals have not changed, it becomes more appealing to the value investor, who is accustomed to searching for just such a scenario. However, as a stock's price rises and the company becomes fairly valued, a trailing stop-loss strategy may allow you to capture extra return from the awakened interest of momentum investors.

Selling a portion of a position when it reaches its fully valued level (target price) captures the paper profits (into cash). Letting the rest of the position have an opportunity to be driven higher by those less sensitive value market participants may allow you to capture additional profits that could otherwise often be left on the table. Setting mechanical or mental stop losses for stocks at this stage of the selling game allows the capture of additional upside and protection of the downside at the same time.

A note of warning: This strategy may not be a good fit for those who don't have a concentrated portfolio of stocks (i.e., 15 to 25 holdings), as they may end up with too many small positions to follow. The largest pitfall of this strategy—emotions—can turn against you, and trying to capture additional profit from "growth investors gone wild" may lead to making an unpleasant round trip in the stock—it may decline considerably, wiping out your earlier paper profits.

Also, this strategy should be applied only to stocks that score very high marks on the Quality and (especially) Growth dimensions, the stocks that growth investors are likely to fall in love with.

SELLING WHEN FUNDAMENTALS HAVE DETERIORATED

> *When the facts change, I change my mind. What do you do, sir?*
> —John Maynard Keynes

Nothing Is Forever

With the exception of diamonds, nothing is forever, or so De Beers leads us to believe. Maybe love is, but that is definitely a discussion for a different book. Defensive moats have different life spans, but they are often finite as companies need to reinvent themselves constantly to retain them. Some companies do this more successfully than others. However, some that still have their original moats in place have simply run out of growth, their respective industries stopped growing, or the company's success led to its capturing significant market share and becoming—de facto—the industry.

If we look at stocks through the Quality, Valuation, and Growth prism, Valuation is usually the most volatile dimension. It is mainly driven by a company's stock price movements, which tend be more volatile than its fundamentals (shift in risk/reward characteristics). Therefore, the Quality and Growth dimensions are usually more stable than Valuation. Whereas Valuation may change on a dime, it usually takes much longer (months or years) for fundamental problems to develop, with the exception of sudden events (e.g., loss of an important lawsuit, invalidation of a patent, hurricane destruction, announcement of change in the regulatory environment of the industry, etc.).

Prenuptial Agreement and Double Secret Probation

Running the risk of being called stock-sexual, I'll write the following: Marry your stocks but with a prenuptial agreement.

Though marrying stocks—falling in love, staying by their side (not selling) for better or worse, in sickness and in health—is not wise in any market, it could be fatal for your portfolio in a range-bound market environment. In a perfect world, a stock-investing paradise, we would buy a portfolio of great companies that would grow consistently, and their prices would appreciate smoothly in line with their earnings, thus maintaining an appropriate margin of safety at all times. Their business would never change, nor would the competitive structure of the industries in which they operate. And their management, being superhumans, would always make wise decisions—wouldn't that be nice? Then we could safely marry all of our stocks and keep them forever. Unfortunately (or fortunately), investing is not a utopian paradise.

You need to strike a balance between excessive promiscuous stock dating—selling after one bad joke—and marriage in its intended sense, namely forever. I don't want to cheapen investing by comparing it to a Hollywood-type marriage where few marriages last a lifetime and the majority last only months or just a few years. But there is a lesson we should learn from our movie stars: Have a prenuptial agreement.

We should buy stocks with an intent to marry them forever (the Warren Buffett approach), but, knowing that there is a chance that it may not work out, at the time of marriage (purchase) we should sign a prenuptial agreement detailing on just what terms the marriage will be ended (stocks will be sold).

The terms of this prenuptial agreement should be specific: You should identify and closely track important variables that constitute a scorecard of a company's fundamental performance (i.e., sales growth, net margins, return on capital, or some industry-specific variables). For retailers, for instance, these variables could be same-store sales growth, inventory turnover, sales per square foot, operating margin, shrink (losses due to theft and spoilage), and so on.

Once these variables stop meeting your expectations, the stock should be put on "double secret probation" to see if they improve, and closely watched. If these variables don't improve in a set time frame (just a few quarters) the stock should be sold (divorced).

If the movie *Animal House* taught us anything, it is the importance of "double secret probation"—singling out a stock and putting it on a higher-priority, under-the-magnifying-glass analysis.

You should take a proactive approach to selling stocks before problems escalate. Keep fundamental underperformers on a shorter leash, sell sooner, and give less time for the company to fix things. And in a range-bound market, where you do not have the pleasant tailwind of secular rising P/Es and widespread confidence, a short leash is important!

I am not advocating setting quarter-by-quarter earnings targets, as that may prove to be a fruitless exercise. Meeting or beating quarterly estimates by a penny, quarter after quarter, is not necessarily an indication of a company's quality or superior fundamental performance. Creative accounting has helped a lot of companies in the past to do so in a very consistent manner, only to be found out later to be achieving this quarterly charade by massaging their numbers or simply cooking their books.

A quarter is just three months, approximately 91 days in the much longer life of the company. Quarterly earnings numbers are a reflection of dozens of variables, many of which are random in nature and took place over a relatively short-term period of time. In fact, I tend to believe that a company that consistently beats the Street's estimates should be closely examined for accounting shenanigans. Contrary to what the Wall Street analysts preach, not meeting the Street's estimates is not the end of the world, and in fact often creates great buying opportunities as the stock prices of corporate disappointers are severely punished. (You, with a longer-term and more rational perspective, can take money from those with short-term, immediate-gratification views.)

Set fundamental performance targets—the marriage vows (or fundamental goals). When the company stops meeting these goals, it should be put on double secret probation. You should consider reviewing your assumptions: If they were incorrect, then evaluate whether the company is still a buy under the revised assumptions. One setback doesn't make the trend; thus double secret probation works as a prioritizing tool for companies that you have to watch like a hawk. Similar to the company reaching a price or valuation target, once a company makes it onto your double secret probation list, its presumption of innocence is forfeited. Guilty until proven innocent! (Yes, I know that sounds un-American.)

Glass Half Empty Mentality Rules

Although the United States is a country of the "glass half full" spirit, a "glass half empty" mentality needs to be at play both in a range-bound market and when reexamining companies that hit your double secret probation list. You should ask two critical questions:

1. Is this problem short-term in nature, or an indication of a long-term trend?
2. Could this escalate into a larger issue?

This is an excerpt from my analysis of U.S. Bancorp's first quarter results of 2005, written for Minyanville.com:

> *Very few positives in this quarter were organic. I am not accusing U.S. Bancorp of using pesticides. There were plenty of one-time items that helped to deliver the bottom line growth. The problem with one-time items is that they are nonrecurring and they don't provide great visibility into the future. This less-than-spectacular performance placed U.S. Bancorp on my "double secret probation" list. If deposits, noninterest income, and assets don't start showing more meaningful growth next quarter, I'll have to part with the stock.*

This is an excerpt from my analysis of U.S. Bancorp's second (following) quarter results of 2005, again written for Minyanville.com:

> *Last quarter, following less-than-spectacular performance, I placed U.S. Bancorp on "double secret probation." Thus I studied U.S. Bancorp's performance with some extra curiosity.... Overall, this quarter was not spectacular, but it provided a favorable glimpse into the future as management demonstrated its ability to grow loans and fee revenues.*

It is crucial to identify important variables (value creators and destroyers) for every company and to closely follow them. For U.S. Bancorp, the ability to grow deposits and loans organically (not through acquisitions) was an important variable, as it was perceived to be an Achilles' heel of the company. There are obviously other important variables that have to be watched when a bank is analyzed (i.e., credit losses, expense ratio, interest margin, and more), but in this case those variables were not in question (at least not as of my 2005 analysis). Its ability to grow was the linchpin impacting U.S. Bancorp's valuation.

To sum up: First you need to find a stock that you would be comfortable marrying forever. The prenuptial agreement is written. At the time of marriage, vows are given—the value creators are identified. Once the company violates its vows, it is put on double secret probation. If fundamental deterioration is determined to be short-term in nature, the stock is kept. But if not, a no-hard-feelings divorce must follow promptly.

Disassociate Yourself from Previous Decisions

The rare ability to draw back from one's circumstance and view it at arm's length, as a stranger might view things, is a valuable skill indeed. A famous example from the mid-1980s was Intel facing new competition from Japan, commoditized memory chips—Intel's bread and butter at the time. This new factor sent Intel from making $198 million in 1984 to making a mere $2 million in 1985. Andy Grove, CEO of Intel, agonized for weeks over the dilemma of what to do, as he recounted in *Only the Paranoid Survive* (Doubleday Currency, 1996):

> *I looked out the window at the Ferris wheel of the Great America amusement park revolving in the distance when I turned back to Gordon [Moore—Intel's founder], and I asked, "If we got kicked out and the board brought in a new CEO, what do you think he would do?" Gordon answered without hesitation, "He would get us out of memories." I stared at him, numb, then said, "Why shouldn't you and I walk out the door, come back, and do it ourselves?"*

Intel refocused its efforts on microprocessors and became one of the most profitable companies in the world, with sales approaching $40 billion and net income exceeding $8 billion in 2005.

By taking an outsider point of view—"If we got kicked out and the board brought in a new CEO, what do you think he would do?"—Andy Grove dumped years' worth of emotional baggage (the financial and emotional costs sunk into an obsolete product strategy) and thus came to a difficult (but critically important) decision. By looking at the problem from an outsider's perspective, he was able to gain unemotional clarity: A new CEO would not have the baggage, so decisions would be forward, not backward-looking.

This example is useful in decision making in many facets of our lives, but it is particularly useful when it comes to investments and especially selling. The baggage of past decisions often haunts us when we attempt to make sell decisions. Selling a stock that is experiencing deteriorating fundamentals forces us to admit that buying that stock was a mistake. We have to accept that not every decision we make will work out. This is just the reality of investments. Paraphrasing my friend Todd Harrison, "If there wasn't risk, it would be called winning, not investing!"

Understanding our behavior when it comes to making investment decisions is important. I said it before, and I'll say it again: Emotions are our worst investing enemy, after all, as they lead us to the opposite of what we should be doing. One of the behavioral traps we fall into is anchoring our current views to our past decisions. For example, the need to feel good about ourselves often causes us to base buy and sell decisions on the past price of a stock. We later anchor our sell decisions to our purchase price in the stock (e.g., if the stock is now down, we hold on hoping to break even). Or we anchor our minds to the past prices of a stock, such as its recent high or recent low.*

You must try to step outside of yourself (as Andy Grove and Gordon Moore did) and ask, "If a new person were to manage my portfolio, what would he/she do?" This attitude should liberate you from your past decisions and focus on the future.

---

*Being a value-sensitive investor, I tend to be agnostic to technical analysis in its pure sense with complete disregard to fundamentals. The stock that "broke out" (i.e., went up) is a less appealing investment to me than the stock that has "broken down" (declined). That said, I have come to respect support and resistance levels, as over time I've found that they are driven by, and then drive, human emotions. As a stock recovers from a prolonged decline, when it comes back to retest the previous highs (resistance levels), many investors who owned the stock last time it approached these levels and failed to sell it will now try to unload the stock in an effort to feel good (or less bad) about themselves. A similar effect occurs in a stock that retests previous lows (support levels). Investors who failed to buy it the last time it hit a previous low will anchor their buy decision at that level; thus they are likely to scoop up the stock once it retests the lows, feeling they are lucky to get a second chance at a perceived bargain.

Although there is nothing logical about support and resistance levels, as long as humans and not computers are in charge of making fundamental buy and sell decisions, their power is likely to persist.

CONCLUSION

Selling is difficult. It is difficult because it often forces us to admit that we made a mistake, or we tend to resist parting with a stock that made us money and thus made us feel good. Sometimes we don't want to experience the regret of selling too soon, or selling requires the further stress of a subsequent (buy) decision that we are not prepared to make. But selling is the seal of success of our buy decisions. The range-bound market requires both disciplined buy and sell strategies. Therefore, you need to become a vigilant seller. Sell when a stock reaches your prior determined valuation level. Sell proactively before fundamentals deteriorate. In other words, sell when a company stops scoring high marks on all dimensions of the QVG framework. Do not hold and hope!

Risk and Diversification

Introduction to Risk
and Diversification

You can probably save a good-sized forest by recycling academic papers that are written on risk and diversification. These concepts are drummed into our heads in academia from day one, but their practical application is usually spoiled by long formulas riddled with Greek symbols. I kept that in mind as I wrote the next two chapters on risk and diversification from the practitioner's point of view. Both concepts are important in any market environment, and therefore I placed them in a separate section.

CHAPTER 13

A Different View of Risk

All of life is management of risk, not its elimination.
—Walter Wriston, former chairman of Citicorp

WHAT IS RISK?

In this chapter I'd like to discuss risk from a slightly different angle, randomness. Before we jump into it we need to agree on a definition of risk. One way to approach risk is from the perspective of volatility: a stock declining in price or returns falling below one's expectations. Another school of thought comes from Warren Buffett and Benjamin Graham; it looks at risk as permanent loss of capital. Are these definitions mutually exclusive? The truth lies somewhere in between.

What risk means to us is shaped by our time horizon. If you are investing for the long run—at least five years—a permanent loss of capital is the risk that you should be concerned with the most. The distinction here is that if you are armed with a long-term time horizon, volatility is a mere inconvenience (and often an opportunity, especially in a range-bound market). Assuming the volatility is temporary in nature, given enough time the investment will come back to its original level.

If you have a short-term time horizon, to you volatility is not temporary. Even a temporary stock decline results in permanent loss of capital, as you don't have the time to wait it out. This is the reason why you should structure your portfolio based on when you'll need the money. As "need the money" time approaches, you should gradually transition the portfolio toward less volatile fixed income securities, which will be the source of liquidity. At that point you cannot afford volatility, as it results in a permanent loss of capital. As an example, suppose you are investing for a daughter's wedding in 24 months. If you invest in stocks and they go down, you must still pay the bills on the expected date. So you must sell at whatever prices are available. If doing so forces you to lock in a loss, your loss of capital is permanent.

Permanent loss of capital is a true risk to the long-term investor, as time will not heal that problem. This book is written for long-term investors, and thus we'll approach risk as permanent loss of capital.

There is another important, although less tangible, issue with volatility: It impacts our emotions and makes us do the wrong things—buy high and sell low. For a very rational, computer-like decision maker, volatility is not an issue. But we are not computers. Therefore, you shouldn't ignore the emotional element of volatility. Make reasonable attempts to minimize its impact on the portfolio through diversification, and/or own stocks whose businesses you understand so that you can be comfortable with their price fluctuations.

PROPERTIES OF RANDOMNESS

What does randomness have to do with risk? If it weren't for randomness, we'd have 100 percent predictability in our forecasting, we'd know a precise outcome for every decision, and investing would be without risk and would therefore have a different name—winning.

When it comes to randomness you should be primarily concerned with two of its properties:

1. *Level of uncertainty*. How much unpredictability is present in a given environment?
2. *Significance of impact*. How deadly is that unpredictability for the final outcome? Stolen lunch in the company fridge—not a big deal. Death or loss of a significant portion of one's capital—a big deal.

Note: The extent of predictability (uncertainty) analysis can be taken even a step further, segmenting the amount of unpredictability into two more aspects: frequency (how often the random event transpires) and predictability (how much forecasting power we have in predicting the event). Identifying frequency and predictability may be important once significance of the impact to you is established.

Once an event is identified as both random and deadly, you need to figure out how to deal with each property:

- What can you do to minimize *exposure to unpredictable events* (i.e., not be there when they happen)?
- What can you do to minimize *exposure to the consequences* of randomness? When it hits the fan, how can you protect yourself?

Identifying the properties of randomness and preparing for it is not a theoretical exercise. You do it on a daily basis—but often you don't realize that you are actually doing it.

When you evaluate a decision to drive or not drive in stormy weather, first you identify that the driving environment will be unpredictable. Second, you evaluate the significance of the impact of unpredictable events; a tree or telephone pole falling, another car swerving on the wet payment and hitting your car—neither is a good outcome.

Once you identify the properties of randomness, you make a decision on how to minimize the exposure to randomness. You may choose not to drive, eradicating the bulk of randomness. Or you could choose to take less busy side roads in hopes of reducing exposure to randomness. Finally, in case luck is not on your side, prepare to minimize the impact of unpredictable events. You may choose to drive a larger car or a car that has airbags (if you have a choice), and fasten your seat belt (have you ever thought of a seat belt as a reducer of the impact of randomness?).

THE CROCODILE HUNTER, RANDOMNESS, AND INVESTING

Steve Irwin—the Crocodile Hunter—seemed like a fun, full-of-life kind of guy. His tragic death by a stingray was very sad. Even beyond the fact that he left a wife and two young children, you wanted him to escape such a fate—just to see what he'd do next.

As Mr. Irwin's life exemplified, randomness by itself is not risky: The event that has a harmful outcome is the risky one. Being exposed to wild animals is not a risky vocation in itself, as wild animals vary in the impact they could have on one's health. For example, being around wild penguins is not a very dangerous vocation. But he was not called the Penguin Hunter. The Crocodile Hunter's producer, John Stainton, made the following comment, published in the *Sydney Morning Herald* on September 5, 2006: "There's been a million occasions where both of us held our breath and thought we were lucky to get out of that one." Mr. Irwin spent most of his time making TV shows in very close proximity to dangerous predators (crocodiles, snakes, spiders, etc.) whose behavior is very unpredictable (random) and potentially lethal.

The Crocodile Hunter seemed to have a lot of fun doing what he did, and maybe that is what life is about. However, there are some investment lessons from his death that we could learn.

Lesson 1: Randomness Can Be Managed—Be in Your Circle of Competence

Nassim Taleb is the author of *Fooled by Randomness* (Texere, 2001), a book that has contributed to our understanding of randomness and the part it plays in our lives. I asked his thoughts on what constituted randomness. As we were having coffee in Bryant Park in Manhattan, he pointed to a pregnant woman seated on a bench reading a magazine. He said, "If you and I were to guess the sex of the fetus, that guess would be completely random to you and me, 50/50 boy or girl. If you were to ask her doctor after he completed an ultrasound, his answer would have a lot less randomness. Though there is still a risk that he's mistaken one body part for another, that risk is very small."

Let me take this a step further; if the same doctor completed a 3-D ultrasound, the predictive power would increase exponentially—the amount of randomness in the forecast would shrink even more. After the birth of the baby, with the benefit of hindsight and many hours of painful labor, the randomness has been completely eradicated and with 100 percent certainty the sex of the baby is known.

Randomness is not absolute—the same event is more random to one person than to another. The extent of randomness decreases with the knowledge we obtain, and not in a linear fashion. The better we understand the business we are exposed to, professionally or through a stock purchase, the less random the environment is to us.

The chance of a significant impact (dying) resulting from being close to a crocodile for an ignorant, inexperienced person like myself (at least when it comes to crocodiles) is very high. Let's say 1 out of 10. The Crocodile Hunter's skill, knowledge, and experience reduced that probability to maybe 1 out of 1,000 for him.

If I was left mano a mano with a crocodile, though, I would know the general direction of the threat—the crocodile's jaws closing on one or more of my extremities. But I would have no idea of what to do to avoid my fate. Stay still? Run in zigzags? Sing a song? Stare him down? Armed with no knowledge and lacking any experience, I'd be dead in one crocodile second—the whole environment would have been random to me.

The Crocodile Hunter's knowledge and experience of dealing with dangerous animals decreased the frequency and significance of impact that randomness had on his life, although they did not eliminate it completely.

He stepped out of his circle of competence. His producer said: "If ever he was going to go, we always said it was going to be in the ocean because there is another element.... On land he was agile, quick-thinking, quick-moving. The ocean puts another element there that you have no control over."

(Though the probability of death from each encounter was much lower for the Crocodile Hunter than for the rest of us, he had a lot more of these encounters, as he was exposed to predators more often than all the rest of us put together times 10,000. Therefore, we can reasonably suspect that it was really a matter of time before something life-ending happened to him.)

Lesson 2: Alternative Historical Paths and Hindsight

One way of understanding how randomness works is by studying alternative historical paths. This means more than just focusing on what took place in the past—the definite (since it already happened), observed history, but one that beforehand was actually still just one of many possible random outcomes. One should focus on what could have taken place, what alternative paths may have existed. This allows us to think creatively about what could have happened, and with that added insight then to predict and prepare for what may happen in the future.

Imagine if the Crocodile Hunter's whole life, day after day in close contact with dangerous predators, could be independently replayed thousands or millions of times. I am sure there would be a few alternative historical paths where luck would be on the Crocodile Hunter's side and he would live until he was 101. But I'll bet a very large portion of these historical paths would lead to an untimely death (if such an event is ever timely). Thus, as sad as it was to see his life end, it was not a surprise. It was just a matter of time before he paid that price for his high exposure to a very random and dangerous environment.

If we were to re-create alternative historical paths for almost any other profession—computer programmer, doctor, administrative assistant—even some of these paths might lead to death, perhaps while driving to work or being crushed by elevator doors. But far, far fewer of them would do so. Unlike constant one-on-one exposure to dangerous predators, these occupations may have plenty of randomness but with more benign outcomes (i.e., a stolen lunch from the refrigerator or running out of coffee).

The dictionary defines hindsight as "understanding the nature of an event after it has happened." Be cautious of hindsight, as it can do the following:

- *Lull you into complacency.* We rarely think that an event could have taken another route, although in so thinking we are wrong. The hindsight of knowing how things transpired provides false clarity and removes any (intellectual) curiosity or desire to know what else could have happened, what other paths events could have taken.

- *Teach you the wrong lesson.* Hindsight usually cements the historical path an event took when it played out, eradicating randomness; however, what happened was just one of a random group of possibilities. If observed history was completely random, then by looking at only one path we learn very little, or, even worse, we learn the wrong lesson.
- *Give you a false sense of control.* Hindsight makes you think you know more than you do, and so you think you control more than you do.

To know the past is essential to being able to predict the future. But the past provides only one (though definitive) version of what could have taken place. Identify other possible pasts.

Always look for hidden risk! A winner is not to be judged—a popular Russian expression. This is a very common attitude when executive decisions, company performance, or investment results are analyzed: If it worked, it must have been a good decision.

Here is an example of how dangerous it is to evaluate decisions by focusing solely on the outcome. Let's say that the CEO of a company that has *all* of its operations in Grand Cayman decided to save a lot of money by canceling its hurricane insurance, saying something to his constituents along the lines of "Why waste millions of dollars on insurance when we can put it into R&D instead?"

With God's help and a little bit of luck there was no hurricane the first year. The company saved a lot of money on insurance premiums and its earnings went through the roof, marking the best year in its history. Now, should the CEO be given a huge bonus for saving millions of dollars on hurricane insurance premiums, or should he be fired?

Hindsight analysis based on observed history would tell us to reward the CEO. He did not waste money on insurance and saved millions of dollars.

But this conclusion completely ignores other very probable alternative paths and risk that has not surfaced—hidden risk. Analysis of what could have taken place, a look at alternative historical paths, would tell us the other, arguably more accurate side of the story. From 1871 to 2004, a hurricane hit Grand Cayman about every two and a quarter years. In other words, there is a 44 percent possibility that a hurricane will hit Grand Cayman in any given year. This estimate is based on 133 years of historical observations, a pretty large data set.

If we gain an understanding of possible alternative historical paths, even if the specific outcome we're looking at was a success, then we will be able to assess the past more accurately—and thus gain a better understanding of the future.

In this example the company's substantially improved profitability was accompanied (actually, generated!) by a very great hidden risk. The CEO had absolutely no control and no predictive/forecasting power over if and when hurricanes would hit Grand Cayman. Unless he accurately predicted about a million different factors that impact the creation and direction of hurricanes, the CEO made a very risky (blind) decision that exposed the company to grave risk, and he just got lucky. Even just several days in advance, meteorologists have a hard time estimating where and when a known, already formed hurricane will make landfall, as many random variables constantly change, impacting other variables.

In the late 1990s, the thinking of investors who owned high-octane technology mutual funds and saw them going nowhere but up was, "Where is the risk?"

Until March 2000 there was no observed risk in Internet stocks or mutual funds that owned them, but there was plenty of hidden risk. By analyzing results in the context of only observed risk, we subject ourselves to the mercy of randomness, because it determines how much risk to show. When evaluations of results are based solely on observed risk, success is often attributed to the skill of the investment or corporate manager, when the credit should have gone to Lady Luck.

Next time you hear a mutual fund or hedge fund manager bragging about outsize returns of his fund and very little (observed) risk, remember our discussion about the randomness, question the alternative historical paths. Maybe it was all skill, but maybe the fund took a lot of risk through significant leverage or placing very large bets on the performance of a single sector. Lady Luck was on his side up to this point, but may or may not be in the future. Think about the cost of being wrong. What if Lady Luck had taken a day or a month off? What would have happened to the fund then?

This is why it is useful to analyze mutual funds or money managers looking at worst-period results, not average longer-term returns; but even that analysis could conceal the embedded hidden risk. For instance, Amaranth, a large hedge fund, had a phenomenal performance until . . . it did not. It placed large leveraged bets on the direction of the price of natural gas in the summer and fall of 2006. It did great until it lost billions of dollars in less than a month.

Long-Term Capital Management (LTCM) was another—a hedge fund whose board of directors and investors included two Nobel Prize winners—Myron Scholes and Robert Merton. LTCM was successful until it was not. It earned "bragging rights" rates of return while employing high leverage.

In 1998, when LTCM's strategy went against it, only four months were needed to wipe out all profits made in the preceding four years, bringing substantial losses to its investors.

Lesson 3: It Is Often Difficult to Spot Randomness

Not all random possible outcomes (random events) will be apparent to us. Ironically, the Crocodile Hunter died from a freak accident, stung in the heart by a stingray. CNN reported that only 17 people have died from stingrays in Australia since 1969. It is hard to say if that number is accurate, but one thing is for certain: death by stingray is extremely rare. Let's assume that a million people swim at Australia's 10,000 beaches every day. From 1969 to 2006 almost 13.5 billion (1 million × 37 years × 365 days a year) people swam in Australia on a daily basis. Using the CNN statistic, the chances of the Crocodile Hunter dying by a stingray on any specific day while swimming in Australia was about 1 in 794 million (13.5 billion divided by 17)—not a statistic one would pay a great deal of attention to when considered in relation to alternative historical paths. Randomness is, after all, random.

Diversification could reduce our exposure to randomness, especially the random event we cannot spot—a lethal random event coming out of left field may destroy a company or two in our portfolio, but the rest of the portfolio would still be intact.

UNDERSTAND THE LINKAGE BETWEEN AND INSIDE QVG DIMENSIONS

Peter Bernstein in his book *Against the Gods* (John Wiley & Sons, 1996) wrote:

> *The essence of risk management lies in maximizing the areas where we have some control over the outcome while minimizing the areas where we have absolutely no control over the outcome and the linkage between effect and cause is hidden from us.*

Taking Peter Bernstein's advice, your objective as an investor should be to own stocks over which you have *some control*—where your knowledge (in-depth research) and expertise make the environment less random. You need to have a clear understanding of:

- *Linkages between variables inside each QVG dimension.* For instance, what is the impact of the loss of a drug patent by a pharmaceutical company on the company's cash flows, its ability to meet financial and contractual obligations, and future earnings growth prospects?
- *Interaction between dimensions.* Taking the example further, as an investor you need to be able to estimate the impact that diminished Quality and Growth dimensions will have on the company's Valuation dimension.

Understanding the linkages inside and between the QVG dimensions will help your buy and sell processes—you'll be a rational decision maker. For instance, if one of your stocks suffers a deterioration in fundamentals, you'll be able to make a rational and unemotional and therefore probably correct decision.

At the other extreme, suppose the linkage between cause and effect is hidden from the "investor" (I use that word loosely in this instance) who is doing no research and buying a loose collection of stocks because "the name sounds cool" or "my brother-in-law owns it." That supposed investor has little or no control over the investment environment, and the behavior becomes irrational as the investor doesn't have solid analytical ground to stand on. Sure, there may be a time when randomness will smile, bestowing outsized returns, as happened in the late 1990s when ignorance was temporarily rewarded. However, in the long run the ugly side of randomness will catch up with such investors as it did in the post-2000 bubble burst.

I'll say it again, all of us have a circle of competence, and therefore we have a circle of incompetence as well. Know your limitations. This key insight is why Warren Buffett avoids technology and other areas he does not think he can really understand well. Armed with knowledge and experience, and with a consistent, well-thought-out investment process in place, you'll have reasonable ability to control a larger portion of the investment environment by intelligent security selection and asset allocation.

IDENTIFY IMPACT OF RANDOMNESS ON VALUE CREATORS

In the previous chapters we discussed the importance of identifying and closely following the value creators and destroyers for each company in the portfolio. In this chapter I suggest taking this analysis a step further and analyzing the impact of randomness on key value creators and destroyers. In other words, we have already determined what makes our companies tick (or blow up); now let's determine how much predictive power we have in forecasting those ticks.

Take the oil industry. Oil companies' profitability and stock performance is heavily dependent on the price of oil. For an oil company, the difference between a $45 and a $25 price per barrel of oil is $20 before tax of pure profitability, and for some it means the difference between profits and losses. Despite that dependency, oil companies have very little control over the price of oil. Even the Organization of Petroleum Exporting Countries (OPEC), a cartel that controls two-thirds of the world's oil reserves, has proved to have very little control over oil prices. To predict future oil prices, one has to accurately forecast the future demand and supply of oil and answer a lot of complex questions:

- Will the demand for oil from China and other developing nations rise as the consumption per capita grows to match that of more developed countries?
- Is the Chinese economy on the verge of economic crises stemming from high indebtedness and significant operational leverage brought on by being a manufacturer to the world, which could mean that a world recession sends the Chinese economy into an economic nuclear winter, curtailing demand for oil?
- Has Saudi Arabia, the world's largest oil producer, reached peak production?
- Are we running out of cheap oil in the ground?
- Will the output of oil from Russia decrease once the government takes greater control over the oil industry?

The fallacy of composition (what applies to a part doesn't apply to the whole) raises the complexity of predicting oil prices even further, as interaction between forces has an impact on where oil prices will settle:

- Will high oil prices create enough political pressure to resume construction of nuclear power plants and increase the number of government-sponsored investments in alternative energy sources?
- Will high energy costs send the global economy into recession?
- Will consumers in large numbers start trading in their gas-guzzling SUVs for gas-efficient Toyota Priuses?
- Will an increase in oil prices lead to discovery of more oil as more money is thrown into oil exploration?

All of these questions should be accompanied by two others: Even if one had the answers to them, determining the timing and magnitude of events (when and with how much impact) is very difficult if not impossible, as they depend on a multitude of other random variables. For instance, to determine whether demand for oil from China will slow or increase, one has to factor in the political situation in China; the demand of U.S. and global consumers for Chinese-made goods; interest rates in China and the rest of the world; the role the Chinese government will be willing to play in managing the Chinese economy; trade, tax, and currency policies; and probably hundreds of other important variables. Though we'd like to believe we have a finger on the pulse of the price of the oil commodity, we don't. It is random for most of us, and its impact on oil company stocks is significant.

What next, then? How do you build the reality of randomness into your portfolio?

The first option is avoidance mode—not to be there when a random event strikes. In this case, that means you can avoid oil stocks altogether.

The second option is a bit more complex but is often the one that looks at risk as an opportunity. Minimize the impact of randomness through the Quality, Valuation, and Growth framework. QVG is a very useful tool, especially from the perspective of managing the impact a random event could have on individual stocks.

A high-quality company will be able to take a beating better than a lower-quality, overleveraged company. Its strong balance sheet will carry it through tough times. And its deeper management is likely to respond more smartly.

The Valuation dimension is important as well. During the 1997 Berkshire Hathaway annual meeting, Warren Buffett said:

> *If you understood a business perfectly and the future of the business, you would need very little in the way of a margin of safety. So, the more vulnerable the business is, assuming you still want to invest in it, the larger margin of safety you'd need. If you're driving a truck across a bridge that says it holds 10,000 pounds and you've got a 9,800-pound vehicle, if the bridge is 6 inches above the crevice it covers, you may feel okay, but if it's over the Grand Canyon, you may feel you want a little larger margin of safety.*

The metaphorical bridge that Buffett described as "6 inches above the crevice" is a bridge with minimal impact in the event random luck runs against you. The greater the potential impact, however, the larger the margin of safety you may need. Returning to oil, what may seem on the surface to be a bad oil company may turn into a good stock depending on its margin of safety. If oil, for instance, is at $45 a barrel, and the bad company stock price has already been discounted for $25 oil prices, you have a nice margin of safety on your hands. Even if oil prices decline from $45 to $25, the stock price should not be impacted much, as a worst-case scenario has already been priced into the stock.

As for the Growth dimension, an oil company with growing earnings and cash flows has time on its side, even if a random event such as lower oil prices removes part of its profitability. With time it will outgrow its problems through higher profitability. You need to focus on companies that are growing their oil production, as this growth will help to overcome lower oil prices by higher volumes. In fact, if you look at the largest exploration and production companies—ExxonMobil, Chevron, BP Amoco, and Royal Dutch/Shell—most of them have shown very little organic growth in production.

THE COST OF BEING WRONG

Randomness is tricky. You'll never get completely rid of it, no matter how diversified you are. Even if you own every single asset class in every single country around the world, you are still exposed to an Armageddon type of event (e.g., meteorite striking the earth, global warming, etc.). Every decision we make has an element of (lethal) randomness attached to it (e.g., driving, flying, eating, operating a lawn mower—people die doing these activities every year), but we cannot keep worrying about those things, and we'll still keep going on with our lives doing them (though I have a guy mowing my lawn because of my laziness).

When we make decisions, we should look at the cost of being wrong (more on this in Chapters 14 and 15). Let's take paying taxes, for example, something we do every year. We make decisions on how much to push the tax envelope. The following ignores morality and our responsibility as citizens. I am approaching this example from John Maynard Keynes' perspective when he said: "The avoidance of taxes is the only pursuit that still carries any reward."

There are gray areas in the tax code that may be open to different interpretations. Every year when we do our taxes we face these decisions (e.g., should we take a full deduction on our cell phone used for both business and pleasure, or "forget" to report that couple of hundred dollars we made on eBay selling Beanie Babies as taxable income?). These decisions (if discovered) usually result in payment of what we were supposed to pay and some penalties and interest payments to Uncle Sam. There are also fraudulent things we can (but should not) do—illegal tax evasion (something among the lines of hiding money in Grand Cayman or devising elaborate tax-avoidance schemes) that could land us, like Al Capone, in jail. Every year, while there is about a 1 in 20 (5 percent) chance that we'll get audited, there is a probably even smaller chance that the Internal Revenue Service (IRS) will discover our little or big ploys.

The probability of being caught is not very high, and let's assume for the sake of argument that it is about the same in each instance. What makes aggressive tax deduction different from committing outright tax fraud? The cost of being caught (being wrong). Most of us can afford the cost of paying back taxes plus penalties even if we have to borrow the money to do that. However, I'd argue that few of us can afford the alternative of spending years in jail for tax fraud. I am not imposing my values, but my logic is that we can always make more money, but we live only once, and it is a lot more fun to be outside of jail. The lesson here, when making decisions, is to always consider the cost of being wrong (or being caught).

This applies to our reputations as well. Warren Buffett said that it takes 20 years to build it and five minutes to lose it. To me the cost of my reputation being damaged by my actions is too high to bear—I love my job and want my kids to look up to me with pride. Therefore, if I consider an action in a gray area, even one that has minuscule probability of being discovered, I just focus on the cost of being caught—something I cannot afford. I ignore the probabilities of reward and focus on the cost.

This applies to leverage. Leveraging your house to buy a high-flying or not so high-flying stock may have a very high potential reward—improved standard of living, kids going to better schools, more family vacations. But it also comes with the possible outcome that you may not be able to afford—living on the street, broken family, kids not going to any college.

CONCLUSION

The investing environment is infested with randomness—it is a professional hazard. Our skill, knowledge, and experience should help to reduce the risk of randomness, but completely eradicating it is impossible since randomness is the nature of the investing jungle. Staying within your circle of competence and doing in-depth research can decrease the amount of randomness and the impact it has on your portfolio. Focus not only on what has happened (which is often random) but also on what could have happened. Learn from the past and judge the actual as well as possible outcomes of what went before. If you encounter a company that has high exposure to random and significant events, make sure that it earns extra-high scores in the QVG framework analysis. Finally, to help protect yourself from randomness—diversify!

CHAPTER **14**

A Different View
of Diversification

In 1965 Steve McQueen starred in The Cincinnati Kid, *the classic poker movie of all time. This movie has so far saved me from becoming ultra broke or ultra rich. The climactic scene in the movie involves a showdown hand of five-card stud between Steve McQueen ("The Kid") and Edward G. Robinson ("The Man"). This scene made an indelible impression on me during my school years. With three cards dealt, Robinson bets heavily on a possible flush, a stupid bet if there ever were one, particularly since McQueen has a pair showing. The pot gets bigger and bigger. McQueen ends up with a full house—aces over tens, which loses to Robinson's straight flush. When Robinson turns his hole card, the jack of diamonds, McQueen looks as though he is going to throw up. He has been wiped out. The movie's soundtrack is throbbing. Sweat is dripping down McQueen's face, as he stares at Robinson's hand in disbelief.*

—Frederick E. Rowe Jr., Forbes

I cannot be in 50 or 75 things. That's a Noah's Ark way of investing—you end up with a zoo that way. I like to put a meaningful amount of money into few things.

—Warren Buffett

It is frequently said that diversification is the only free lunch an investor will ever get, as this risk-reduction strategy doesn't need to lead to subsequent reduction in return. Or does it? Warren Buffett disagrees: "Diversification is a protection against ignorance. It makes little sense for those who know what they are doing."

Both statements are correct. In one extreme, investors often fail to diversify, holding just a handful of companies and subjecting themselves to unnecessary risk. Kenny, our investor with a great chunk of his net worth in five fantastically overpriced technology stocks, learned that lesson the hard way. In this situation you should ask yourself if you can afford to see one (or more) of your stocks lose the bulk of their value overnight—a real possibility. However, what a finance book will not tell you is that a portfolio consisting of just a handful of stocks also enormously impairs your ability to make rational decisions at the time when that ability is needed the most—under pressure. Managing this emotional reality is one of the more subjective aspects of risk management through diversification. And traditional finance textbooks and courses ignore it, since they see the world as always rational.

DON'T BET THE FARM!

The following happened to a good friend of mine. Let's call him Jack (though his name is Brian). He and his wife both worked for the largest insurance broker in the world, Marsh & McLennan. It was a much-respected firm with a market capitalization over $20 billion and revenue in excess of $12 billion—not a flaky start-up with a lot of unknowns ahead of it, but a Wall Street darling—a bellwether. Over the years, Jack and his wife accumulated a large position of Marsh's stock, which they were reluctant to sell.

Sometime in 2000 he asked me what I thought of their financial situation, having all this wealth in Marsh's stock. I commented that although I didn't see Marsh going out of business anytime soon, I would not recommend having all their net worth in one company. Employees of Enron, MCI, or Lucent did not foresee their 401(k)s disappearing just months before they did so. Although the probability of Marsh disappearing was very, very small, this couple's lack of diversification was just not worth the risk, especially considering that both their personal income streams (paychecks) also came from Marsh. Jack listened to my advice and agreed with it. He did not feel the urgency to do anything about it, though, got busy with his day-to-day life, and did not take action, until . . .

Several years later, one sunny day (at least it was sunny on my side of Denver), I was driving to work when I got a call from Jack, who asked, "Did you see what happened to Marsh?" I had not. Jack explained that Eliot Spitzer (the state attorney general of New York at the time) had filed a lawsuit against Marsh accusing the company of bid rigging, insinuating that Marsh was not acting in clients' best interests when it charged (often undisclosed) contingent commissions. Marsh's stock was almost halved on the news, as contingent commissions accounted for a large portion of company profits. Talks about bankruptcy were in the air. To my surprise, Jack was very calm (considering that Marsh stock was his entire net worth at the time) and asked my thoughts on what he and his wife should do about their Marsh stock.

In this type of situation, when all hell is breaking loose, you need to weigh the probabilities of possible outcomes. Bankruptcy, which was an improbable outcome for Marsh a day before the lawsuit was filed, suddenly became a lot more probable. Or at least the odds went from one in a gazillion to a remote but imaginable outcome. Marsh's debt did not seem high, at about 30 percent of total assets; however, without contingent commissions (whose future was very uncertain and which carried almost 100 percent gross margin), Marsh was barely profitable (if at all). Also, this had a similar smell to a recent Arthur Andersen debacle, since both firms were in the intellectual capital or trust business in which a lawsuit could trigger a massive client exodus and put the company out of business.

If Marsh was just another stock (one of 15 or 20) in a diversified portfolio, the remote risk of its bankruptcy—the worst-case scenario—would be considered as one of the risks with appropriate attribution of probabilities to each outcome coming to fruition. But this is what theory doesn't tell you: In the situation in which one cannot afford a low-probability outcome (and Jack could not afford it), one starts treating that outcome as having a much increased probability.

Jack was not diversified, and he did not have the luxury of looking at the worst-case Marsh scenario as just one of the low-probability outcomes, as it was a possible outcome whose consequences he could not afford.

P.S. After our conversation, Jack sold a good portion of his Marsh stock at a significant loss. At the time the Marsh debacle was taking place, he was going to buy a new house, but he had to break the contract. He lost a large portion of the down payment, plus he was not sure if he and his wife would have their jobs down the road. Luckily, neither of them lost their jobs. Several months later he took a job (a promotion) with another insurance broker to diversify his income stream (plus working for Marsh was not the same anymore). I bet he'll never look at diversification with the same complacency again.

TOO MANY EGGS OR TOO MANY BASKETS

At the other extreme, investors holding hundreds of stocks incur another cost—ignorance. The dictionary defines ignorance as the condition of being uneducated, unaware, or uninformed—the cost Buffett is referring to. A very large number of companies in investors' portfolios makes it impossible for them to know these companies well. Lack of knowledge leads to an inability to make rational decisions, which then causes investors to behave irrationally and hurt portfolio returns. Another side effect of (over-) diversification is indifference to individual investment decisions. In a portfolio of hundreds of stocks, an individual position might represent 1 percent (or less) of the total portfolio. The cost of being wrong is very small (if, for instance, it goes up or goes down 20 percent, the overall impact on the portfolio is only 0.20 percent on either side), but so is the benefit of being right. This breeds a semi-indifference to incremental decisions common among overdiversified buy-and-hold investors.

You need to strike an appropriate balance, weighing the consequences of either extreme. Academics disagree on the exact number of uncorrelated stocks needed in a portfolio to eradicate individual stock risk, but the number is usually given as somewhere between 16 and 25 stocks. This is another case where being vaguely right is better than being precisely wrong. I found that a portfolio of around 20 stocks is manageable and provides an adequate level of diversification; at this level, the price of being wrong is not too high, but every decision matters.

Taking diversification a step further, stress testing a portfolio (playing out different what-if scenarios) for probable risks coming to fruition is critical, as it exposes the weaknesses of the portfolio in the event possibility turns into reality. For example, during mid-2006 my firm was stress testing our clients' portfolios for exposure to a consumer and housing slowdown, slowdown in Chinese and emerging market economies, weakening/rising U.S. dollar, rising/falling oil prices, and rising/falling interest rates. Once stress testing reveals exposure (or underexposure) to a certain risk or event, we are equipped with information to realign the portfolio accordingly and unemotionally.

MENTAL ACCOUNTING AND DIVERSIFICATION

Robert (not his real name) is a successful businessman with both street and book smarts. He built a prospering multimillion-dollar business from scratch. He made good money in real estate, investing when times were tough and nobody would touch condos and houses with a long pole.

Robert knew enough about stocks to realize that he didn't have the time, training, or experience to handle his stock portfolio. He outsourced management of his portfolio—to my firm. However, Robert was not just a regular client. He was my partner's very old friend.

That was in the early 1990s. My firm has done a good job for Robert. In 1999 the stock market went crazy and the NASDAQ briefly touched 5,000. The new economy stocks were doubling every three months or so. However, our stodgy, unexciting stocks that lacked ".com" in their names generated great cash flows (to their detriment, by the standards of that time), traded at very attractive valuations—and did not budge in price. Robert did not mind our underperformance. He hired us to invest, not to speculate. In 2000 our patience was rewarded, as his portfolio went up by double digits as the dot-coms and other bubbly stocks tanked. Having a ".com" in the name became a liability, and being stodgy and having cash flows came back into fashion again.

In 2002 Robert's stock portfolio was pushing $2 million, and that was when the market melted down. This time the market collapse was widespread; there was no place to hide other than being in cash. At one point his portfolio declined 15 percent, down by $300,000 to $1.7 million. Robert called his money manager (his old friend, my partner), and told him that he was obsessed with his stock losses. He said, "I know it is not you—it is the market. I know I am probably marking the bottom in the stock market, but I have to get out of stocks. Their decline is impacting my life. I cannot sleep at night."

My partner explained to him that it was the wrong thing to do. But at the same time, not wanting to infringe on their 30-year friendship, he tried only lightly to persuade him to remain in stocks and not to sell. Robert clearly, and right now, wanted nothing to do with stocks. At the time there was no way to dissuade him from selling out. We obliged. I am not sure if that phone call took place on the lowest day for the stock market in 2002, but it was the lowest week for sure. The stocks have gone up significantly since.

Several years passed. My partner and Robert (still great friends) were going to a baseball game and Robert stopped by our office. I was leaving to teach my class. With a kind smile, Robert inquired on the subject of that night's lecture. Ironically, it was on behavioral finance. Robert was genuinely interested in the subject and somehow our conversation switched to his decision to liquidate his stock portfolio in 2002. Robert smiled and said, "I know my sell marked the bottom of the market. But I just could not take it. It caused me too much pain. I don't know what it is, but when it comes to stocks I cannot stomach losing money. I am sure the value of my business and my real estate portfolio fluctuates a lot short-term. But I don't see those numbers printed in the newspaper or on TV on a daily basis, nor do I get a monthly statement from the custodian. Plus I feel more in control when it comes to my business and real estate." When those words came out of his mouth, it hit me. Although his statement was very accurate, I knew there was a more important point that Robert has missed.

Robert fell into what is called in behavioral finance the *mental accounting trap*. He had segmented his wealth into mental accounts: stocks, real estate, bonds, and business. He evaluated short-term performance of each asset class in isolation and failed to notice their interaction in the context of the total portfolio.

His overall portfolio was not down 15 percent, but a mere 3 percent. Let me explain. Robert's net worth at the time was $10 million. His business was worth at least $4 million, his real estate holdings (excluding his house) were pushing $3 million, he had about $1 million in high-quality short-term bonds, and his stock portfolio had just declined from $2 million to $1.7 million. Thus, when that decline hit ($300,000), his total wealth had declined by a mere 3 percent ($300,000 ÷ $10 million). I'd argue that his total wealth probably increased that year despite stocks being down, as his business was growing at a double-digit rate, and the values of his real estate and bond portfolios increased.

Robert failed to look at his stocks' performance in the context of his total portfolio. His common sense led him to diversification among four loosely correlated asset classes, but his entrapment in a mental accounting error precluded him from reaping the fruits that diversification had given him. His diversified portfolio worked as it was supposed to, but it did not matter, as his wrongly framed perception crowded out reality.

What is the lesson to be learned? I'll borrow the answer from an excellent book by Gary Belsky and Thomas Gilovich, *Why Smart People Make Big Money Mistakes* (Simon & Schuster, 1999): "Every financial decision should result from a rational calculation of its effect on our overall wealth."

MENTAL ACCOUNTING AND RANDOMNESS IN A STOCK PORTFOLIO

Robert was not the only person to ever step into the mental accounting trap; it is one of the most frequently visited potholes in investing, usually located somewhere near the *value* and *relative value* problems. The mental accounting trap can be taken a step further, as well, from asset class to the individual stock level. It is important to be diligent in your analysis, but it is more important to accept that you just will not be right all the time on every stock. Even if your analysis and investment process was right on the money, unpredictable (random) events may turn what was supposed to be a good investment into a loser. Over time investors make mistakes—that is a reality of investing. Even Warren Buffett, whom many consider the god of investing, occasionally loses money on individual stocks. Ironically, the original Berkshire Hathaway, the textile company bought in 1962 that Buffett later turned into a vehicle for his investments, was an investment that went bad. Buffett bought Berkshire Hathaway on the cheap, but the fundamentals of the textile business were deteriorating at a faster rate than he estimated.

There is a reason for a diversified portfolio of stocks—to allow room for losers (though not too many). When we make mistakes, we should try to learn as much as possible from them (assuming there is something to learn) and move on. If we let a mistake drive us crazy, the rest of the portfolio will suffer, as it will obscure our judgment. In my personal experience, it is an active process to force myself to concentrate on the overall portfolio—not something that comes naturally for most of us, myself included, since we analyze each stock individually before they make it into the portfolio.

I encourage you to pay close attention to fundamentals (value creators/destroyers) and not be overly sensitive to individual short-term stock *price* action, as more often than not it is a manifestation of random noise.

Nassim Taleb in *Fooled by Randomness* provides a great example. Using a Monte Carlo simulation engine, he created a virtual (hypothetical), normally distributed portfolio that goes up 15 percent a year and has a standard deviation (volatility) of 10 percent—a return/volatility combination most investors would kill for, especially in a range-bound market. Here's his probability projection for making money over different time horizons, based on statistical probabilities:

1 year	93%
1 quarter	77%
1 month	67%
1 day	54%
1 hour	51.3%

If it were not for volatility, the investor would observe no noise (i.e., ratio return to volatility), as the portfolio would go up by 0.0383 percent a day (or 1.17 percent a month, 3.55 percent a quarter, or 15 percent a year). However, in the real world, 10 percent standard deviation sprays some uncertainty into the portfolio—introducing noise to the mix.

The amount of noise observed by the investor increases with the shortening of the observed time period. Even though an investor holding the portfolio described has a 93 percent chance of making money in any given full year, looking at the portfolio on a more frequent basis—let's say every hour—the investor would observe the portfolio making money only

51.3 percent of the time—a tiny 1.3 percent advantage (the difference between 51.3 percent and 50 percent) over breaking even or losing money. In other words, even though over the course of an entire year this investor has only a 7 percent chance of seeing an overall loss in the portfolio, the same portfolio observed on an hourly basis would disappoint the investor with losses 48.7 percent of the time. In fact, that small 1.3 percent edge for making money on an hourly basis will probably not be noticed by our data-overloaded investor, as the pain of losses has a greater negative emotional utility than the joy of gains.

This example is right on the money. However, stock investors will observe more noise than is shown in this example, for two reasons: Returns from stocks are not normally distributed; thus the fluctuations are sharper. And second, individual stocks are more volatile than a portfolio of stocks. If you focus on the performance of individual stocks on a short-term basis, rather than on the overall portfolio, you will observe even more short-term volatility (noise).

In the short run, we observe volatility of the portfolio and individual stocks, but not the returns. I implore you—don't act on noise! Focus on the stock in the context of the total portfolio, and focus more on whether the company QVG is still on track, rather than on daily or weekly share prices.

A properly diversified equity portfolio should consist of stocks from different industries, of various sizes (from large-capitalization to small-capitalization), growth rates, valuations, and countries. At times the market will fancy a certain characteristic over another, which is what markets do and is at least in part why investors diversify: to lower *overall* volatility. I say "in part" because there are two more reasons: first, and the most important, to limit exposure to the true risk—a permanent loss of capital; second, to be able to maintain a rational state of mind. As mentioned earlier, a portfolio should have a small enough number of stocks that every decision matters, but not so few that the cost of being wrong in a stock is unbearable. All that having been said, don't make marginal (buy) decisions for the sake of diversification.

RANDOMNESS COULD BE YOUR FRIEND

Randomness can work to your advantage, as it may at times drive stocks you own above their intrinsic values, providing you with an opportunity to sell earlier than you originally expected at the time of purchase. It may also drive totally fine stocks below their intrinsic values, providing an opportunity to buy more. I sometimes find myself guilty of missing this unique opportunity. When I look for new buying opportunities, my natural tendency is to start looking outside of my portfolio first. But this makes me neglect to formally consider buying more of stocks that I have already researched, even though I still believe the fundamentals are intact but for some random reason the stock has declined. Perhaps a good check and balance on this common tendency would be to pretend I was 100 percent in cash and had the entire universe of eligible attractive stocks from which to choose.

CHAPTER **15**

Conclusion and Implication

In a strict sense, there wasn't any risk—if the world had behaved as it did in the past.

—Merton Miller, Nobel laureate

I COULD BE WRONG, BUT I DOUBT IT

Could I be wrong? Maybe the range-bound market I've described is not in the cards. Maybe we are about to embark on the biggest bull market in U.S. history. In *Fooled by Randomness*, Nassim Taleb writes, "I can use data to disprove a proposition, never to prove one. I can use history to refute conjecture, never to affirm it." Looking at history, we can study the conditions that preceded different markets, learn from them, and thereby form an educated forecast. Although conditions that preceded previous range-bound markets are firmly in place and the probability of a range-bound market unfolding over the next dozen years is high, it is clearly not certain.

Every strategy should be evaluated not just on a "benefit of being right," but at least as importantly on a "cost of being wrong" basis, and I intend to do just that. The Active Value Investing strategy has the lowest "cost of being wrong"!

Let's examine the probable performance of our Active Value Investing strategy in three possible secular market environments: bull, range–bound, and (true) bear. We'll compare Active Value Investing to a buy-and-hold strategy (which I lump into the same category as passive indexing); to a high-beta (I thought I'd please modern portfolio theory buffs), momentum, growth-stocks-on-steroids strategy; and to a simple bonds-only strategy.

EXHIBIT 15.1 The "Cost of Being Wrong" and the "Benefit of Being Right" in Secular Markets

	Bull	Range-Bound	Bear	
			High Inflation	Deflation
Active Value Investing	On Par with Stock Market or Slightly Less	Decent (Above Stock Market) Returns	Smaller Decline Than Stock Market	Smaller Decline Than Stock Market
Buy-and-Hold (Passive Indexing)	On Par with Stock Market (Plus or Minus)	Zero Price Appreciation + Dividends	Market Decline Plus or Minus	Market Decline Plus or Minus
High-Beta Growth	Better Than Stock Market	Zero or Negative Price Appreciation + Small Dividends	Greater Decline Than Stock Market	Greater Decline Than Stock Market
Bonds	Considerably Worse Than All Above	On Par with Stock Market Plus or Minus (Depend on Direction of Inflation and Interest Rates)	Worse Than All Above	Better Than All Above

I have to warn you that I'll be generalizing about these strategies, as they come in different flavors and vary from investor to investor.

Exhibit 15.1 shows the rough performance of each equity strategy versus holding a portfolio of bonds during secular bull, range-bound, and bear markets. Since the bond portfolio would perform very differently in an inflationary versus a deflationary bear market, I subdivided bear market returns into those two types.

BULL MARKETS

In the unlikely case of a secular bull market now unfolding (especially at a time when stock valuations are still at the level where the previous range-bound market started and when we no longer have the tailwind of declining interest rates), Active Value Investing will not punch the lights out of a more aggressive, albeit riskier, strategy—owning higher-valuation, higher-growth stocks. Active Value Investing will not get you inducted into the hall of investing fame, but it should produce solid returns. After all, you will own good companies that are growing earnings, maybe even paying fat dividends, and you will have bought them at the right prices—with an appropriate margin of safety.

Active Value Investing has some natural disadvantages to buy-and-hold and high-beta strategies in a bull market, but for the most part you could overcome them:

■ *You'll sell too soon.* This is not the worst problem to have. As successful investor Bernard Baruch said, "I made my money by selling too soon." Selling will free up your cash to reinvest in better risk/reward opportunities. The "growth investors gone wild" strategy (i.e., selling a portion of the position and keeping the rest, albeit with a disciplined trailing stop loss in place) will mitigate this problem, at least partially. Also, "too soon" will be evident to us mortals only in hindsight (sorry).

■ *You'll have too much cash.* As we saw in the "Why Not Bonds?" section of Chapter 4, cash (short-term bonds, money market funds) is your enemy in a bull market, as its returns pale in comparison to the ones from stocks whose earnings are growing and P/Es are expanding. If cash is just a by-product of the lack of attractive investment opportunities (i.e., you cannot find enough stocks that score high on all QVG dimensions), I'd argue there is no such thing as too much cash in such a market environment. Cash is better than a marginal stock that doesn't pass your QVG test. However, you can mitigate the cash problem by doing two things:

1. Beef up your stock discovery process (without compromising on your QVG standards). Make sure that you do a good job canvassing the market for opportunities—all strategies we discussed in Chapter 10.

2. Integrate looking overseas for opportunities as a natural part of your stock discovery process. Of course, international markets could be overpriced as well in which case you'll have a larger cash position. But you'll have more sanity, too. Arguably, being invested for the sake of being invested is not a coherent, sane strategy.

The high-beta growth strategy will likely outshine Active Value Investing in a full-blown secular bull market. Although buy-and-hold is likely to underperform a riskier high-beta strategy, it should still do well in a bull market. But the cost of being wrong by using these strategies if a range-bound or a bear market turns out to be the environment will be devastating to your wealth (especially during a bear market). And since our lives are short, damage later in life is especially dangerous. The small level of underperformance of the Active Value Investing strategy against the buy-and-hold and high-beta strategies in a bull market is a small insurance premium to pay to avoid failure in a range-bound or bear market.

BEAR AND RANGE-BOUND MARKETS

Although we do have one-half of the components in place for a bear market to start—high valuation—the chances are, unless we have a tremendous *wRong!*

deterioration in the economy, a bear market is unlikely to show its sharp claws.

However, in case it does, high-beta stocks should experience greater declines than the overall market will, due to P/E compression. Investors who held high-beta aggressive mutual funds or stocks in 2001 discovered the risk of this strategy in a very painful, money-losing way. Aside from the fact that investors tend to overpay for high earnings growth rates, high valuation and lack of meaningful dividend yield (a by-product of the high starting valuation and lower dividend payouts predominant in growth stocks) set up this strategy for failure in a bear market from the get-go. It has the highest cost of being wrong if a bear market unfolds; add a likely higher P/E compression exhibited by these stocks, and this strategy should result in substantial losses. The impact of a range-bound market on this strategy should be less dramatic than that of the bear market, but still it is likely to produce zero or negative price appreciation and minuscule dividends.

Buy-and-hold will generate marketlike negative returns in a bear market. Its returns in a range-bound market will not be exciting, either, as it will result in approximately zero price appreciation plus dividends—returns that are far below the expectations of most investors. In the event of a bear or range-bound market, this strategy has a very high cost of being wrong. A buy-and-hold strategy in this climate, with its low total returns, will look bad on a risk-adjusted basis against being in some combination of cash and bonds.

It is difficult to make money in declining (bear) markets—period— unless you are in the rare minority who can short sell successfully. But Active Value Investing is a superior strategy to the traditional buy-and-hold, passive indexing, or "high octane beta" strategies for these reasons:

- Companies that scored high marks on all three QVG dimensions should suffer a smaller P/E compression for three reasons: First, they'll have a higher margin of safety, absorbing some of the P/E compression. Second, investors' risk senses are much sharper during a bear market, and investors will likely seek safety, which is just a bear market code word for quality. Finally, earnings growth will help to fight back against P/E compression.
- Higher dividend yields should mitigate some of the P/E contraction. In addition, dividends provide you with a relatively constant cash income, which in turn will allow you to reinvest in stocks at times when they are trading at ridiculously low valuations. As the market later recovers you'll come out stronger, as you'll own more shares at a lower cost basis—thanks to dividends!

- Cash rules. Your higher cash position, created as a by-product of your stock-selection discipline, should soften the blow of the declining market.
- Exposure to international stocks that scored high marks on the Quality, Valuation, and Growth framework may open a sea of opportunities when the opportunity well dries up in the United States.

In a range-bound market this active buy-and-sell process should work to your advantage in a market that is not going anywhere but has plenty of two-sided volatility. Cash being a residual of your investment decisions should only help you, providing a much-needed dry powder to strike when future opportunities (stocks meeting all QVG dimensions) present themselves. High-dividend-yielding stocks will be the source of an important portion of your portfolio's returns as they have been in the previous range-bound markets. Finally, a careful look across the pond or the border should present additional investment opportunities and expose you to markets that may be entering a bull cycle.

BONDS?

There is another alternative often viewed as safer—bonds. Though bonds may be perceived to be safer than stocks, this is true only in the (low-inflation) short run. We know that in the long run, over a full market cycle, passive buy-and-hold equity strategies (and index funds) beat bonds. But during past range-bound markets, passive indexing (S&P 500) had a marginal and not a consistent supremacy against bonds. If you factor in bonds' lower volatility, that preference was marginalized further.

Range-bound markets bring a buy-and-hold investor a return of about zero price appreciation plus dividends—and that assumes the investor actually has the fortitude to hold through the scary volatility. A bond-only strategy's performance in the range-bound stock market may slightly outperform or underperform buying and holding. The bottom line will greatly depend on what interest rates and inflation do during that time period.

The Active Value Investing strategy should be superior to buy-and-hold and passive indexing strategies and therefore should produce greater returns than a bond-only strategy in the range-bound market.

The only bear market scenario where an Active Value Investing strategy or stocks in general would underperform bonds is a recession that coincides with (or is caused by) deflation (e.g., Japan's latest bear market). Default-free Treasury bonds should do well in that environment; however, corporate bonds below those of top quality probably will not do well, as default rates are likely to skyrocket. Corporate bonds that are issued by companies that have large fixed costs should suffer the highest default rates. These companies perform worse than others in a deflationary environment, as their nominal sales drop due to deflation, but their costs are fixed and thus remain more or less the same, rapidly eroding their profitability.

In a bear market caused by or coinciding with high inflation (a rare scenario—Germany during World War I) bonds should do considerably worse than stocks. If we have an environment of high inflation and/or rising interest rates, bonds will deliver terrible real returns; in this case, the cost of being wrong will be high (especially long-term bonds, as their cash flows are fixed for a long period of time, dramatically eroding their real purchasing power).

NO, I AM NOT WRONG

The cost of being wrong using Active Value Investing is much lower than pursuing buy-and-hold, passive indexing, high-beta, or bond-only strategies. However, Active Value Investing is even more superior to those strategies if you factor in the probabilities of each type of market transpiring over the next dozen years. Looking at history as a guide, the probability of the current range-bound market staying for quite a while is high, but the probability of a bull or bear market rearing its head is very low. The Active Value Investing should be your strategy of choice!

APPENDIX

Years to Bull Market

EXHIBIT A.1 Years to Bull Market? Earnings Growth 7 Percent

								Starting Price to Earnings											
Ending Price to Earnings	**37**	**36**	**35**	**34**	**33**	**32**	**31**	**30**	**29**	**28**	**27**	**26**	**25**	**24**	**23**	**22**	**21**	**20**	**19**
18	10.6	10.2	9.8	9.4	9.0	8.5	8.0	7.6	7.0	6.5	6.0	5.4	4.9	4.3	3.6	3.0	2.3	1.6	0.8
17	11.5	11.1	10.7	10.2	9.8	9.3	8.9	8.4	7.9	7.4	6.8	6.3	5.7	5.1	4.5	3.8	3.1	2.4	1.6
16	12.4	12.0	11.6	11.1	10.7	10.2	9.8	9.3	8.8	8.3	7.7	7.2	6.6	6.0	5.4	4.7	4.0	3.3	2.5
15	13.3	12.9	12.5	12.1	11.7	11.2	10.7	10.2	9.7	9.2	8.7	8.1	7.6	6.9	6.3	5.7	5.0	4.3	3.5
14	14.4	14.0	13.5	13.1	12.7	12.2	11.7	11.3	10.8	10.2	9.7	9.1	8.6	8.0	7.3	6.7	6.0	5.3	4.5
13	15.5	15.1	14.6	14.2	13.8	13.3	12.8	12.4	11.9	11.3	10.8	10.2	9.7	9.1	8.4	7.8	7.1	6.4	5.6
12	16.6	16.2	15.8	15.4	15.0	14.5	14.0	13.5	13.0	12.5	12.0	11.4	10.8	10.2	9.6	9.0	8.3	7.6	6.8
11	17.9	17.5	17.1	16.7	16.2	15.8	15.3	14.8	14.3	13.8	13.3	12.7	12.1	11.5	10.9	10.2	9.6	8.8	8.1
10	19.3	18.9	18.5	18.1	17.6	17.2	16.7	16.2	15.7	15.2	14.7	14.1	13.5	12.9	12.3	11.7	11.0	10.2	9.5
9	20.9	20.5	20.1	19.6	19.2	18.7	18.3	17.8	17.3	16.8	16.2	15.7	15.1	14.5	13.9	13.2	12.5	11.8	11.0
8	22.6	22.2	21.8	21.4	20.9	20.5	20.0	19.5	19.0	18.5	18.0	17.4	16.8	16.2	15.6	15.0	14.3	13.5	12.8

EXHIBIT A.2 Years to Bull Market? Earnings Growth 6.5 Percent

Starting Price to Earnings

Ending Price to Earnings	37	36	35	34	33	32	31	30	29	28	27	26	25	24	23	22	21	20	19
18	11.4	11.0	10.6	10.1	9.6	9.1	8.6	8.1	7.6	7.0	6.4	5.8	5.2	4.6	3.9	3.2	2.4	1.7	0.9
17	12.3	11.9	11.5	11.0	10.5	10.0	9.5	9.0	8.5	7.9	7.3	6.7	6.1	5.5	4.8	4.1	3.4	2.6	1.8
16	13.3	12.9	12.4	12.0	11.5	11.0	10.5	10.0	9.4	8.9	8.3	7.7	7.1	6.4	5.8	5.1	4.3	3.5	2.7
15	14.3	13.9	13.5	13.0	12.5	12.0	11.5	11.0	10.5	9.9	9.3	8.7	8.1	7.5	6.8	6.1	5.3	4.6	3.8
14	15.4	15.0	14.6	14.1	13.6	13.1	12.6	12.1	11.6	11.0	10.4	9.8	9.2	8.6	7.9	7.2	6.4	5.7	4.8
13	16.6	16.2	15.7	15.3	14.8	14.3	13.8	13.3	12.7	12.2	11.6	11.0	10.4	9.7	9.1	8.4	7.6	6.8	6.0
12	17.9	17.4	17.0	16.5	16.1	15.6	15.1	14.6	14.0	13.5	12.9	12.3	11.7	11.0	10.3	9.6	8.9	8.1	7.3
11	19.3	18.8	18.4	17.9	17.4	17.0	16.5	15.9	15.4	14.8	14.3	13.7	13.0	12.4	11.7	11.0	10.3	9.5	8.7
10	20.8	20.3	19.9	19.4	19.0	18.5	18.0	17.4	16.9	16.3	15.8	15.2	14.6	13.9	13.2	12.5	11.8	11.0	10.2
9	22.4	22.0	21.6	21.1	20.6	20.1	19.6	19.1	18.6	18.0	17.4	16.8	16.2	15.6	14.9	14.2	13.5	12.7	11.9
8	24.3	23.9	23.4	23.0	22.5	22.0	21.5	21.0	20.5	19.9	19.3	18.7	18.1	17.4	16.8	16.1	15.3	14.6	13.7

EXHIBIT A.3 Years to Bull Market? Earnings Growth 6 Percent

Ending Price to Earnings	Starting Price to Earnings																		
	37	36	35	34	33	32	31	30	29	28	27	26	25	24	23	22	21	20	19
18	12.4	11.9	11.4	10.9	10.4	9.9	9.3	8.8	8.2	7.6	7.0	6.3	5.6	4.9	4.2	3.4	2.6	1.8	0.9
17	13.3	12.9	12.4	11.9	11.4	10.9	10.3	9.7	9.2	8.6	7.9	7.3	6.6	5.9	5.2	4.4	3.6	2.8	1.9
16	14.4	13.9	13.4	12.9	12.4	11.9	11.4	10.8	10.2	9.6	9.0	8.3	7.7	7.0	6.2	5.5	4.7	3.8	2.9
15	15.5	15.0	14.5	14.0	13.5	13.0	12.5	11.9	11.3	10.7	10.1	9.4	8.8	8.1	7.3	6.6	5.8	4.9	4.1
14	16.7	16.2	15.7	15.2	14.7	14.2	13.6	13.1	12.5	11.9	11.3	10.6	10.0	9.3	8.5	7.8	7.0	6.1	5.2
13	18.0	17.5	17.0	16.5	16.0	15.5	14.9	14.4	13.8	13.2	12.5	11.9	11.2	10.5	9.8	9.0	8.2	7.4	6.5
12	19.3	18.9	18.4	17.9	17.4	16.8	16.3	15.7	15.1	14.5	13.9	13.3	12.6	11.9	11.2	10.4	9.6	8.8	7.9
11	20.8	20.3	19.9	19.4	18.9	18.3	17.8	17.2	16.6	16.0	15.4	14.8	14.1	13.4	12.7	11.9	11.1	10.3	9.4
10	22.5	22.0	21.5	21.0	20.5	20.0	19.4	18.9	18.3	17.7	17.0	16.4	15.7	15.0	14.3	13.5	12.7	11.9	11.0
9	24.3	23.8	23.3	22.8	22.3	21.8	21.2	20.7	20.1	19.5	18.9	18.2	17.5	16.8	16.1	15.3	14.5	13.7	12.8
8	26.3	25.8	25.3	24.8	24.3	23.8	23.2	22.7	22.1	21.5	20.9	20.2	19.6	18.9	18.1	17.4	16.6	15.7	14.8

EXHIBIT A.4 Years to Bull Market? Earnings Growth 5 Percent

Ending Price to Earnings	Starting Price to Earnings																		
	37	36	35	34	33	32	31	30	29	28	27	26	25	24	23	22	21	20	19
18	14.8	14.2	13.6	13.0	12.4	11.8	11.1	10.5	9.8	9.1	8.3	7.5	6.7	5.9	5.0	4.1	3.2	2.2	1.1
17	15.9	15.4	14.8	14.2	13.6	13.0	12.3	11.6	10.9	10.2	9.5	8.7	7.9	7.1	6.2	5.3	4.3	3.3	2.3
16	17.2	16.6	16.0	15.4	14.8	14.2	13.6	12.9	12.2	11.5	10.7	10.0	9.1	8.3	7.4	6.5	5.6	4.6	3.5
15	18.5	17.9	17.4	16.8	16.2	15.5	14.9	14.2	13.5	12.8	12.0	11.3	10.5	9.6	8.8	7.8	6.9	5.9	4.8
14	19.9	19.4	18.8	18.2	17.6	16.9	16.3	15.6	14.9	14.2	13.5	12.7	11.9	11.0	10.2	9.3	8.3	7.3	6.3
13	21.4	20.9	20.3	19.7	19.1	18.5	17.8	17.1	16.4	15.7	15.0	14.2	13.4	12.6	11.7	10.8	9.8	8.8	7.8
12	23.1	22.5	21.9	21.3	20.7	20.1	19.5	18.8	18.1	17.4	16.6	15.8	15.0	14.2	13.3	12.4	11.5	10.5	9.4
11	24.9	24.3	23.7	23.1	22.5	21.9	21.2	20.6	19.9	19.1	18.4	17.6	16.8	16.0	15.1	14.2	13.3	12.3	11.2
10	26.8	26.3	25.7	25.1	24.5	23.8	23.2	22.5	21.8	21.1	20.4	19.6	18.8	17.9	17.1	16.2	15.2	14.2	13.2
9	29.0	28.4	27.8	27.2	26.6	26.0	25.3	24.7	24.0	23.3	22.5	21.7	20.9	20.1	19.2	18.3	17.4	16.4	15.3
8	31.4	30.8	30.3	29.7	29.0	28.4	27.8	27.1	26.4	25.7	24.9	24.2	23.4	22.5	21.6	20.7	19.8	18.8	17.7

EXHIBIT A.5 Years to Bull Market? Earnings Growth 4.5 Percent

Starting Price to Earnings

Ending Price to Earnings	37	36	35	34	33	32	31	30	29	28	27	26	25	24	23	22	21	20	19
18	16.4	15.7	15.1	14.4	13.8	13.1	12.4	11.6	10.8	10.0	9.2	8.4	7.5	6.5	5.6	4.6	3.5	2.4	1.2
17	17.7	17.0	16.4	15.7	15.1	14.4	13.6	12.9	12.1	11.3	10.5	9.7	8.8	7.8	6.9	5.9	4.8	3.7	2.5
16	19.0	18.4	17.8	17.1	16.4	15.7	15.0	14.3	13.5	12.7	11.9	11.0	10.1	9.2	8.2	7.2	6.2	5.1	3.9
15	20.5	19.9	19.2	18.6	17.9	17.2	16.5	15.7	15.0	14.2	13.4	12.5	11.6	10.7	9.7	8.7	7.6	6.5	5.4
14	22.1	21.5	20.8	20.2	19.5	18.8	18.1	17.3	16.5	15.7	14.9	14.1	13.2	12.2	11.3	10.3	9.2	8.1	6.9
13	23.8	23.1	22.5	21.8	21.2	20.5	19.7	19.0	18.2	17.4	16.6	15.7	14.9	13.9	13.0	12.0	10.9	9.8	8.6
12	25.6	25.0	24.3	23.7	23.0	22.3	21.6	20.8	20.0	19.2	18.4	17.6	16.7	15.7	14.8	13.8	12.7	11.6	10.4
11	27.6	26.9	26.3	25.6	25.0	24.3	23.5	22.8	22.0	21.2	20.4	19.5	18.7	17.7	16.8	15.7	14.7	13.6	12.4
10	29.7	29.1	28.5	27.8	27.1	26.4	25.7	25.0	24.2	23.4	22.6	21.7	20.8	19.9	18.9	17.9	16.9	15.7	14.6
9	32.1	31.5	30.9	30.2	29.5	28.8	28.1	27.4	26.6	25.8	25.0	24.1	23.2	22.3	21.3	20.3	19.2	18.1	17.0
8	34.8	34.2	33.5	32.9	32.2	31.5	30.8	30.0	29.3	28.5	27.6	26.8	25.9	25.0	24.0	23.0	21.9	20.8	19.7

EXHIBIT A.6 Years to Bull Market? Earnings Growth 4 Percent

Ending Price to Earnings	Starting Price to Earnings																		
	37	36	35	34	33	32	31	30	29	28	27	26	25	24	23	22	21	20	19
18	18.4	17.7	17.0	16.2	15.5	14.7	13.9	13.0	12.2	11.3	10.3	9.4	8.4	7.3	6.2	5.1	3.9	2.7	1.4
17	19.8	19.1	18.4	17.7	16.9	16.1	15.3	14.5	13.6	12.7	11.8	10.8	9.8	8.8	7.7	6.6	5.4	4.1	2.8
16	21.4	20.7	20.0	19.2	18.5	17.7	16.9	16.0	15.2	14.3	13.3	12.4	11.4	10.3	9.3	8.1	6.9	5.7	4.4
15	23.0	22.3	21.6	20.9	20.1	19.3	18.5	17.7	16.8	15.9	15.0	14.0	13.0	12.0	10.9	9.8	8.6	7.3	6.0
14	24.8	24.1	23.4	22.6	21.9	21.1	20.3	19.4	18.6	17.7	16.7	15.8	14.8	13.7	12.7	11.5	10.3	9.1	7.8
13	26.7	26.0	25.3	24.5	23.8	23.0	22.2	21.3	20.5	19.6	18.6	17.7	16.7	15.6	14.5	13.4	12.2	11.0	9.7
12	28.7	28.0	27.3	26.6	25.8	25.0	24.2	23.4	22.5	21.6	20.7	19.7	18.7	17.7	16.6	15.5	14.3	13.0	11.7
11	30.9	30.2	29.5	28.8	28.0	27.2	26.4	25.6	24.7	23.8	22.9	21.9	20.9	19.9	18.8	17.7	16.5	15.2	13.9
10	33.4	32.7	31.9	31.2	30.4	29.7	28.8	28.0	27.1	26.3	25.3	24.4	23.4	22.3	21.2	20.1	18.9	17.7	16.4
9	36.0	35.3	34.6	33.9	33.1	32.3	31.5	30.7	29.8	28.9	28.0	27.0	26.0	25.0	23.9	22.8	21.6	20.4	19.1
8	39.0	38.3	37.6	36.9	36.1	35.3	34.5	33.7	32.8	31.9	31.0	30.1	29.1	28.0	26.9	25.8	24.6	23.4	22.1

EXHIBIT A.7 Years to Bull Market? Earnings Growth 3.5 Percent

Ending Price to Earnings	Starting Price to Earnings																		
	37	36	35	34	33	32	31	30	29	28	27	26	25	24	23	22	21	20	19
18	20.9	20.1	19.3	18.5	17.6	16.7	15.8	14.8	13.9	12.8	11.8	10.7	9.5	8.4	7.1	5.8	4.5	3.1	1.6
17	22.6	21.8	21.0	20.1	19.3	18.4	17.5	16.5	15.5	14.5	13.4	12.4	11.2	10.0	8.8	7.5	6.1	4.7	3.2
16	24.4	23.6	22.8	21.9	21.0	20.1	19.2	18.3	17.3	16.3	15.2	14.1	13.0	11.8	10.5	9.3	7.9	6.5	5.0
15	26.2	25.4	24.6	23.8	22.9	22.0	21.1	20.1	19.2	18.1	17.1	16.0	14.8	13.7	12.4	11.1	9.8	8.4	6.9
14	28.3	27.5	26.6	25.8	24.9	24.0	23.1	22.2	21.2	20.1	19.1	18.0	16.9	15.7	14.4	13.1	11.8	10.4	8.9
13	30.4	29.6	28.8	27.9	27.1	26.2	25.3	24.3	23.3	22.3	21.2	20.1	19.0	17.8	16.6	15.3	13.9	12.5	11.0
12	32.7	31.9	31.1	30.3	29.4	28.5	27.6	26.6	25.6	24.6	23.6	22.5	21.3	20.1	18.9	17.6	16.3	14.8	13.4
11	35.3	34.5	33.6	32.8	31.9	31.0	30.1	29.2	28.2	27.2	26.1	25.0	23.9	22.7	21.4	20.1	18.8	17.4	15.9
10	38.0	37.2	36.4	35.6	34.7	33.8	32.9	31.9	30.9	29.9	28.9	27.8	26.6	25.4	24.2	22.9	21.6	20.1	18.7
9	41.1	40.3	39.5	38.6	37.8	36.9	36.0	35.0	34.0	33.0	31.9	30.8	29.7	28.5	27.3	26.0	24.6	23.2	21.7
8	44.5	43.7	42.9	42.1	41.2	40.3	39.4	38.4	37.4	36.4	35.4	34.3	33.1	31.9	30.7	29.4	28.1	26.6	25.1

EXHIBIT A.8 Years to Bull Market? Earnings Growth 3 Percent

Starting Price to Earnings

Ending Price to Earnings	37	36	35	34	33	32	31	30	29	28	27	26	25	24	23	22	21	20	19
18	24.4	23.4	22.5	21.5	20.5	19.5	18.4	17.3	16.1	14.9	13.7	12.4	11.1	9.7	8.3	6.8	5.2	3.6	1.8
17	26.3	25.4	24.4	23.4	22.4	21.4	20.3	19.2	18.1	16.9	15.7	14.4	13.0	11.7	10.2	8.7	7.1	5.5	3.8
16	28.4	27.4	26.5	25.5	24.5	23.4	22.4	21.3	20.1	18.9	17.7	16.4	15.1	13.7	12.3	10.8	9.2	7.5	5.8
15	30.5	29.6	28.7	27.7	26.7	25.6	24.6	23.4	22.3	21.1	19.9	18.6	17.3	15.9	14.5	13.0	11.4	9.7	8.0
14	32.9	32.0	31.0	30.0	29.0	28.0	26.9	25.8	24.6	23.4	22.2	20.9	19.6	18.2	16.8	15.3	13.7	12.1	10.3
13	35.4	34.5	33.5	32.5	31.5	30.5	29.4	28.3	27.1	26.0	24.7	23.4	22.1	20.7	19.3	17.8	16.2	14.6	12.8
12	38.1	37.2	36.2	35.2	34.2	33.2	32.1	31.0	29.9	28.7	27.4	26.2	24.8	23.4	22.0	20.5	18.9	17.3	15.5
11	41.0	40.1	39.2	38.2	37.2	36.1	35.1	33.9	32.8	31.6	30.4	29.1	27.8	26.4	25.0	23.4	21.9	20.2	18.5
10	44.3	43.3	42.4	41.4	40.4	39.4	38.3	37.2	36.0	34.8	33.6	32.3	31.0	29.6	28.2	26.7	25.1	23.4	21.7
9	47.8	46.9	45.9	45.0	44.0	42.9	41.8	40.7	39.6	38.4	37.2	35.9	34.6	33.2	31.7	30.2	28.7	27.0	25.3
8	51.8	50.9	49.9	49.0	47.9	46.9	45.8	44.7	43.6	42.4	41.2	39.9	38.5	37.2	35.7	34.2	32.6	31.0	29.3

Acknowledgments

It seems to me that a book is like wine: Though created by a winemaker, he is only part of the process (an instigator), while the external environment—the minerals in the soil, the sunlight, the humidity, the temperature, the rainfall—has to be on his side for the wine to be fine. I'll let you be the judge of how fine this book really is, but the perfect conditions were in place for this vintner, as I received a tremendous amount of support and feedback on the book from the fantastic people I am about to mention (if you find this book being less than fine, the fault lies solely with me).

I've spent almost one-third of my life at Investment Management Associates (IMA), at first as an employee and later as a partner. Michael Conn, the company's founder and president, has been my boss (though he never behaved like one, and despite being 30 years my senior always treated me as an equal), my teacher, my mentor, my chess sparring partner, and my friend. I can safely say that Michael has shaped me as an investor and I am in great debt to him. A lot of the ideas in this book either came from the discussions Michael and I had over the years or were simply instigated by him and expanded by me.

I am also thankful to the following wonderful people for their feedback, discussions, and inspiration, or simply for being sounding boards for ideas in this book (the names are listed in a random order):

Joe Pecoraro, in addition to providing very detailed, prescient feedback on the manuscript, he is the reason I got into investing—he gave me my very first job; Ed Stavetski helped with many chapters of this book and especially with Chapter 7's story of Tevye the Milkman; Greg Collins—planted the idea of this book; Michelle Leder kindly guided me through the book-writing process; Susan Lakatos—my first editor at TheStreet.com, the first person to tell me that I have what others want to read; Ben Thomas; Ned Sunderman; Kevin Depew; Hewitt Heiserman; Jeffrey Scharf ; Raja Ziady; Marianne Plunkert; Mark Bauer; Stanley Wolpoff; Anil Tahiliani; Craig Jacobson.

Cristy Reid and Theresa Lewingdon, my coworkers at IMA, victimized many times by my insistence that they read and provide feedback on barely readable early drafts.

My circle of trust (see Chapter 10)—John McCorvie, Fil Zucchi, Brian Gilmartin, Geoffrey Johnson, Robert Kizik, Greg Denewiler, Mathew Emmert, and Giles Fox.

Marat Oganesyan, my best friend whom I met a week after I moved to the United States, we have been best friends since, for his patience and support.

Folks at Standard & Poor's (J. P. Tremblay, Brad Daggett, Fred Manio, Doug Dashiell, and A. J. Wellman) for providing tremendous help with Backtester, which was instrumental for Chapter 7.

I am grateful to John Wiley & Sons' excellent team, Jennifer Mac-Donald and Mary Daniello, and especially my amazing editor, Pamela van Giessen, for providing brilliant, insightful, and brutally honest (the best kind) feedback.

My teachers at the University of Colorado at Denver—Larry Johnston, Marcelle Arak, and John Turner; and my students at the University of Colorado, as many of the ideas in this book came from our classroom discussions.

I am flattered to have luminaries for whom I have a tremendous respect for endorse this book: Doug Kass, Tom Brown, James Montier, James Altucher—I read every article they pen; David Einhorn—one of the brightest minds in value investing; Aaron Brown, his *Poker Face of Wall Street* brought a great insight on gambling and investing; Bill Mann and Philip Durell are my favorite Fools (*The Motley Fool* analysts/newsletter writers); Todd Harrison, founder of one of a kind Minyanville.com (a financial community committed to enhancing human potential through financial understanding), to which I am a proud contributor; Jeff Macke—a terrific analyst and writer (whose writing style I tried to plagiarize for years) and a contributor to CNBC's *Fast Money*, he is responsible for my nickname at Minyanville: "Red"; Nassim Taleb's book *Fooled by Randomness* and our walk in Bryant Park in Manhattan shaped my views on randomness and were instrumental for Chapter 13; Ed Easterling—his book *Unexpected Returns* and our discussions provided great insight into market cycles; Donald Cassidy, founder of the Retirement Investment Institute (r-i-i.org, on whose board I serve), one of the kindest people I ever met in my profession, his book *It's When You Sell That Counts* is a must read for anybody who is serious about investing.

I cannot thank adequately Eric Wagner, my marvelous friend, who as I became acclimated to American culture, had great conversations with me, ranging from the rules of baseball to the ethics behind the TV series $M*A*S*H$ (the rest of my American immigrant story is found in the Author's Note, should you care to read it). Eric volunteered to make this book readable (before it got into Pamela's hands at Wiley), a great undertaking, to say the least. His contribution to this book is simply enormous.

I am forever indebted to my incredible family. Though my dear mother passed away when I was 10, I can still feel her love and think of her every day. My father always saw a hidden (it was really hidden) potential in me and cultivated it. He is a true Renaissance man: In addition to having a PhD in electrical engineering, he is an accomplished artist (one of his paintings is on the jacket of this book). A son cannot ask for a better role model! My dear aunt Natulya (my mother's sister), despite living in Russia and not speaking or reading a word of English, insisted on seeing the book so she could have it translated and read it in Russian. She is the closest person I have to a mother. My brothers: Leo, for believing in me and protecting me when we were kids; Alex, for his unconditional love and, as he would say, for raising me (Alex drew Exhibit 7.1, but don't blame him for that as I asked him to draw it as Tevye would have done); and Igor, for always(!) being there. My stepmother—for not living up to her "step" title. My wife Rachel for loving, for her eternal kindness, and for taking care of our wonderful spin-offs while "daddy was writing his book at the bookstore" on Saturdays and Sundays. My son Jonah and my daughter Hannah for being who they are—amazing kids.

AUTHOR'S NOTE

I spent my youth in Murmansk, a city in the northwest part of Russia (located right above the Arctic Circle). Murmansk owes its existence to the port that, due to the warm Gulf Stream, doesn't freeze during the long winters, providing unique access to Russia from the north. During the Cold War, Murmansk's coordinates must have been on the speed dial of the U.S. military, as it is the headquarters of the Russian Northern Navy Fleet (the headquarters actually are in Severomorsk, a town 20 miles away, but the distinction is rarely made). Fans of Tom Clancy's *The Hunt for Red October* may remember Murmansk as the home base for the submarine *Red October*.

The city revolves around its port, and its academic institutions are geared toward producing a workforce for the fishing and merchant marine industries. Since I was very young it was assumed that I'd attend either the Marine College or the Marine Academy. Both were semi-military schools where the students (cadets) had to reside in dormitories, wear navy uniforms, follow strict military-like rules, and take orders from navy officers (and ask no questions). The major difference between them was that the college accepted students after eighth grade and the academy after tenth grade (at the time, Russia had a 10-year education system).

Russia has a draft army. It is not concerned about recruiting and thus treats its soldiers very poorly (an understatement). The pay is only high enough for soldiers to afford the postage to write home asking for money. Russian youth look at serving in the Russian army as akin to a two-year prison sentence (at least when I was there). The army avoidance in the late 1980s was not about fear of death, as the war in Afghanistan was over, but came from the dread of losing years of one's youth and the dismay of humiliation, as the older soldiers commonly abused the younger ones. My very sane friend entered a psychiatric institution and faked mental disease just to avoid serving in the army.

My father and both of my older brothers graduated from the Murmansk Marine Academy. My father also taught electrical engineering at the academy for 27 years. Neither my brothers nor I had any dreams about being seamen. Quite to the contrary, my oldest brother could have been a philosopher (now he is a technology engineer); my other brother wanted to be anything but an electrical engineer (he is now a successful real estate broker in Denver). Our choices were limited: either attend one of these two semi-military schools or join the Red Army.

By the time I was finishing eighth grade, the law had changed: Cadets from the Marine Academy lost their draft exemption, but college cadets were spared. I enrolled in the Marine College and dreaded every moment I spent there, but the alternative was even worse.

My father has two younger sisters; one lived all her life in Moscow, while the other moved with her family from Moscow to Siberia in 1979. For a long time I wondered why my aunt and my cousins in Siberia never visited or called us. It seemed so uncharacteristic of our family, who were always very close. In the summer of 1988 my father finally told me that my aunt did not really move to Siberia—she immigrated to the United States of America. My immediate reaction was resentment toward her. The first words out of my mouth were "traitor" and "spy."

It sounds a bit silly now, but you have to understand I was a child of the Cold War. A couple of times a month my class walked to the movie theater (this was before VCRs) and watched propaganda documentaries about decaying capitalistic America, infested with the homeless, where black people are lynched, the poor are exploited by the rich, and people are poisoned by hamburgers (later, of course, I learned that the part about hamburgers was not a complete lie).

Russian movies showed Americans as evildoers, usually spies whose single goal in life was to destroy Mother Russia—the whole country was brainwashed. When I was nine years old, I attended a pioneer camp and went on a field trip. A foreign tourist, mesmerized by my smile and internal beauty (okay, that is just a wild guess), gave me bubble gum. My camp teacher, in horror, took it away, yelling that I was lucky to be alive as it was probably poisoned.

But back to my aunt. My father was not a bit surprised to hear the words "traitor" and "spy" come out of my mouth. He calmly explained that despite being well educated, his sister's family had lived in poverty because they had faced the invisible anti-Semitic wall that is so often encountered by Jewish people in Russia. Though my parents always tried to shield us from anti-Semitism, I was often made aware that there was something wrong about me being Jewish, as even as a little child I often encountered a second-class-citizen attitude toward me.

My father also explained that he hid the truth about my aunt's whereabouts from me (and my brothers) because the consequences of the truth leaking out to local authorities would have been dire. My mother and he could have lost their jobs, and my brothers and I would never be permitted to leave the borders of the country, which for (future) seamen would have been devastating. In fact, his sister who stayed behind was demoted due to the other sister's departure for the United States—she was deemed guilty of betrayal by association.

After the glasnost reform (transparency, openness) of 1985, the decades of brainwashing were slowly supplanted by the truth. In the late 1980s few people could afford VCRs, but little VCR movie theaters were popping up on every corner. These movie theaters were usually in the basement of an apartment building: just several TV sets hooked up to a VCR. Unlike state-owned theaters, they were not censored and had the freedom to choose their repertoire. Picture and sound quality was terrible, as VHS tapes were copied dozens of times before they made it into a VCR. Movies were dubbed by one monotone voice that translated all characters. But all that did not matter; we were hungry for variety, and American cinema was it. After watching hundreds of these flicks, it became painfully obvious that America and capitalism were not so rotten after all, and despite what my camp teacher told me, Americans did not really have any intention of poisoning little kids.

Just a few years earlier it would have sounded absurd, but after my "Siberian" aunt's invitation in 1990, we decided to immigrate to the United States. As my father says, he looked at his kids and saw no future for us in Russia. On December 4, 1991, we landed in New York City. Our new and in many ways harder (at least at first) life started, and we never regretted leaving Russia. Opportunity had a new meaning for us, and we've been calling the United States our country ever since.

I am forever grateful to this wonderful country. This book would not have been possible were it not for the United States!

Notes

Chapter 1   Introduction: Range-Bound Markets Happen

1. Jeremy Siegel, *Stocks for the Long Run*, 3rd ed. (New York: McGraw-Hill, 2002), 26, 27.
2. Ibid., 18–22.
3. http://www.sjsu.edu/faculty/watkins/hyper.htm#GERMANY.
4. Siegel, *Stocks for the Long Run*, 21–22.
5. Peter Bernstein, *The Power of Gold* (New York: John Wiley & Sons, 2000), 3–4.
6. Siegel, *Stocks for the Long Run*, 10.
7. Dalbar, Inc., "Market Chasing Mutual Fund Investors Earn Less Than Inflation, Dalbar Study Shows," July 16, 2003, www.dalbarinc.com/content/printerfriendly.asp?page=2003071601.

Chapter 2   Emotions of Secular Bull, Bear, and Range-Bound Markets

1. François Trahan, Kurt D. Walters, and Caroline S. Portny, "Asset Bubbles: A Look at Past and Future Manias," Bear, Stearns.
2. John Steele, *The Great Game: The Emergence of Wall Street as World Power, 1653–2000* (New York: Scribner, 1999), page 236.
3. Masahiro Kawai, "Reform of the Japanese Banking System," http://ideas.repec.org/p/hst/hstdps/d05-102.html.

Chapter 3   Stock Market Math

1. www.answers.com/topic/fed-model-1.
2. This is an excerpt from the article I wrote for The Motley Fool titled "The Profit Margin Paradigm" on March 1, 2006, www.fool.com/investing/value/2006/03/01/the-profit-margin-paradigm.aspx.

Chapter 5   The "Q" — Quality

1. Paul Krugman, "Housing Gets Ugly," August 25, 2006, http://select.nytimes.com/gst/abstract.html?res=F30F10F7385A0C768EDDA10894DE404482&showabstract=1.
2. This is an excerpt from the article I wrote for Minyanville.com titled "Toll's Bias" on August 25, 2006, www.minyanville.com/articles/index.php?a=11078.
3. CallStreet.com, transcript of Costco's third quarter 2004 earnings call.
4. CallStreet.com, transcript of Lionsgate Entertainment Corporation's first quarter 2007 earnings call.

Chapter 6   The "G" — Growth

1. This is an excerpt from the article I wrote for Minyanville.com titled "Mailbag: Dividends and Buybacks" on November 9, 2005, www.minyanville.com/articles/index.php?a =8922.
2. This is an excerpt from the article titled "Westwood: One to Avoid," which I wrote for The Motley Fool on April 4, 2006, www.fool.com/investing/high-growth/2006/04/06/westwood-one-to-avoid.aspx.
3. http://online.barrons.com/article/SB108216598657085442.html?mod=b_this_weeks_magazine_main.
4. Jeremy Siegel, *The Future for Investors: Why the Tried and the True Triumph over the Bold and the New* (New York: Crown Business, 2005), 148.
5. Robert D. Arnott and Clifford S. Asness, "Surprise! Higher Dividends = Higher Earnings Growth," *Financial Analysts Journal* 59, no. 1 (January/February 2003): 70–87, www.cfapubs.org/doi/abs/10.2469/faj.v59.n1.2504.
6. David Dreman, *Contrarian Investment Strategies: The Next Generation* (New York: Simon & Schuster, 1998), 201.

Chapter 7   The "V" — Valuation

1. This is an excerpt from the article I wrote for The Motley Fool titled "Why Are Banks' P/Es So Low?" on February 10, 2006, www.fool.com/investing/dividends-income/2006/02/10/why-are-bank-pes-so-low.aspx.
2. http://online.barrons.com/article/SB108216598657085442.html?mod=b_this_weeks_magazine_main.
3. Benjamin Graham, *The Intelligent Investor: A Book of Practical Counsel* (New York: HarperCollins, 2004), 295. Value = Normal Earnings × (8.5 + Twice Expected Annual Growth Rate).

Chapter 9   Buy Process — Fine-Tuning

1. Mohnish Pabrai, *Mosaic: Perspectives on Investing* (Irvine, CA: Grammar Buff, 2006).

Chapter 10   Buy Process — Contrarian Investing

1. http://money.cnn.com/2000/03/28/mutualfunds/q_funds_notebook/.

Chapter 11   Buy Process — International Investing

1. www.pwc.com/gx/eng/about/svcs/corporatereporting/SandD_05.pdf.
2. This an excerpt from the article I wrote for The Motley Fool titled "Russia: We Don't Need the West Anymore," published January 24, 2007, www.fool.com/investing/international/2007/01/24/russia-we-dont-need-the-west-anymore.aspx.

Chapter 12   Sell Process — Make Darwin Proud

1. This is an excerpt from the article titled "The 'Buy and Forget to Sell' Investor," which was first published on Minyanville.com on February 20, 2007, www.minyanville.com/articles/index.php?a=12196.

Index

Note: Page numbers in italics indicate exhibits.